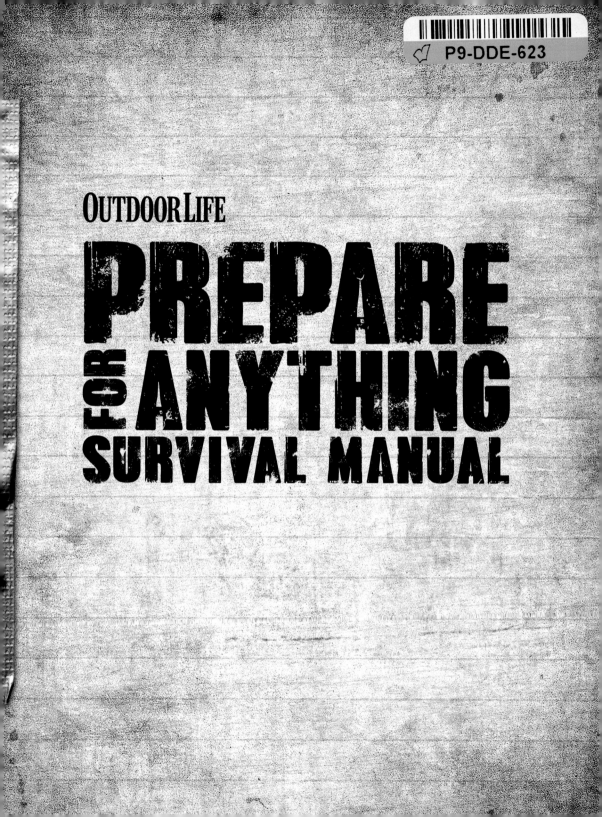

OUTDOOR LIFE

PREPARE FOR ANYTHING SURVIVAL MANUAL

OUTDOOR LIFE

TIM MACWELCH
and the editors of OUTDOOR LIFE

PREPARE FOR ANYTHING SURVIVAL MANUAL

weldon**owen**

CONTENTS

- Introduction from *Outdoor Life*
- Introduction from the Author

1 | Understand Situational Awareness
2 | Sharpen Your Strategy
3 | Know the Steps
4 | Color Code It
5 | Know What You're Preparing For
6 | Understand the Crisis
7 | Get Familiar with the Scope
8 | Learn Your Task
9 | Create Your Family Emergency Plan
10 | Conduct Drills

GEAR

11 | Pack a BOB for Any Situation
12 | Stock a Home Survival Kit
13 | Pack Something Weird
14 | Make a Fire Kit
15 | Waterproof Your Matches
16 | Be Fire Smart
17 | Know Your Fire Types
18 | Check Home Safety Basics
19 | Stay on Comm
20 | Know Your Region
21 | Stock the Right Supplies
22 | Disaster-Proof Your Home
23 | Fool the Bad Guys
24 | Reinforce Your Home
25 | Don't Forget the Garage
26 | Bar the Door for Real
27 | Shop Smart

28 | Start with the Basics
29 | Power Up with Protein
30 | Go Carb Crazy
31 | Stash Some Little Luxuries
32 | Pack It in PETE
33 | Plan for the Long Haul
34 | Don't Forget FIFO
35 | Count Your Calories
36 | Store Food Right
37 | Go Cuckoo for Coconut
38 | Sleep On It
39 | Figure Out How Much Water You'll Need
40 | Be Chemical Safe
41 | Harvest the Rain
42 | Let the Sun Shine In
43 | **This Could Happen To You:** Wild Auto Repair
44 | Hold Your Water
45 | Think Outside the Sink
46 | Banish Bacteria
47 | Pool Your Resources
48 | Suit Up for Safety
49 | Get Wild and Woolly
50 | Walk Tall
51 | Be Your Own Bootblack
52 | Dress for the Occasion
53 | Build Your Tool Kit
54 | Get Creative with Your Toolbox
55 | Rip It Up with a Hammer
56 | Make Fire with a File
57 | **Don't Get Caught Without:** Vodka

SPOTLIGHT ON: Evan & Scot Hill

58 Meet the Hill Brothers
59 Get the Gear of the Hill People
60 Stick to Your Guns

61 Grab a Gun (Or Two)
62 Be Gun Safety Savvy
63 **This Could Happen To You:**
   Paracord Escape
64 Own 8 Essential Knives
65 Tie 7 Simple Knots
66 Have a Financial Plan
67 Shelter Your Funds
68 Stash Your Cash
69 Know the Right Amount
70 Understand Your Fuel Types
71 Know Your Color Codes
72 Make It Last Longer
73 Store Fuel Right
74 Determine How Much Fuel You Need
75 Burn This, Not That
76 Live on Solar Power
77 Get the Most from a Propane Stove
78 Make Recycled Briquettes
79 Get Ready to Get Around
80 Buy the Best Vehicle
81 Upgrade Your Ride
82 Charge It Yourself
83 Provide All the Air
84 Get the Tools for Your Car
85 **Don't Get Caught Without:** Paracord

SKILLS

86 Know Basic Life Skills
87 Revisit Home Ec
88 Build Your Survival Skills
89 Build Your First Aid Kit
90 Improvise Medical Supplies
91 Level Up
92 Check Vital Signs
93 Assess and Control Bleeding
94 Bandage a Wound
95 Disinfect a Wound
96 Know CPR
97 Treat for Shock
98 Set Broken Bones
99 Identify and Treat Burns
100 Perform the Heimlich Maneuver
101 Build a Fire in the Rain
102 Get the Best Materials You Can Find
103 Make Char Cloth
104 Learn the Tricks to Tinder
105 **Don't Get Caught Without:** Sardines
106 Know Your Water
107 Disinfect with UV Light
108 Disinfect with Boiling Water
109 Keep Clear
110 Use Your Canner to Distill Water
111 Build a Solar Still
112 Double Up
113 Dig Your Own Well
114 Get the Water Up
115 Make a Gypsy Well

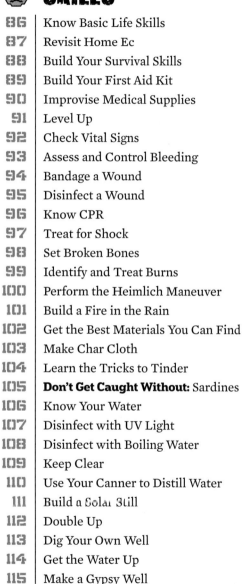

116 | Boil in a Bottle
117 | Maintain Your Perimeter
118 | Be Your Own Chimney Sweep
119 | Keep Your Fortress in Good Shape
120 | Stock Your Home Plumbing Toolbox
121 | Clean with the Basics
122 | Start Outside, Then Bring It All Inside
123 | Stock Your Safe Room
124 | Grab the Popcorn
125 | Don't Forget Your Pets
126 | Alert the Authorities
127 | Board Up
128 | Stock a P.B.O.B.
129 | Prepare to Leave Them Behind
130 | Train for Disaster
131 | **This Could Happen To You:** Rooftop Escape
132 | Do Your Research
133 | Pick the Right Spot
134 | Get the Dirt
135 | Place Your Plants
136 | Go Urban
137 | Take It Easy
138 | Build a Food Wall
139 | Grow the Right Veggies

140 | Build a Raised Bed Garden
141 | Feed a Family of Four
142 | Scare Off Critters
143 | Grow Your Own Medicine Chest
144 | Make a Self-Watering Container Garden
145 | Know Fido's Risks

SPOTLIGHT ON: Rod Morey, Medicine Man
146 | Take Charge of Your Own Wellness
147 | Brew Rod's Favorite Remedies
148 | Know Three Essential Herbs

149 | Build a Backyard Chicken Farm
150 | Raise Chicks
151 | Get a Good Egg
152 | Feed Free-Range Chickens
153 | Kill a Chicken Humanely
154 | Prepare Your Chicken
155 | Consider Other Fowl
156 | Include Quail in Your Homestead
157 | Avoid Salmonella
158 | Find the Right Feed
159 | Raise Rabbits
160 | Breed Rabbits the Right Way
161 | Build a Rabbit Hutch
162 | Raise a Cavy
163 | Kill Small Animals Humanely
164 | Build a Barrel Abattoir
165 | Dress a Rabbit
166 | Create a Conflict-Free Homestead
167 | Don't Forget the Poop

168	Make Goat's-Milk Cheese		196	Build a Bicycle-Powered Generator
169	Avoid Cattle, No Bull!		197	Power Up
170	Make a Canning Kit		198	Brew Coffee Without Power
171	Can in a Water Bath		199	Make Power with Water
172	Learn to Pressure-Can		200	Build a Water Turbine
173	Get a Lift		201	Consider the Biodiesel Switch
174	Yes You Can . . . Meat		202	Know Your Diesels
175	Plant a Canning Garden		203	Make the Conversion to Bio
176	Follow These Golden Rules for Pickling Produce		204	Get Running on French-Fry Oil
			205	Turn the Right Oils into Fuel
177	Jam or Jelly Your Favorite Fruits		206	Be Safe with Home Chemistry
178	Dry Out Your Fruits		207	Get the Supplies
179	Drop Some Acid		208	Learn the Process
			209	Be Biodiesel Smart
	SPOTLIGHT ON: Rick "Hue" Hueston		210	**This Could Happen To You:** Cougar Face-Off
180	Survive the End Times with Hue		211	Avoid Conflict
181	Forage Hue's Top 10 Wild Foods		212	Throw a Power Punch
182	Cook Hue's Squirrel Stew		213	Hit the Spot
			214	Block and Counter
183	Make a Cardboard Box Smoker		215	Choose the Right Knife
184	Smoke Out Your Vegetarians		216	Stand and Deliver
185	Get Fishy		217	Get a Grip
186	Make Jerky		218	Throw a Knife
187	Brew Your Own Alcohol		219	Sharpen Your Blade
188	Brew Mead		220	Don't Get in a Knife Fight
189	Craft an Amber American Ale		221	Make a PVC Bow
190	Make Blackberry Wine		222	Fletch Your Own Arrows
191	Tie 7 Helpful Knots		223	Shoot Your Bow Properly
192	Improvise a Solar Lightbulb		224	**Don't Get Caught Without:** Duct Tape
193	Make Your Own Fuel			
194	Assemble an Oil Lamp		225	Learn Safe Gun Handling
195	Make Candles		226	Stand and Shoot

227 | Avoid Four Common Trigger Mistakes
228 | Drill Home Accuracy
229 | Build Your Own Blowgun
230 | Use What's Close

 **SURVIVAL**

231 | Chart Your Survival Priorities
232 | Assess and Respond to Emergency
233 | Survive Anything
234 | Obey the Rule of Threes
235 | Develop an Attitude
236 | Decide Whether to Stay
237 | Ask for—and Give—Help
238 | Share Your Skills
239 | Plan Your Bug-Out Camp Supplies
240 | Embrace the Plastic
241 | Create Order with Areas
242 | Make Camp Life Easier
243 | Signal to Rescuers
244 | Turn On the Radio
245 | Use a Survival Mirror
246 | **Don't Get Caught Without:** Space Blankets
247 | Understand Major Blackouts
248 | Create Flare Contingencies
249 | Don't Panic After a Pulse
250 | Laugh in the Face of Darkness
251 | Employ People Power
252 | Understand EMP Danger
253 | Protect Electronics with a Faraday Cage
254 | Charge a Cell Phone in a Blackout

255 | Hack Your C-Cell
256 | Be Ready for Storms
257 | Prepare for Hurricanes and Cyclones
258 | Fight Back Against Flooding
259 | Find a Quake-Safe Spot
260 | **This Could Happen To You:** Natural Disaster
261 | Get Ready for a Fall
262 | Stock Up for the Crash
263 | Build a Team
264 | Hail the New Chief
265 | Understand the Real Threat
266 | Choose the Right Leader
267 | Don't Screw It Up
268 | Lead like the Great Ones
269 | Spot a Sociopath
270 | Pick a Compound
271 | Remember the Basic Tenets
272 | Build a Defensive Perimeter
273 | Create Observation Posts
274 | Build a Basement Bunker
275 | Make a Bucket Bathroom
276 | Create Layers of Security
277 | Keep It Breathable
278 | Have Some Comms Handy
279 | Keep It Dry

SPOTLIGHT ON: Kirk Lombard
280 | Catch a Weird Fish
281 | Poke Pole for Eels
282 | Follow Kirk's Foraging Tips

283 | Select Your Trap

284 | Cover Your Scent
285 | Build a Deadfall
286 | Bait Your Trap Correctly
287 | Know Your Neighborhood Animals
288 | Bag a Backyard Buck
289 | Break the Law (If You Must)
290 | Hunt Better with Bait
291 | Catch Live Critters
292 | Tan Your Hides
293 | Use Your Brain
294 | Smoke Tanned Hides
295 | Enjoy Sun-Dried Foods
296 | Dry It in the Dark
297 | Whip Up Some Hardtack
298 | Make Your Own Pemmican
299 | Make a Good Trade
300 | Get Your Balance

SPOTLIGHT ON: R.P. MacWelch
301 | Survive Like Dad
302 | Learn an Art
303 | Develop New Skills

304 | Spark It Up
305 | Make Fire from Rocks
306 | Build a Fire Like a Pro
307 | Use a Fire Plow
308 | Make Charcoal from Firewood
309 | Mix Your Own Gunpowder
310 | Build Your Own Backyard Forge
311 | Forge Your Own Knife
312 | Heat with the Sun
313 | Warm Up Safely

314 | Use Bricks and Stones to Heat Your Home
315 | Consider These Heaters
316 | Master 6 Advanced Knots
317 | **Don't Get Caught Without:** Beer
318 | Multitask Your Meds
319 | Stockpile Essential Meds
320 | Repurpose Street Drugs
321 | Deliver a Baby
322 | Use an EpiPen
323 | Apply a Tourniquet
324 | Don't Try This at Home
325 | Save a Toe (or Finger, or More)
326 | Save an Eye
327 | Don't Spill Your Guts
328 | Open an Airway
329 | **This Could Happen To You:** Airway To Go
330 | Survive a Gunshot Wound
331 | Take Care of an Impaled Victim
332 | Decompress a Chest Wound
333 | Suture a Wound
334 | Survive with Nothing
335 | Know Your Lines of Shelter
336 | Scrounge for Nourishment
337 | Diagnose and Treat Ailments
338 | Keep It Positive

• Closing Statement
• Index
• About the Author/Credits

BE PREPARED.

Such a clear commandment. But like so many imperatives ("Eat your vegetables!"), it's been diluted by repetition, and some people may associate those two words more with merit badges and Boy Scout jamborees than with personal protection.

But that couplet is the purpose of this book, and it's a directive that we hope guides you through our unpredictable, chaotic, and sometimes turbulent world. Whether it's enduring a Category 4 hurricane, protecting yourself and your family from a regime-toppling mob, or simply making it through an extended blackout with your sanity and possessions intact, this book is your ultimate what-if insurance policy.

We show you how to disaster-proof your home, stock a pantry (and why a bottle of vodka should be part of it), bar your front door, make a duct-tape belt, and stash your emergency cash. Learn how to grow a survival garden, should your grocery store be leveled, or build your own bicycle-powered generator, should your lights go out for good.

While those are critical survival techniques, *Prepare for Anything* is also a primer in workaday skills that every well-rounded human should know—whether or not the apocalypse is coming. These include how to throw a knife, start a fire, filter water, make your own jerky (and beer), dress a rabbit, tie down a tarp, and deliver a knockout punch.

Survival instructor Tim MacWelch is your guide and mentor through all these topics. For MacWelch, who operates a wilderness-skills school in Virginia and blogs on disaster preparedness for *Outdoor Life*, survival isn't accidental. It's the result of preparation and knowledge. His favorite skill is fire building, but he's also an expert on emergency shelters, water and food gathering, and backcountry medical skills. We asked him to open his kit and teach us everything we need to know to survive a weekend—or a year.

Want to learn how to make an oil lamp? Read on. How about using a signal mirror? That's here, too, along with the reasons to keep a tin of sardines in your pack. Learn how to shoot a shotgun, build a blowgun, and fletch your own arrows, plus hundreds more skills and perspectives. Plus, if the shit does hit the fan, it's a great read while you wait for the end to arrive. And when it does, the pages burn pretty well.

Be prepared. Because it's much, much better than the alternative.

Andrew McKean
Editor-in-Chief, *Outdoor Life*

ARE YOU READY TO SURVIVE?

It's a simple question, but to answer it correctly, you have to know what you're up against. There's a core set of basic requirements for staying alive: security, shelter, water, medical care, and food. But then there are the extras—things you might need depending on specific scenarios—and they are vast and plentiful. You may need a weapon to survive an attack, medical gear to make it through a traumatic injury, or a respirator to survive a chemical spill. But do you need all of those items? What about everything else? Deciding what you need is a major part of preparing yourself for emergency survival situations. During a passing emergency, issues like shelter, medical care, and water are paramount. But in an extended state of disaster, the pursuit of food, security, communications, and energy could become a struggle.

You want to be prepared for anything, but where to begin?

That's where this book comes in. Within these pages, you'll find the gear, guidance, and plans you need to make it through many different types of emergency scenarios. Along the way, you'll pick up some new skills, gain some perspective on survival, become more self-reliant, and learn from those who have been there and done that. On the surface, this book is about emergency preparedness and disaster survival, but dig a little deeper and you'll find that this book is about self-sufficiency, taking charge of your fate, and maintaining a survivor's attitude.

The skills presented herein will empower you—something sorely needed in today's world. It's easy to feel overwhelmed when you consider all the hardships that could befall us. Pondering the likelihood of EMPs, superstorms, terrorist attacks, and earthquakes can leave a person feeling vulnerable and powerless. But that's not the case—you have the power. You are in control of your reaction to these situations and your preparations for these possibilities. Your preparedness reclaims your strength. This book isn't a list of all the things that can go wrong in the world—it's a list of all the things that you can do right.

You can survive, with some good disaster planning and a little luck. And there's no better time to plan than right now.

Tim MacWelch

1 Understand Situational Awareness

Situational awareness is the combined ability to pay attention to details, process the information you gain, use this information to identify threats, and create plans to handle or avoid these threats. The easiest way to explain this feat of mental multitasking is to imagine the mental state of police officers on duty. They are paying attention to everything around them, especially the things that look like trouble. While their training may not be available to the public, we can all take steps to develop a more alert mental state. And it's well worth your time, as it can be a lifesaving ability.

2 Sharpen Your Strategy

Though situational awareness is more of a mind-set than a skill set, awareness should be practiced often and supported by further studies, the same way you would develop most other skills. You'll never run out of opportunities to practice, either. The concrete jungle and an actual jungle both contain threats to your safety, making situational awareness a mental priority everywhere you go. Enhance your own natural powers of observation by performing these three simple actions.

ELIMINATE DISTRACTIONS Chatting on your cell phone or listening to music through headphones may seem harmless enough, but they are poison to situational awareness. These activities and other distractions are likely to rob you of the attention you should be paying to your surroundings.

LOOK AT PEOPLE Don't make excessive eye contact with strangers (who may perceive your stare as a threat), but check out those around you wherever you go. Try to sum individuals up in one concise phrase (biker dude, soccer mom, business guy, burger flipper, possible criminal), as any of these labels will help you to pay attention to the body language and actions of the people around you.

LOOK AT YOUR SURROUNDINGS Whether you are in the city or in the wild, it makes sense to pay attention to the "lay of the land." Understand where you are, where you are going, and which way to go if you need to backtrack. While you're at it, assess all possible dangers. The dark alleyway of the city and a predator-rich forest in the wilderness can both be dangerous to an unaware person.

3 Know the Steps

BE OBSERVANT	RECOGNIZE ANY THREATS	MAKE A JUDGMENT OR PLAN	ACT ON IT!	DON'T PANIC OR FAIL TO ACT

1 Pay attention to the sights and sounds you notice when you are fully alert and aware.

2 Determine any threats based on observations, experience, and the feeling that "something's not right."

3 Make a decision based on your training, experience, and imagined outcome to the situation.

4 Take control of the situation before it takes control of you.

5 Panic or mental paralysis could be the death of you.

4 Color Code It

Assigning corresponding colors to situational awareness levels helps to classify where you fall—and where you should fall—on the spectrum.

WHITE
You are oblivious. You wouldn't notice if anything dangerous was unfolding around you, nor would you be prepared to react. This can be caused by mental states such as distraction, apathy, and a false sense of security. Physical issues like sleep deprivation, pain, stress, alcohol, and drugs (or any medication) can also take their toll on awareness. This white level of awareness is like being drowsy behind the wheel of your car.

YELLOW
You are aware of your surroundings, calm, and alert. This is how a soldier or someone in law enforcement moves through his or her life. At this level of awareness, you are observant of things close and distant, large and small. You are aware of people, weather, animals, and the layout or terrain of an area. You could react quickly if your situation were to change. This is similar to the level of alertness needed for normal defensive driving on a busy road.

ORANGE
You are aware that there may be a problem. You're starting to process information that causes concern for your safety. At this level, you're processing clues that something is wrong, and you're formulating plans to deal with problems that may arise. This would be an ideal time to move to a safer location or change what you're doing before things get ugly. Consider this alertness level similar to that needed for driving in very bad weather or on an icy road.

RED
You are in trouble. You are aware that you need to fight or flee. The time for debating and assessing is over. Don't succumb to "analysis paralysis," which involves thinking too much and failing to act (see code black). Pick a target or an escape route and move! This level is like your reaction to a car pulling out in front of you when you are traveling at high speed in bad weather. You have a split second to decide whether to hit the car or swerve for the ditch.

BLACK
You are in panic mode. This level is worse than the first level. You may be paralyzed with fear or indecision, or you may be exhibiting panicked behavior (whether or not you're aware of it). This level is where your mind was when you froze behind the wheel on the freezing roadways, hit the other car, and flipped over. You may not even know what just happened or why you're upside down. You're lucky to be alive because you just blacked out!

5 Know What You're Preparing For

Volcanic eruptions, superstorms, tsunamis, tornadoes—this is the world we live in, but different areas are prone to different risk factors. Look up your area's flood history, seismological data, and other geological information, and prioritize the events and crises you most need to prepare for. It's time to take stock of the threats to your area, and take action.

Understand the Crisis

Being prepared for disaster means knowing the possibilities. Sometimes, a full-blown state of emergency is just a more extreme version of the minor inconveniences you've faced once (or many times) before.

LEVEL 1	LEVEL 2	LEVEL 3	LEVEL 4
Power outage	Rolling brownouts	Weeklong blackout	Grid failure
Aftershocks	Minor quakes	Major quakes	The Big One
Volcanic ash interferes with air travel	Heat and ash cause health issues	Evacuations/ local destruction of cities	Megavolcanic eruption

Learn Your Task

Preparation is a significant part of surviving unforeseen emergencies. You can't predict the future, but you can feel confident in your ability to face it. Some preppers may indeed be readying themselves for the end of the world; most are simply taking steps to reduce their dependency on infrastructures that won't last forever.

No matter where you live, you should know what you can do in emergency situations and how you can arm yourself—mentally and physically—for disaster. Survival and emergency-preparedness skills will assist in any situation from power failures and the breakdown of public services to devastating hurricanes and government collapse.

Get Familiar with the Scope

With all these potential disasters, you may be wondering where to start. Let's look at the reach of each type of crisis.

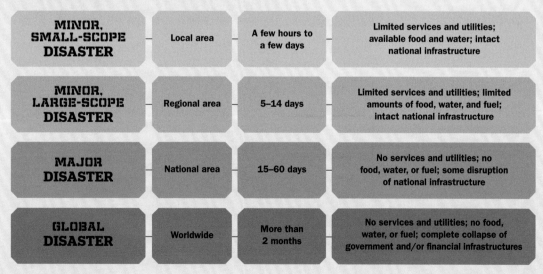

MINOR, SMALL-SCOPE DISASTER	Local area	A few hours to a few days	Limited services and utilities; available food and water; intact national infrastructure
MINOR, LARGE-SCOPE DISASTER	Regional area	5–14 days	Limited services and utilities; limited amounts of food, water, and fuel; intact national infrastructure
MAJOR DISASTER	National area	15–60 days	No services and utilities; no food, water, or fuel; some disruption of national infrastructure
GLOBAL DISASTER	Worldwide	More than 2 months	No services and utilities; no food, water, or fuel; complete collapse of government and/or financial infrastructures

Create Your Family Emergency Plan

In the event of an emergency, a well-thought-out family emergency plan can eliminate stress, limit confusion, and save a great deal of wasted time. Instead of wondering what to do or when to do it, you can put your emergency plan to work right away, bringing sanity and safety to dangerous situations.

Your plan should include the following.

- ☐ Maintaining up-to-date contact information cards or sheets for each family member
- ☐ Communication strategies to keep in touch, with options in case the phones are out
- ☐ Ways to assist or care for family who have mobility or medical issues, communication difficulties, or special needs
- ☐ The maintenance, inspection, and rotation of emergency supplies, such as nonperishable food, water, first aid, lighting, and communication equipment
- ☐ The maintenance of specialized supplies for any infants, young children, or elderly members of your family
- ☐ A plan and supplies for the care of pets and livestock
- ☐ The knowledge and tools to shut off your utilities
- ☐ Self-sufficiency skills and supplies, should you have to shelter in place without utilities
- ☐ Evacuation plans and routes, should you have to leave your home
- ☐ Learning and practicing safety skills, such as first aid, CPR, and fire prevention

10 Conduct Drills

Mark some dates on your calendar to perform emergency drills with your family. They may not want to participate, but find a way to get them involved nevertheless. Here are some emergency drills that can keep a family's skills sharp.

DISTANT CONTACT Have each family member contact a friend or family member who lives outside your area—without using a phone (cell or landline). This could be done through e-mail, social media, satellite phone, ham radio, or even a carrier pigeon. Get creative!

SUPPLY SHAKEDOWN Pull out all of your emergency supplies, take inventory, check expiration dates, use up older items, replace them with new supplies, and make sure you end up with a few more items than you started with.

FIRE DRILL For starters, perform a classic fire drill, evacuating the home at an unexpected time. Make sure you have a planned meeting spot outside the home, and have everyone low-crawl out of the house. For more practiced families, eliminate the easy exits and add some obstacles. Also, round out the exercise with some stop, drop, and roll each time you have a fire drill.

EVAC Take the fire drill exercise one step further with a mock evacuation. Tell everyone that they have 2 minutes to grab some clothes and supplies and get to the family vehicle.

GEAR

If you don't think that tools and supplies are important, just try going without them. Gear makes almost every task easier, and when you're staring down the barrel of a life-or-death scenario, easier is always better.

Imagine yourself in a survival situation without any gear. Perhaps you went for a hike with nothing in your pockets or pack. People do it all the time and rarely face tragedy. But you're tempting fate by heading off without any emergency supplies—and if we add an injury or wrong turn to this situation, your simple walk in the woods may be the last trip you ever take. Now consider this scenario with a little survival gear in hand—a whistle to call for help, or a space blanket to stave off hypothermia. Maybe all you have is a lighter—well, then you have warmth and a way to signal distress. A little bit of gear can make the difference between getting home in one piece or never getting home at all.

And survival is not always about the wilderness. Just ask the survivors of Katrina, Fukushima, or Chernobyl. Life-ending events can happen anywhere, and you'll need the right resources to have the best chances of enduring both natural and man-made disasters.

In our first chapter, we are going to look at the value and benefits of everyday items as well as some specialized survival equipment. Don't look at these items as a list of goodies that you hope to someday have; treat the chapter like a shopping list, and get the items relevant to your situation now! Your first acquisitions should be for the most pressing dangers and the survival situations you anticipate in your area. Then add to your supplies by preparing for less-likely situations as well.

Mid-crisis is not the time to pick up some gas jugs, start pricing generators, or consider which types of weapons would be most effective against a mugger. The point of supplies is to have them before you need them. We've all heard the adage, "It's better to have it and not need it than to need it and not have it." Make that your mantra next time you're at the store, prioritize your needs, and get prepared.

11 Pack a BOB for Any Situation

A BOB (bug-out bag) is a collection of goods that you would need to survive if you had to flee your home with no guarantee of shelter, food, or water during an emergency. Think of the BOB as your survival insurance policy for any disaster or mayhem. There may not be one perfect, universally agreed-upon set of equipment, but with a good core set of items (similar to those used in backpacking) you can put together a BOB suited for a wide variety of situations. Most people use either a backpack or a duffle bag as a container for their goods, which should include basic survival essentials and a few irreplaceable items. Fill up your BOB with a minimum of the following things, with most items sealed in zip-top bags to prevent damage:

- Shelter items like a small tent and sleeping bag, or a tarp and blanket
- A couple quarts (or liters) of drinking water, and purification equipment to disinfect more water
- High-calorie, no-cook foods like protein bars, peanut butter, trail mix, etc.
- First-aid, sanitation, and hygiene supplies
- Several fire-starting devices
- A small pot for boiling water or cooking
- A few basic tools like a knife, duct tape, rope, etc.
- Extra clothes appropriate for the season
- Flashlight with extra batteries
- Cash
- A digital backup of all your important documents and artifacts. This could be a thumb drive with your bank info, insurance documents, wills, and family photos and videos

Keep your main BOB safe and ready to go in a secure location, with modified versions in your car and office. It's also a good idea for you to have "everyday carry" (EDC) items—survival essentials that you can carry in your pocket or purse. Here's a breakdown for these different types of kits.

	HOME/CAR	OFFICE	EDC
High-calorie, no-cook foods	○	○	
Bottled water	○	○	
Tent or tarp	○		
Sleeping bag	○		
Lighter or fire-starting gear	○		○
Change of rugged clothing	○	○	
Flashlight & extra batteries	○	○	○
Pocket knife	○	○	○
Can opener	○		
Heavy cord	○		
Battery-operated radio	○		
Battery-op or solar/crank cell-phone charger	○		
First aid kit	○		
Sanitation items	○		
Meds, eyeglasses, hearing aid batteries, etc.	○		
Snare wire	○		
Signal mirror	○		○
Whistle	○	○	○
Change of shoes & socks	○	○	
Small pen & paper	○		
Duct tape	○		
Razor blades	○		
Water filter	○		
Water purification tablets	○		
Adhesive bandages	○	○	
Disinfectant wipes	○		
Fishing kit	○		
Bouillon cubes	○		
Tinfoil	○		
Small shovel	○		
Snow chains or a sand bag	○		
Car-safety items including jumper cables, flares, reflective sign, tow strap, ice scraper	○		

12 Stock a Home Survival Kit

One of the first steps toward being prepared for anything is having a multipurpose, day- or week-appropriate survival kit stocked and ready in your home. It's always a good idea to have certain essentials at hand whenever possible—you never know just where you'll be when disaster strikes.

Here are a few essentials that will help meet your needs (and those of your family) in a hunker-down scenario. Store the kit somewhere easy to access, and make sure everyone knows where to find it.

- [ ] **A three-day supply of nonperishable food per person**
- [ ] **Small camping stove**
- [ ] **Kitchen tools, including a can opener**
- [ ] **A three-day supply of water—that's 1 gallon (3.75 l) per person, per day**
- [ ] **Water-purification tablets**
- [ ] **Bleach (a mild disinfectant with water, or purifier in the right amounts—see item 46)**
- [ ] **Portable, battery-powered radio/TV and extra batteries**
- [ ] **Flashlight and extra batteries**
- [ ] **Battery-operated, hand-cranked, or solar-powered cell-phone charger**

13 Pack Something Weird

Opinions about survival gear and bug-out bag (BOB) contents (see item 11) are as varied as political views these days. Everybody has his or her own version of the right and wrong stuff to carry.

But what about the weird stuff—those bizarre items that you might not think to carry? Most people don't spend much time on the unusual things that could be (or should be) in your survival kits and BOBs. Here are my top five "under the radar" essentials:

CONCENTRATED ENERGY DRINK If you are a caffeine addict, then these little bottles of nectar will go down smoother than spinach in Popeye's throat when coffee isn't an option. When you're running out of steam, knock back an energy drink and keep plugging away. It also helps to stave off caffeine-withdrawal headaches.

CIGARETTES Even if you don't smoke, think of all the smokers out there who would instantly become your

best friend if you had spare smokes to hand out. They also make for good, lightweight tinder.

VODKA One of those little airline-size bottles can serve as a wee nip to swallow for courage or as a disinfectant used with your medical gear. For more ways vodka can help out in a pinch, see item 57.

CANDY Vodka won't solve everything. Keep some hard candy in your survival pack. Sugar is great short-term fuel, and a few sweets can lift the morale of both grown-ups and kids in a group.

NOTEPAD AND PENCIL. Communicate or signal for help. Keep a journal. Take handy notes for your survival situation. Use the paper as tinder. The list goes on.

14 Make a Fire Kit

Fire building is one of those skills that can make or break you in a survival situation. With so much riding on your ability to produce flame, it makes a lot of sense to plan for your own success by building a dedicated fire-starting kit. It's easy and fun to do, and you probably already have all the stuff lying around the house.

The three basic parts of this kit are the container, the heat/ignition sources, and the fuels. Note that the last two are plural—you're going to want some extra insurance in the form of multiple fire-starting implements and several fuels.

CONTAINER The container can be anything that's watertight and easily transported. This can range from a small Pelican case or similar waterproof box to a small, wide-mouth plastic bottle or even a zip-top freezer bag.

IGNITION At a minimum, your kit should include a lighter, a box of matches, and a spark rod. The lighter is the best of the bunch for most fire-building situations. The open flame can be used to dry out damp tinder and kindling, catching it ablaze without much trouble. There really isn't a situation in which matches are a better ignition source than a lighter, but I like the matchbox for redundancy and for the fact that those matchsticks can double as kindling. Lastly, the spark rod will serve as an indestructible backup ignition source. It won't light the variety of materials that matches and lighters will, but it will work when the lighter and matches have failed.

FUEL Dry cotton balls, dryer lint, or gauze can take the role of tinder (your initial fuel for fire). I also like a candle nub and a tube of petroleum jelly.

The candle can be lit and used as a fire starter by itself, or the wax can be dripped onto the tinder or kindling for a wet-weather fire boost. The petroleum jelly can be smeared into the cotton balls to make long-burning fire starters, plus the jelly is helpful for a number of first-aid and survival chores.

You could pre-assemble the petroleum jelly cotton balls, but the summertime heat can cause the jelly to melt and seep through all but the most watertight containers. Melted jelly has ruined enough boxes of matches for me that I now carry the tightly sealed tube and the cotton balls separately.

15 Waterproof Your Matches

You can buy waterproof matches, but they're going to cost you—and they're not the kind of thing you want to waste if you need to toast a marshmallow and can't find the regular matches. But the good news is that you can turn everyday matches into waterproof ones with a few easy techniques.

TURPENTINE The easiest and most foolproof way to waterproof matches is with turpentine. Soak them for 5 minutes in enough fluid to cover them, then put them on newspaper to dry for 30 minutes. You'll have a set of waterproofs that will last 3–6 months.

NAIL POLISH If you or your loved ones happen to have some clear nail polish lying around, dip the head of the match and part of the stick into the polish. Let dry on the end of a counter so the head hangs off and won't stick to anything.

CANDLE WAX Let a candle burn until a small pool of wax forms around the wick. Blow it out, and dip the head of your match in the melted wax until the wax is about 1/3 inch (8.5 mm) of the way up the matchstick. Remove the match instantly and blow on it to cool the wax, or it will soak too deeply.

16 Be Fire Smart

Residential fires are a far greater danger than, say, home invasions, and more likely as well. Have you thought about preventing and fighting fires in your home? Here are some things to consider.

GET ARRESTED If you have a fireplace, be sure you've got a spark arrester installed. In addition, inspect your chimney regularly, and keep it clean—chimney fires are common in older homes.

BE READY Kitchens are typically where home fires begin. Keep a fire extinguisher in plain sight, so that anyone can use it in the event of a fire. It's also wise to keep a fire extinguisher in a secondary location—perhaps one that would be fire-prone as well, such as a room with a fireplace or a home workshop.

GEAR UP Smoke hoods can also be a smart investment. These breathing filters fit over your whole head and protect your lungs from dangerous smoke. Keep one at the bedside of each family member, and practice using them so that you'll be ready to escape quickly and safely if they're ever needed.

SCREEN IT If you live in forest fire country (or anywhere, really—can't be too careful), cover any external vents with a fine metal screen to keep sparks from an external fire from entering your home.

17 Know Your Fire Types

If you have a fire in your home or garage, you'll obviously want it put out pronto. But not all fires are created equal, and so there are a variety of fire extinguishers to choose from. Be sure you get the right one for the "right" fire. Various extinguishers often have a rating for the size of the fire (based on the extinguisher's size and contents), and its type, denoted by a colored geometric symbol.

 CLASS A Marked with a green triangle, these extinguishers are for fires fueled by ordinary flammable materials: wood, paper, and some plastics.

 CLASS B Extinguishers for this class, involving combustible liquids like gasoline or oil, and some gases (like acetylene or butane), bear a red square symbol.

 CLASS C Electrical equipment, wiring, outlets, and appliances are the source of this class of fire. A blue circle is found on Class C fire extinguishers.

CLASS D Usually found in chemical laboratories or machine shops where combustible metals are used (like magnesium and sodium), this type of extinguisher is marked with a yellow star.

 CLASS K You'll find a black hexagon on fire extinguishers for this type of fire, which includes kitchen fires that involve cooking oils or fats.

Class A extinguishers just use water—they won't stop some fires and may make them worse. Combined B/C-class extinguishers use carbon dioxide or a dry chemical powder. You can also find multipurpose foam or dry chemical extinguishers for class A, B, and C fires. Class D fires require special dry agents, and class K fires use dry powders or CO_2. Another, rare fire type is class E, involving radioactive materials, which should be handled by skilled hazmat personnel.

19 Stay on Comm

Being able to call for help in an emergency situation can mean the difference between life and death. So many of us rely on our cell phones for everything these days, but you might want to consider keeping that landline. When mobile service goes out, the landlines may well still function. If you do go this route, be sure to have a corded phone—that cordless will lose power quickly and be as useless as your cell.

You'll also want to get a battery-powered cell phone charger (and be sure you have a car charger in every vehicle). A solar phone charger is a nice option, but of course you'll need sunshine in order to use it.

18 Check Home Safety Basics

When we think about home safety, it's easy to jump into the really intense stuff—panic rooms, home defense, moats and alligators (well, maybe not the last one). While it's important to consider strategies for serious disasters or social upheavals, assessment of your home's safety and security should start with the basics. Carbon monoxide monitors may not be very exciting in the moment, but "essential" and

"exciting" aren't always the same thing.

In other words, it's important to take a good hard look at the safety of your home, even if you're not preparing for a disaster. Fire, injury, and other emergencies can happen at any time. While we cannot control many of the things that happen in our lives, we can at least take control to make our residence a safer place to live.

20 Know Your Region

Wherever you live, you probably think that you know what you need to worry about. But do you really? Especially if you're a recent arrival, it makes sense to do some research. For instance, if you live in California, you know to be well prepared for earthquakes. But did you know that the state has also been hit by tsunamis? Or that earthquakes often lead to fires? Similarly, Missouri residents know to prep for tornadoes—but many may not know that their state has also experienced powerful earthquakes in the past. Luckily, there is a lot of overlap in the supplies and survival priorities you'd need to make it through most natural and manmade disasters. In preparing for one potential disaster, you end up preparing for most scenarios.

21 Stock the Right Supplies

An easy way to think of life after a disaster is to imagine living in the 1800s. You have some comforts, but most tasks are accomplished with a lot more work than in modern times. Assuming you didn't have to abandon your home in a disaster, you'd only need the basics for that home to remain livable. You still have your clothes, bedding, and pots and pans, though the utilities could be out for a while.

WATER Since water may be unavailable or possibly contaminated after a disaster, keeping a supply of safe, drinkable water is key to survival. A few factory-sealed water cooler jugs will stay safe for a year or more, ready to drink if needed. One 5-gallon (20-l) jug per family member is a good start. Also, plan to resupply with a water filter or disinfection tablets.

FOOD You'll need some no-cook or easy-to-cook food. Keep at least a week's supply of nonperishable food per family member, and throw in a manual can opener. Have a way to cook, like a camping stove with abundant fuel, if you have a safe place to operate it; a hot meal can be morale-boosting and easier to digest.

EXTRAS What else? Check this handy checklist. Stash everything except the water in a big plastic bin, so you can transport it if you have to evacuate your home.

- ☐ Multiple flashlights
- ☐ Extra batteries
- ☐ Battery-powered or hand-cranked radio that has NOAA Weather bands
- ☐ Utility shut-off wrench, which can turn off gas and water, if needed

Last, don't forget things like a favorite treat, good book, or inspirational item to help keep your spirits up.

22 Disaster-Proof Your Home

Okay, full disclosure. You can't disaster-proof your home, at least not against *every* disaster, no matter how drastic. That said, there's a lot you can do to ensure that it comes through relatively unscathed. And a lot of this is basic stuff you really should be doing anyway.

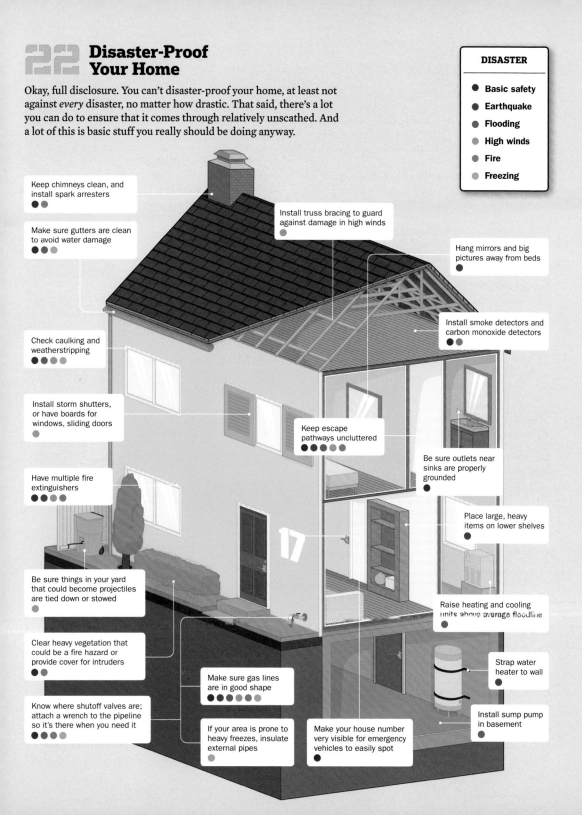

DISASTER

- ● Basic safety
- ● Earthquake
- ● Flooding
- ○ High winds
- ● Fire
- ● Freezing

Keep chimneys clean, and install spark arresters ●●

Make sure gutters are clean to avoid water damage ●●●

Install truss bracing to guard against damage in high winds ●

Hang mirrors and big pictures away from beds ●

Check caulking and weatherstripping ●●●●

Install smoke detectors and carbon monoxide detectors ●●

Install storm shutters, or have boards for windows, sliding doors ●

Keep escape pathways uncluttered ●●●●●

Be sure outlets near sinks are properly grounded ●

Have multiple fire extinguishers ●●●●

Place large, heavy items on lower shelves ●

Be sure things in your yard that could become projectiles are tied down or stowed ●

Raise heating and cooling units above average floodline ●

Clear heavy vegetation that could be a fire hazard or provide cover for intruders ●●

Strap water heater to wall ●

Know where shutoff valves are; attach a wrench to the pipeline so it's there when you need it ●●●●

Make sure gas lines are in good shape ●●●●●●

If your area is prone to heavy freezes, insulate external pipes ●

Make your house number very visible for emergency vehicles to easily spot ●

Install sump pump in basement ●

Fool the Bad Guys

It's a law-enforcement truism that criminals look for easy targets. If your home appears badly defended, you're making it that much more likely that something might happen. A few simple steps can make a world of difference in your home and family's safety.

BEWARE OF DOG Even if you don't have a dog, or your dog is pocket-size, get a large dog bowl and large chew bone to leave by your back door or other ground-level entrances. Write a thief-frightening name on the dish, such as Killer, Diablo, or something else that implies great size and bad temperament. Just the idea of an "attack" dog will change many burglars' minds.

INSTALL SENSORS Lights or even water sprayers that are motion-sensitive can surprise both burglars and pests who might wander through your property at night. These are typically affordable and easily installed, but they won't help if the power is out.

HIDE THE KEY Don't just slip a spare key under your front doormat. Hide the key in a spot where no one would ever look for it, far away from the door. Loose rocks and bricks, hard flower pots and lawn gnomes can also be used as window-breaking "keys" to gain entrance. Reconsider landscaping and decoration, and get rid of things that looters could use to break windows or doorknobs.

24 Reinforce Your Home

Nothing is going to stop a Mad Max–style gang of marauders from tearing their way into your home during the apocalypse, but you can toughen up your home against common thieves and make it harder for them to gain entry.

LOCK THE DOORS Solid-core doors and beefy deadbolts are a great way to discourage break-ins. Yes, these can be pricey, but they should add value to your dwelling and a little more peace of mind to your night's sleep. Sliding-glass doors are extremely vulnerable; be sure they have a locking steel pin to keep them from being forced open, or go low-tech with a length of dowel or 2x4 that you can place in the door's tracks to keep it from being forced open by intruders.

BE WINDOW SMART If any of your external doors has a glass pane in it, make sure it's made of shatterproof plastic or safety glass. Be sure that all of your windows lock (however, also be sure they're easy to unlock from the interior, for fire safety).

GET THE REAL DEAL Get a home security service. It's hard to beat an actual alarm service and monitoring. Modern services even include fire detection, carbon monoxide monitoring, and other features. If the cost is deterring you, sit down and write down what your life is worth. It should be worth more than what the alarm service costs.

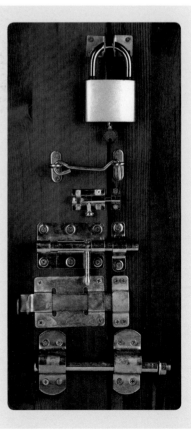

25 Don't Forget the Garage

Your garage door is a particular point of weakness, since most of them have rather flimsy construction. If you have a security system, be sure it covers the garage (you'd be surprised how many people forget this step).

If you have an automatic garage-door opener, you can reprogram it to be different than factory settings. Contact the manufacturer for details—it's usually very simple and adds an extra layer of security.

If you're going out of town (or want to be extra secure overnight, or when home alone), you should consider installing a slide-bar latch or a padlock to keep the door from being manually rolled up. You can also cut a piece of wood to fit snugly into the door's track, and clamp it in place, preventing it from rolling up. Disable the opener beforehand, so that if you forget and try to open it, you won't damage the door.

26 Bar the Door for Real

Barring your front door (if it's inward-facing) may seem a little medieval or excessive, but if you live in a crime-prone neighborhood, or are concerned about home invasion before, during, or after a major disaster, they're worth considering. You can buy a commercial prefab kit, but it's not that hard to install some sturdy brackets into the studs on each side of the door frame (go for the top, middle, and bottom just to be safe), and keep three sturdy 2x4s at the ready for when you need to hole up securely.

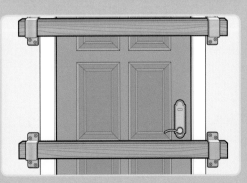

27 Shop Smart

Get 10 different survival experts together and you'll hear at least 10 different ideas to fill the perfect survival pantry. Factors include what emergency you're preparing for (earthquake? economic crash? the end times?), how many folks you need to feed, and what you like. Your postapocalyptic pantry shouldn't be all beer and cheese puffs (although the latter are great fire starters), nor do you want to spend weeks, months, or years gnawing on hardtack and tofu jerky. A good pantry plan balances out storability, nutrition, and taste. The following pages have a few checklists to get you started.

You'll probably want to make your first trip to one of the big warehouse stores, since they tend to stock large bulk packages and have great prices. However, selection can be spotty. So, in order to fill in the gaps, look online and in specialty stores for additional items to round out your supplies.

A lot of people get superexcited about prepping and feel like they need to stock up on everything immediately. It makes more sense to build your stash a bit at a time, being sure to get what you really want and need, rather than what's on sale this week at the MegaloMart.

28 Start with the Basics

It's debatable what's absolutely essential for your survival pantry, and what's a "nice to have," or even a "you stocked up on what?" Here are some pretty inarguable staples everyone should at least consider.

SALT It makes your food taste better, helps you preserve meats, and lasts pretty much forever. Almost all salt sold commercially is iodized—but check just to be sure. You need that iodine for thyroid health.

BAKING POWDER This pantry essential is used in cooking, but it's also good for cleaning, deodorizing, or other household chores.

FATS & OILS Tubs of solid vegetable shortening have fairly long shelf lives. Olive oil is healthy and versatile but tends to go bad more quickly, so buy it in smaller bottles and open as needed. Coconut oil is a surprising favorite (see item 37).

SUGAR & OTHER SWEETS White sugar can be stored for a very long period if packaged right (see item 36). Honey and molasses are also good to have on hand for cooking and for livening up oatmeal and the like.

BEANS Sure, beans and rice are practically a prepper cliché, but most clichés exist for a reason. Dried, beans can last for up to 30 years, they're full of nutrients, and when cooked right, they're really pretty tasty.

RICE Like beans, rice is one of those go-to staples that has kept large portions of this planet's population alive through good times and bad. Combine with beans to boost nutrients.

VITAMINS No matter how well your pantry is stocked, you may not get the variety that would be ideal in your diet. Supplement with a good multipurpose vitamin and mineral pill just to be sure.

CANNED GOODS Stock up on a good selection of fruits and vegetables—choose whatever you and your family like best, but be sure to get a variety for extra nutrition and to prevent boredom if you're eating out of your stockpiles for a while.

COFFEE AND/OR TEA Some people might class these beverages under luxuries, not essentials, but those people have never seen an addict at 6 a.m. without caffeine. Even if you're not a giant fan of coffee, it can be a fantastic trade good, so you should stock at least a few cans just in case.

DRIED FRUIT A great way to store fruit for the long-term, and a fantastic source of concentrated nutrition. A handful of raisins can sweeten your morning cereal, and some dried apricots make a nice portable source of energy. Buy them in bulk or make your own (see item 178 for instructions).

29 Power Up with Protein

Protein is absolutely essential to your everyday health, and many of us already eat less than we should . . . even without the additional stress of trying to survive heavy weather or other challenges. Here are some key protein sources to keep on hand.

HARD CHEESE In Europe, people stash cheeses for months or even years inside cool, dark caves. The secret? A good coating of wax. It's not easy to find hard, waxed cheeses in the United States, but they are available, and the little search to find a wax-clad wheel of Parmesan will be worth it in 10 years when you grate it on your postapocalyptic pasta.

JERKY Dried meat or fish is close to 100 percent protein, and it lasts a long, long time (Native Americans and other cultures made jerky for long-term use and for easier transport). Buy all-natural products that have fewer additives—the same stuff that keeps it "moist" also makes it spoil more quickly. You can also make your own (see item 186).

CANNED & DRIED FISH Stock your pantry with canned tuna and salmon, as well as surprisingly versatile sardines (see item 105). All fish are a great source of omega-3 fatty acids, and any fish that has tiny, edible bones, such as kippers, also provides a good dose of calcium.

WHEY PROTEIN Protein powder isn't just for gym rats! It has a long shelf life and a very high protein content—a small scoop can have as much protein as a whole steak. Stir into water or milk for a high-protein, on-the-go meal replacement.

NUTS & NUT BUTTERS Nuts can go bad relatively quickly, but they're a good source of protein, healthy fats, and calories, so it makes sense to have some on hand. Buy peanut butter in smaller jars so you only have to open and use as needed.

DEHYDRATED MILK It's nutritious and long-lasting when nitrogen-packaged, and can be used in cooking or to add to that coffee you hoarded. You did remember to hoard the coffee, didn't you?

30 Go Carb Crazy

The modern fear of carbs is just that . . . modern. For most of history, humans have relied on starchy foods for energy, comfort, and nutrients. And the All Grapefruit Supermodel Diet has no place in a disaster situation.

WHOLE-WHEAT FLOUR Whole-grain flour does spoil more quickly than the white stuff, but it also has a lot more nutrients. Store it carefully.

DRIED CORN This American Indian staple has a very long shelf life and can be ground up to make grits, polenta, and cornbread. Or if you want to get really old-school, look into making masa harina (or just buy some premade for your pantry). This corn flour processed with lime is used to make nutritious corn tortillas.

OATMEAL Buy the whole, steel-cut oats and you have a versatile staple that can be cooked up for breakfast or used in baking to add nutrients and fiber.

CRACKERS You don't get a lot of nutrition from crackers, but they have a long shelf life, are easy to eat, and can be a good snack for kids (or grown-ups!) who need some sense of normalcy in a tough situation. Never underestimate the calming power of peanut butter and saltines!

PASTA & NOODLES Dried pasta lasts virtually forever and, if you buy the fortified kind, can be a source of some vitamins as well. Ramen noodles aren't terribly good for you, but they're easy to cook and can be a nice comfort food.

31 Stash Some Little Luxuries

Man (and woman and especially child) doth not live by whey powder and canned tomatoes alone. If you're going to be eating from your pantry for more than a few days, you really want to be sure it will provide variety and enjoyment as well as sheer nutrition. Even Soylent Green tastes better with a little horseradish.

HERBS & SPICES A dash of hot sauce or a sprinkling of oregano can make a bland survival dish into a real meal. Grow fresh herbs and chile peppers in your kitchen garden (see item 137), and stock your pantry with some versatile basics. Tabasco and soy sauces last virtually forever, cinnamon and ginger spice up desserts and tea, and spice blends ("Italian seasoning," "Chinese five-spice powder," etc.) make cooking easy.

CONDIMENTS Most condiments spoil pretty quickly, so buy them in smaller-size bottles, and open as needed. Flavored vinegars have a very long shelf life and can liven up all kinds of dishes.

SWEETS Bags of chocolate chips and bars of high-quality chocolate last well if stored in a cool place. Cocoa powder and chocolate syrup are also good treats in tough times.

PERSONAL FAVORITES While making your bulk purchases of those essential canned tomatoes, corn, beans, and peaches, throw in some quirky indulgences that will brighten your day even if the power's out and the water's rising. That might be fancy stuffed olives in a jar, hearts of palm, pumpkin pie filling, or whatever else might lift your spirits after a week or two of oatmeal and bean soup.

32 Pack It in PETE

For long-term storage of dry goods, consider using bottles made of PETE (polyethylene terephthalate) plastic. Many standard bottles out there are made of PETE (check for these letters under the recycling symbol), but you want to buy fresh ones, not reuse old food or drink packaging. A lot of plastic is too flimsy or porous to moisture, oxygen, and pests, but PETE, when used in combination with oxygen-absorbing packets, does the job. Only use this kind of packaging for dry foods—moist foods must be handled much more carefully to avoid the danger of botulism (see item 33 for more information). Bottles should be no bigger than 1 gallon (4 l) for optimal effectiveness.

STEP 1 Test your bottle's seal by closing it tightly, placing it under water, and pressing on the lid or cap. If any bubbles escape, that means the seal is faulty;

don't use it for long-term storage.

STEP 2 Place an oxygen absorber (a packet of iron powder that helps keep food fresh, available at home storage stores or online) in the bottle.

STEP 3 Fill your bottle with dry goods (wheat, corn, dry beans, etc.).

STEP 4 Wipe the bottle's top sealing edge clean with a dry cloth, and screw on the lid tightly.

STEP 5 Store the sealed bottle in a cool, dry location away from direct light. If you use a bottle's contents, add a new oxygen absorber when you refill it.

33 Plan for the Long Haul

Certain foods, if properly stored, can last up to 30 years or more in your pantry. Remember, do not try these long-term storage methods with even very slightly moist foods, to avoid the risk of botulism.

STORE FOR UP TO 30 YEARS IN PETE BOTTLES

Wheat • White rice • Dried corn • White sugar • Pinto beans • Rolled oats • Dry pasta • Potato flakes • Nonfat powdered milk

NOT SUITABLE FOR LONG-TERM STORAGE

Pearled barley • Jerky • Nuts • Dried eggs • Brown rice • Whole-wheat flour • Milled grain • Brown sugar • Granola

Not sure if a foodstuff is dry enough? Try this test. Place it on a piece of paper and whack it with a hammer. If it shatters, it's dry. If it squishes, it definitely isn't. And if it breaks but leaves a little spot of water or oil, it's still too moist. Err on the side of safety—your family's life is literally on the line.

35 Count Your Calories

We're accustomed to reading food labels to make sure they don't have too many calories, too much fat, or too many carbs. In a short-term emergency, you turn this wisdom on its head. Your body needs fuel, and fat and sugar are the fastest ways to fuel up. Your BOB and short-term food stashes should include things like protein bars, MREs, peanut butter, jelly, crackers, and other calorie-dense, easy-to-eat items. That doesn't mean your best survival foods are pork rinds and soda pop—you should strive for some nutritional value, which is why nutrition bars are a good, reasonably priced staple.

34 Don't Forget FIFO

A basic rule of any food pantry is "First In, First Out." What that means: Keep track of the expiration dates on items, and swap them out as they approach culinary old age. That bagged rice is good for a year? After 11 months, replace it with a new bag and enjoy a nice jambalaya. You should never have to throw anything away, just keep using ingredients and replacing them as needed. That way, if and when disaster does strike, dinner's not going to be expired okra served over bug-infested rice.

36 Store Food Right

How you store your food has a great bearing on its longevity. Anyone storing more than a week's worth of food in his or her home should consider these points:

KEEP COOL (AND DRY) Find a cool place to prevent food loss from heat. A dry basement is ideal, but a closet can also work. Metal cans with food-safe desiccant packs are a great way to save food from moisture, light, insects, and rodents. Food-grade buckets are pretty handy, and oxygen-absorbing packets can also extend the life of stored food.

LIGHTS OFF This part is easy; most containers are lightproof. But if you do end up with a stock of food in clear jars or plastic containers, keep the storage area dark to prevent light from reacting with the food.

BUG OUT Rodents and bugs can play havoc in your food. Metal canisters or glass jars can keep them out.

KEEP TIME Depending on the food item and type, it could be nitrogen-packed, freeze-dried, or in a vacuum-sealed package for best shelf life. Otherwise, go with canned food and rotate your stock often. Put the new cans in the back, and use the older cans first.

BE CREATIVE Stash your goods in basements, closets, or garages, or create storage spaces under furniture.

FREEZE SMART Dry goods can stay frozen indefinitely, but not wet-packed foods. Avoid breaking or exploding containers by keeping your stuff from freezing.

BE STRONG Make sure any shelving is sturdy; your jars of food won't help anybody when they have smashed everywhere due to a flimsy shelf or a cheap, collapsed bookcase. Don't keep your food where it can be easily stolen. And in earthquake-prone areas, keep the food in bins on the ground.

37 Go Cuckoo for Coconut

Coconut water seems to be the trendy beverage of the moment. Thing is—for once, those hipsters may be onto something. Coconuts are amazingly healthy and versatile, and they have a special place in your pantry (and medical kit!).

OIL One problem with storing oils in a long-term survival pantry is that most oils go bad really fast, especially in the heat. Coconut oil lasts for up to two years without going rancid and, since it's solid at room temperature, it doesn't need to be refrigerated. That all sound good? Well not only can you cook with it, it's a great skin moisturizer and

has been touted as a topical cure for pinkeye and even for head lice.

WATER Coconut water is high in electrolytes and great for hydration. Store single-serving cans or pouches for a quick, refreshing treat after exertion in the hot sun. As a bonus, this will help you preserve your water stores for other purposes.

MILK Coconut milk is rich in taste and calories, and a delicious addition to rice, stews, and soups. Use it instead of water to boil your rice and not only will it taste better, it will also cook more quickly.

38 Sleep On It

If your pantry is literally overflowing with emergency supplies, congratulations! You're a prepping superstar. That said, you might want to take some pressure off those groaning shelves (and free up space for your everyday groceries) with this crafty storage system. As a bonus, it keeps your stash hidden from intruders.

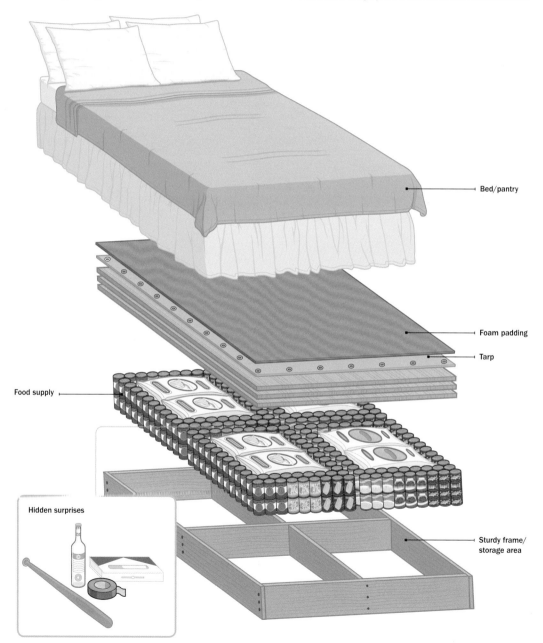

Bed/pantry

Foam padding

Tarp

Food supply

Hidden surprises

Sturdy frame/ storage area

39 Figure Out How Much Water You'll Need

Survival guides will tell you to store enough water for a week or more, but how do you know what that means? Look at the figures below, then multiply the daily numbers by 14 for adults, children, elderly, infants, and the sick or wounded to calculate your family's water storage requirements for a two-week emergency.

ACTIVITY LEVEL ▶	BARE BONES	SOME ACTIVITY	DRY CLIMATE OR VERY ACTIVE	DRY CLIMATE AND VERY ACTIVE
ILL, BURNED, OR WOUNDED ADULT	2 gal (8 l)	3 gal (11 l)	4 gal (15 l)	5 gal (19 l)
AVERAGE ADULT	1 gal (4 l)	1.5 gal (6 l)	2 gal (8 l)	3 gal (11 l)
CHILDREN & ELDERLY	.75 gal (3 l)	1 gal (4 l)	2 gal (8 l)	2 gal (8 l)
INFANTS	.5 gal (2 l)	1 gal (4 l)	1.5 gal (6 l)	2 gal (8 l)

40 Be Chemical Safe

You may remember the old ad that reminded us that without chemicals, life would be impossible. That's true. But it's also true that if you don't properly respect and understand the chemicals you're working with, you can do yourself a world of harm. Consider the following when disinfecting water.

TAKE YOUR TIME This is powerful stuff, so don't rush it. Never take shortcuts with water safety, it's worth doing right. After all, the last thing you need in an emergency situation is a case of dysentery on top of everything else.

KEEP IT SIMPLE Never mix chemicals when disinfecting water. Choose one method and stick to it, as some mixtures can be dangerous.

KNOW THE RISKS Avoid using iodine to purify the water if anyone who will be drinking it is pregnant or nursing, or has thyroid problems.

BE EFFICIENT Counterintuitively, tincture of iodine 2% is actually much stronger than the 10% Povidone iodine solution that's sold as a disinfecting agent, so you'll use less of it. An added benefit to any iodine product is that you can use iodine for wound disinfection (never use chlorine for this!).

41 Harvest the Rain

One of the most obvious sources of water is what falls from the sky. You shouldn't make rainwater the linchpin of your strategy, but if you live in an area that gets a decent amount of rain, it can't hurt to take advantage of this, er, windfall.

Some areas have laws against collecting rainwater, generally targeted at those who divert large amounts that would have fed into reservoirs (most common in drought-plagued Western states), so look into local ordinances. A kiddie pool is a good vessel; it'll collect about 18 gallons (69 liters) in a modest rainfall. You can also place buckets beneath your downspouts to collect water that runs off the roof.

All water gathered using these methods should be purified before drinking—even "pure" rainwater can have contaminants.

42 Let the Sun Shine In

If you have a clear glass or plastic bottle, some water, and a sunny day, you can use the sun's light to make your water much safer to drink. Largely advocated for developing countries, solar water disinfection is gaining some traction in the survival-skills crowd; and it's a great fit for equatorial countries with abundant strong sunlight but few other resources.

The most common solar disinfection technique is to expose clear plastic bottles full of questionable water to the sun for a minimum of one day. The sun's abundant UV light kills or damages almost all biological hazards in the water. This method has many advantages: It's easy to use; it's inexpensive or free; and it offers good (but not complete) bacterial and viral disinfection.

There are some problems, though. You need sunny weather (or two days of overcast sky) to reach the maximum effectiveness. You cannot use it in rainy weather. It offers no residual disinfection. It may be less effective against bacterial spores and cyst stages of some parasites. Both the water and the bottle need to be very clear. And finally, it only works with bottles that are 2 liters (0.5 gallons) or smaller.

While solar disinfection isn't 100 percent effective, it's still a lot better than taking your chances by drinking raw water.

IT WAS A COLD DAY IN OCTOBER WHEN I DECIDED TO GO FOUR-WHEELING IN A RARELY-TRAVELED SECTION OF WOODLANDS IN NORTH CAROLINA.

SOON, THE TRAIL MERGED INTO AN OLD RAILROAD GULLY, TOO NARROW TO EVEN TURN THE TRUCK AROUND.

AND THAT'S WHEN THE ENGINE FINALLY STOPPED. "NO WAY!" I BELLOWED. I WAS ILL-PREPARED TO SPEND A LONG, COLD NIGHT IN A BROKEN-DOWN TRUCK.

REMEMBERING AN OLD ARMY SURVIVAL GUIDE I HAD PORED OVER AS A KID, I REALIZED THAT VINES HAVE WATER INSIDE, AND WATER CONDUCTS ELECTRICITY.

ALL I NEEDED TO DO WAS CARVE IT DOWN TO SIZE.

*Story from Wes Massey, Chapel Hill, North Carolina

AFTER PLUNGING THROUGH A PARTICULARLY DEEP MUD HOLE, THE ENGINE BEGAN RUNNING VERY ROUGH.

BRAP

KRAK

THIS WAS THE LAST THING I NEEDED IN A REMOTE AREA AT THE END OF A LONG DAY. AS I PUSHED ON, THE SUN DROPPED, AND I JUST KEPT HOPING TO MAKE IT BACK TO A ROAD.

AFTER CHECKING OUT THE ENGINE, I REALIZED THAT THE IGNITION COIL WIRE HAD BURNED UP, SO I SWAPPED IT WITH ONE OF THE SPARK PLUG WIRES.

BUT THIS LEFT ME RUNNING ON JUST A FEW CYLINDERS. I NEEDED A PLUG WIRE, BUT WHAT COULD REPLACE IT?

THE TRUCK STARTED AND RAN WELL ENOUGH TO GET BACK TO THE PAVED ROAD.

I REPLACED THE PLUG WIRE WITH THE VINE, AND WRAPPED IT IN ELECTRICAL TAPE TO INSULATE IT.

44 Hold Your Water

Water is a top survival priority, so get the right containers to fulfill this necessity.

GALLON JUGS Glass wine jugs or juice jugs can be a nice choice for household storage—until you break them. Plastic 1-gallon (4-l) water jugs are more resistant to breakage, but they are vulnerable to leakage and chewing rodents. Don't reuse milk and juice jugs, as they're hard to sanitize and often grow more bacteria.

WATERBOB This 100-gallon (400-l) water bladder can be laid in a bathtub and filled from the tub's faucet in 20 minutes. It's a great thing to deploy if you know that trouble is coming, such as a hurricane heading for you.

SODA BOTTLES It's totally okay to use reclaimed 2-liter soda bottles. Make sure the containers are stamped with HDPE (high-density polyethylene) and coded with

the recycle symbol and a number 2 inside. HDPE containers are FDA-approved for food and water storage.

WATER COOLER JUGS The Holy Grail of water containers, the 5-gallon (19-l) jug can hold a lot of water and stay portable. Buy them factory-filled; they'll be safe to drink for a year or more.

55-GALLON (210-L) DRUMS Designed specifically for water storage, these big blue monsters will hold a week's worth of water or more. But they can be difficult to transport if you have to move them when full. Make sure it's a food-grade water barrel. Other barrels may create chemical interactions between the water and the plastic.

45 Think Outside the Sink

It doesn't take much to disrupt municipal water—earthquakes can break pipes, floods can overwhelm the system, and so forth. And sometimes it takes the city a while to get the taps back on. If the water stops flowing to your home, you do have a few options to consider before you start sucking on your last ice cubes. There's abundant water hidden in the average dwelling, if you know where to look for it.

THE PIPES Even in a utility outage, water can be found lying in the pipes. Open the highest faucet in the house, then open the lowest faucet or spigot, catching the water in some clean containers.

THE HOT WATER HEATER You may find 40 to 80 gallons (150 to 300 l) of drinkable water simply by opening the drain valve at the bottom of the unit and catching the water in a pan or shallow dish. Use this water soon, as the warm water heater is a great bacterial breeding ground. Turn off the power to electric water heaters, as they will burn up with no water in the unit.

THE TOILET TANK To clarify, we are talking about the tank, not the toilet bowl. The tank of every toilet has a gallon (4 l) or more of perfectly clean water in it.

THE FISH TANK A freshwater fish tank can be claimed as a water source, along with koi ponds, fountains, and other water features. Treat this water with chemicals or by boiling for 10 minutes to make it safe to drink.

THE GUTTERS The gutter system on your home can provide many gallons of water from just a light rain shower. Divert your downspouts into rain barrels or other large containers to take advantage of free water from the rainfall.

46 Banish Bacteria

As unlikely as this may sound, you can actually disinfect your drinking water safely and effectively with common household items. Just be aware that chemical disinfection doesn't remove salt, toxins, or fallout—it just kills the living pathogens that would make you sick.

FILTER Any water you get from a rain barrel, your pool, or a nearby creek should be considered contaminated and in need of disinfection. Water that is visibly dirty or muddy should be filtered through a coffee filter or a cloth. This won't make it safe to drink, but it will help the following disinfection methods to work more effectively.

CHLORINE BLEACH Add 2–4 drops of ordinary chlorine bleach per quart (or liter) of water. Use 2 drops if the water is warm and clear. Go to 4 drops if it is very cold or murky. Put the bottle cap back on and shake the container for a minute. Then turn the bottle upside down and unscrew the cap a turn or two. Let a small amount of water flow out to clean the bottle threads and cap. Screw the lid back on tight, and wipe the exterior of the bottle to get the chlorine on all surfaces. Let it sit for one hour in a dark place and it will be ready to drink.

TINCTURE OF IODINE Use 5–10 drops of tincture of iodine 2% in one quart (or liter) of water. Flush the threads, wipe down the bottle, and allow it to sit in the shade one hour, as with chlorine. Use 5 drops tincture of iodine for clear warm water, and up to 10 drops for the cold or cloudy variety of water.

POVIDONE IODINE You'll need 8–16 drops per quart (or liter) of water with this form of iodine. Add 8 drops for nice-looking water and 16 drops for swamp water. Clean the bottle threads, and wait an hour, as with the other methods.

47 Pool Your Resources

Your swimming pool or spa can yield a wealth of water, but be sure to disinfect it first, as any open water collects algae and bacteria. Chlorinated water can be relatively safe to drink, but be careful. The same UV rays that can disinfect bottled water will also be breaking down the pool's chlorine, but test it before you drink; chlorine is a potent chemical. Normally, the chlorine level of a properly maintained pool is kept at about 3 to 5 ppm (parts per million); 4 ppm or less is considered safe to drink. Test strips are cheap and easy to get; keep some on hand to check the water's drinkability.

48 Suit Up for Safety

People joke about having a full hazmat suit at the ready "just in case," but this isn't practical for all kinds of reasons—the main one being that high-quality hazmat suits are very costly, and in any situation where you and your family might actually need them, there will be so many other serious issues that the suits themselves aren't likely to save you (they also require support and maintenance that won't likely be available to you).

That said, in a number of disaster scenarios, you may want to be protected from airborne or environmental pathogens or contaminants. A solution is to buy Tyvek safety suits and respirators at a home-improvement store and add them to your kit. These suits and masks are very inexpensive; they're basically disposable protection for housepainters and construction workers. They certainly won't protect you from radiation or a chemical attack, but they will offer a layer of protection. For another layer, search online for "chemical protection suits," which can offer a higher level of protection against a variety of radioactive particles and at least some chemically dangerous or toxic subtances.

49 Get Wild and Woolly

You'll note that a lot of the "must-have" clothing for survival is wool. There's a reason for this—wool is soft, breathable, resists odor, dries quickly (and keeps you warm even when it's wet), is resistant to fire, and offers some good UV protection. Unless you're allergic to it, wool is one of the more comfortable fabrics. In the old days, trappers wore their wool undies for months at a time and, while that's really not recommended, there aren't many fabrics that would stay comfy and (relatively) fresh under those conditions.

Look for pure merino wool for long-lasting and comfortable clothing. It's not going to be cheap, but given the benefits and how long wool clothing lasts, it's almost certainly worth the investment.

Any emergency situation almost certainly involves some walking, whether you're hiking out of the wilderness, crossing a storm-devastated cityscape, or fleeing civil unrest (or hordes of zombies). That means you need good shoes. Don't go cheap—buy a sturdy, comfy pair of hiking or combat-type boots (real combat, not club fashion!). Break them in well and take care of them. High-tech synthetic material is lighter and easier to break in but won't last as long. Real leather takes more work but, cared for properly, can last forever.

51 Be Your Own Bootblack

Caring for your shoes isn't just about style, it ensures a much longer life for them. As soon as you get hold of a new pair of leather boots, waterproof them with mink oil (sold where you buy good leather products). Rub it in well with a soft cloth, then carefully remove any excess. Then, clean and polish your boots whenever they get dirty or scuffed.

STEP 1 Clean the surface of the shoes well with a soft cloth. Use an old toothbrush to reach any hard-to-reach spots.

STEP 2 Lightly apply polish, using a circular motion. Work it into any cracks, to condition dry leather. Let the polish set for a couple of minutes to fully dry.

STEP 3 Buff with a horsehair brush, using a back-and-forth motion and following the leather's grain.

52 Dress for the Occasion

Your extended survival kit should include practical, sturdy clothing for a range of conditions. Remember that, within reason, you get what you pay for, and when clothing will have to stand up well to the elements and maybe last a good long while, it's worth an investment. That said, smart shoppers will find much of what they need at big box or surplus stores. If you do winter sports and/or a lot of camping, you may already have a number of these items. Just be sure they're easily accessible when you need them. Here are some absolute basics.

- ☐ Waterproof shoes and/or boots
- ☐ Wool socks (they chafe less and have some natural waterproofing); pack more socks than you think you'll need.
- ☐ Comfortable underwear made of quick-drying fabric
- ☐ Women should consider wearing well-constructed sports bras as a basic undergarment, as they can be more comfortable for long-term wearing, as well as more versatile
- ☐ Wool-based long john–style bottoms
- ☐ Moisture-wicking long-sleeve top
- ☐ Long-sleeve wool top
- ☐ High-collared button-up wool shirt
- ☐ Sturdy jeans
- ☐ Insulated waterproof jacket
- ☐ Rain poncho
- ☐ Cold-weather gloves
- ☐ Work gloves
- ☐ Knit hat with rain visor
- ☐ Shatterproof sunglasses
- ☐ Balaclava or waterproof face mask
- ☐ Several bandanas (good for dust masks and head coverings, can be soaked in water and tied around neck to cool down, and more)
- ☐ Repair items such as a sewing kit (including awl for heavy-duty repairs), zipper-repair tools, shoe-repair glue, and heel savers for shoes
- ☐ Superconcentrated washing soap and a small brush to help get stains out when hand-washing

53 Build Your Tool Kit

Everybody should have some basic hand tools around the house to fix things up when your castle starts feeling more like a hovel. Take this list on your next trip to the hardware store.

- ☐ Claw hammer (for carpentry and home repairs)
- ☐ Handsaw (get one for wood cutting; a higher "tooth" count makes clean cuts)
- ☐ Hacksaw (for cutting metal and plastic)
- ☐ Screwdriver set (get an assortment of sizes and types)
- ☐ Duct tape (you can fix just about anything with duct tape)
- ☐ Utility knife (get extra blades so you always have a sharp tool)
- ☐ Superglue (fixes what the duct tape cannot)
- ☐ Tape measure (for the obvious reason, measuring)
- ☐ Pliers (get several sizes for plumbing and mechanical work)
- ☐ Crescent wrenches (get several sizes for a variety of repair needs)
- ☐ Nails and screws (a variety of diameters and lengths will come in handy)
- ☐ 100 feet (30 meters) of cordage (for tie-downs and bundling jobs)
- ☐ A standard and metric socket set (for mechanical repairs)
- ☐ A small pry bar (for opening doors and windows, and for carpentry)
- ☐ Rasps and files (to repair and sharpen other tools and items, focus on metal files)

54 Get Creative with Your Toolbox

When times are tough, you may not have the luxury of popping on down to your local superstore to find just the right item for the job. That's when you think like the pioneers—what would Pa Ingalls have done? Here are a few ideas. We bet if you look at your workshop with a creative eye, you'll come up with a few more.

CARRY DRYWALL Big sheets of drywall, plywood, or even heavy cardboard can be a real hassle to carry around if you don't have arms like a chimpanzee. Use a pry bar as an arm extender to grab the bottom of the sheet. No ape sounds needed, but go for it if you like.

PULL ELECTRICAL STAPLES It can be tough to pull out those staples that hold down cables without damaging the actual line. Diagonal cutting pliers make the job easy.

REMOVE STUBBORN NAILS If your hammer just can't grab that nail—or, worse, if its head has broken off—use locking pliers to grab it. Clamp the nail and pull downward to curl the nail out of the wood.

TIE IT SECURELY When you need to hold together something big or unwieldy, like a coiled extension cord or a rolled-up tarp, a few lengths of copper wire can be really handy. It's easy to cut and bend, and you just have to twist it once to get it to hold.

HOLD A SMALL NAIL Needle-nose pliers can hold that tiny nail in place better than your stubby fingers . . . and won't scream if you hit them with the hammer by accident.

FAKE A HEMOSTAT Those needle-nose pliers also come in handy when you need to create the kind of flexible lock that hemostats make for cheap. Great for holding wires to solder or cable when you don't have enough hands, one can be made with a pair of pliers and a rubber band.

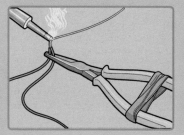

55 Rip It Up with a Hammer

You know that when all you have is a hammer, everything looks like a nail? Not always so. If you happen to have a "rip hammer," which is one with a straight rather than curved claw, you've got a surprisingly multifaceted tool. Sure, you can use it to pull and pound nails, but that's not all.

SPLIT LUMBER Let's say you need a 2x2 but all you have is 2x4s. No problem! Or if you need to split a wood block or otherwise get rid of a bit of wood along the grain. The straight end of your hammer can act like a little mini axe. It's not a precision instrument, but most often it doesn't need to be.

MAKE A ROUGH MEASURE A lot of time it doesn't matter exactly how high something is off the ground (think electrical boxes, for instance), just that it's consistent. If you have a basic idea of your hammer's length (insert the dirty joke of your choice here), you can skip pulling out the measuring tape.

DO A DEMO If you need to pull out some drywall or disassemble woodwork, the claw end of your hammer (especially if it has a long handle) is almost as good as a pry bar. It'll do in a pinch, anyway.

HIT THE GARDEN When breaking up hard soil, your hammer's claw is better than most of those little hand tools, as it's more ergonomic and packs more of a punch. Once you've broken up the turf you can bring in fertilizer and pull out the more conventional rakes and trowels.

SAVE A SAW BLADE Thin saw blades bend easily. You can pinch the blade in your hammer's claw and carefully bend it back to true. Or you can try laying it down on your work table and pounding it straight.

MAKE LIKE A MOUNTAIN CLIMBER This is one of those tricks you hope you never have to use—and that you're quick-thinking enough to remember if you do need to. Up on the roof working on the shingles and slip? If you have the presence of mind to turn the hammer around and slam the claw into the roof, you may well arrest your fall. We've heard it's been done. We don't want to test it.

56 Make Fire with a File

If you have bastard files (the roughest cut in metal files) in your toolbox, char cloth (see item 103) in your survival kit, and a good rock, you have a good backup fire starter.

STEP 1 Grab your file—a mill bastard file is best due to its carbon content.

STEP 2 Get a nice chunk of flint, quartz, or jasper.

STEP 3 Put the char cloth on a good surface, then strike the file firmly with your rock. Sparks should fly and catch the char cloth. Add more tinder to those sparks, and you'll have a fire in no time!

57 Don't Get Caught Without: VODKA

Wait, what? It's true, the idea of sipping screwdrivers after the apocalypse might seem a little strange, but hear us out. As a clear spirit, vodka has a surprising number of uses. In addition to those below, booze can make a great trade good or way of befriending your neighbors. And after a hard day's labor in the summer heat, that screwdriver is going to sound mighty refreshing.

❶ MOUTHWASH
With its antibacterial qualities, vodka can help keep your teeth and gums in good shape. If you're really feeling fancy, you can even infuse it with mint leaves or extract.

❷ PAIN RELIEF
No, not like that! Dab on cold sores or blisters to help them heal.

❸ MOSQUITO REPELLENT
Spray yourself down to discourage mosquitoes and other pests (does not work on hobos).

of Sweden
RON

Citron is created
Swedish winter
pristine well water.
ingredients and
hundred years of
making experience.
Absolut classic.

750ML
SWEDEN

4 TREAT SMELLY FEET
Nobody likes a stinky dude in a small bunker. Wipe down smelly feet and shoes.

5 ITCH TREATMENT
Helps soothe the discomfort from poison ivy and even jellyfish stings.

6 GET RID OF MOLD
Mold isn't just ugly, it can make you all kinds of sick—to get rid of it, spritz full-strength vodka on it, then scrub to remove.

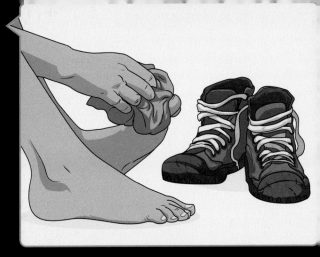

7 DEODORIZE CLOTHING
Put vodka in a spray bottle; use it to kill the bacteria that make your clothes stinky.

8 ICE PACK
A half mug each of water and vodka frozen together makes for a good reusable ice pack.

9 CLEAN LENSES
Use unflavored vodka to clean off eyeglasses, camera lenses, binoculars, or your rifle scope.

10 MAKE A MUSCLE RUB
Fill a glass jar with lavender flowers, then top off with vodka. Let steep in the sun three days, then strain through a coffee filter. Voila! A soothing linament—or a really gross cocktail.

Evan and Scot Hill are the owners and operators of Hill People Gear (hillpeoplegear.com), a family-owned outdoor gear company that produces simple, modern, and reliable gear for those living close to the land.

58 Meet the Hill Brothers

I sat down with Evan to talk gear, motivations, and how he and Scot got into this business.

EVAN: I've always been an engineer at heart. I started sewing outdoor gear when I was 12. Most of it I didn't use for very long because my fabrication skills weren't up to snuff! I majored in anthropology in college, but I was excited by the Web's potential for empowering people in very fundamental ways. I'm a Luddite at heart and was never in love with the technology itself, just the ways that it could make the world better. I was in software management for a decade and a half, which trained me to design things more systematically. I also learned a lot about small start-up businesses, because those were the types of companies I gravitated toward.

When my oldest daughter was about to go into school, I decided to move my family to a more rural town. That was pretty much death for my software career, though it stayed on life support another eight years. But having ready access to the backcountry opened up a part of myself that had been closed for so long that I'd forgotten it existed. A Diné friend of mine calls it "getting back to my natural way."

While underemployed in my new town, I learned that meaningful side projects help keep your sanity and spirits up while job hunting. Fabric is cheap, and it takes time to make a nice piece of outdoor gear: Perfect! I ended up turning out quite a few pieces of kit that I used regularly. Other people saw and wanted their own. I thought to myself, why not?

From the beginning, I knew I needed someone more pragmatic and detail-oriented than myself involved. Scot was a natural choice. He also brings his own common-sense outlook and "why can't it do this" questions to the design process.

And Hill People Gear was born.

59 Get the Gear of the Hill People

Hill People Gear has a fleet of loyal customers, not excluding its creators. I asked Scot and Evan about their favorite and most popular pieces of gear.

SCOT: Our most popular item is the Kit Bag, and of those probably the Original sells the best—it's the most versatile. The Kit Bag really fills a niche—while there are some excellent chest holsters and belt-mounted options out there, as well as some other chest rigs available currently and historically, there is nothing quite like the Kit Bag. It allows ready access to a handgun and gear—whether or not you have a pack on and no matter what you're doing. However, I have to say that the Mountain Serape is probably my favorite piece of gear. It doesn't get used on an almost-daily basis like my Kit Bag, but it just plain works better than anything else out there, and it fulfills so many roles with its multiple configurations. If I could only have one piece of our gear, it would be a hard choice between those two.

EVAN: My favorite tends to change based on what I'm using at a particular time—and I don't even remember life without my Kit Bag. That being said, I've really been loving my Tarahumara lately. It's funny, because I think of the Tara as a luxury as packs go, but when you put smart design and our shoulder harness together you get a really nice little pack that disappears on your back. I also think it is the most aesthetically pleasing thing I've done. Since I'm more of an engineer than a designer, I appreciate that aspect of it.

60 Stick to Your Guns

I asked the brothers if they ever get suggestions that they'd never follow up on.

SCOT: We are constantly looking for better ways to do something, but we balance all the data points, not just a single one, and some people tend to get caught up in one aspect—like the color. We want our products to work for everyone, which is why you see good solid earth tones that can blend well in multiple environments. Ranger Green is our most popular color by a wide margin.

EVAN: If I hear another critic say, "If you switched to this other material you'd save 3 ounces," I'm going to lose it. Not really, but I fantasize about it. The answer that we're too polite to give those folks is that if they spent as much time using their gear in the real world as they did reading the specs, their opinion would count for more.

For us, ease of use and versatility are our primary goals with any design—not data points. It takes experience to recognize those attributes, and they're going to vary in value. We're not building gear that specs out so the internet pundits like it. We're building gear that works well. When we get positive feedback from guys who are truly living with the backcountry, who aren't still trying to "cheat the mountain," I'm satisfied. As our friends at Lester River Bushcraft say, "Shut up and get it dirty."

61 Grab a Gun (Or Two)

Whether you own a handgun, a rifle, or a shotgun, keeping any firearm in your home is a very serious responsibility—but it could save your life in the right situation. You should consider various factors when choosing a firearm, such as ease of use, reliability, and ammunition. The most powerful, top-of-the-line gun will be of little use if it's hard to maintain, troublesome to carry or operate, or if it runs out of ammo to shoot.

Whatever choice you make in this process, be sure you know everything about properly operating and maintaining your firearms, and keep them safely and securely stored when not in use.

HANDGUNS

While some handguns can be used for hunting purposes, these guns are primarily meant for self-defense in close quarters. Your best bet is to go with newer-model semiautomatic types.

Common cartridge sizes include 9mm, .38, .357, .40, .44, and .45.

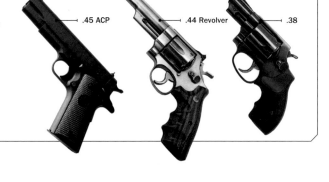

.45 ACP · .44 Revolver · .38

RIFLES

There are an endless variety of rifles, from lever-action to bolt-action to semiautomatic "AR" type (so named after the original Armalite manufacturer), and no shortage of accessories to choose from, to fit any hunter's needs. Keep it simple with a basic semiauto like an AR-15, or even simpler, a magazine-fed, bolt-action model (some versions can even be quickly disassembled to fit into a BOB). Look for common ammunitions like .22 LR, .223, .30-06, and .308.

.22

AR-7

AR Rifle

.308

Useful for both hunting and home defense, a shotgun is a versatile, if short-range, choice of personal firearm. Break-action models are simple to operate, but they only fire once or twice before reloading. Pump-action models are nearly ubiquitous, however, and, along with their larger magazine (usually 5 to 7 shots), offer the same ability to fire birdshot, buckshot (for hunting or defense), or slugs. Most common shell sizes: 12- and 20-gauge, in varying lengths.

Tactical

Double-barreled

Semi-automatic

62 Be Gun Safety Savvy

You should know how to safely handle and care for your firearms. If you have a gun, be sure to invest in a way to take care of it and store it, and definitely know how to use it.

A basic gun-cleaning kit usually consists of a set of brushes, cloths, and solvents that are used to remove gunk that sticks to the interior of your gun's barrel and other workings after use—copper fouling from bullet jackets, burnt propellant, etc. Over time, a buildup of these substances can make a firearm not only difficult to use but unsafe. Keep it clean and in working order and your gun will remain with you for years to come.

When not in use, your firearms should be placed somewhere safe and secured, and out of reach of others, especially children. Invest in a gun safe or, at least, a lock that obstructs the action, magazine, or trigger to keep it from being loaded and fired. Keep

your gun unloaded and your ammunition stored separately when not in use.

Last, remember the basic tenets of safe gun handling: Always assume a gun is loaded. Always point the gun in the safest direction possible when not in use. Always be aware of what's beyond your target. And always keep your finger off the trigger unless you are ready to fire. If you're interested in additional training, there are various classes from gun basics up to self-defense and combat courses.

I'D JUST GOTTEN HOME FROM A HIKE.

MAN, WAS I TIRED! WITHOUT EVEN TAKING MY BOOTS OFF, I SAT DOWN TO RELAX.

THE ROBBERS OVERPOWERED ME AND ZIP-TIED MY HANDS.

I REMEMBERED TO FLEX MY WRISTS SO THEY COULDN'T TIGHTEN THEM DOWN ALL THE WAY.

I QUICKLY TIED A BOWLINE AT ONE END, AND SLIPPED IT OVER THE TOE OF MY BOOT.

THEN FED IT THROUGH THE ZIP TIES, TIED IT TO MY OTHER BOOT. . .

* The following *This Could Happen To You* stories are based on real events and represent real-life scenarios that you should be prepared for.

64
Own 8 Essential Knives

The frontiersmen may have used the same knife to skin game, eat dinner, and shave—but that doesn't mean it was a good idea. Here are eight basic knives that everyone should own, and why.

1 EVERYDAY CARRY The classic pocket knife is often a folding knife, but it can just as easily be a fixed-blade knife. This is your go-to blade for most cutting jobs and the most likely tool that you'll be keeping on your person (in your pocket). The newer-model folders can often have assisted-opening features such as spring assist and thumb studs on the blade's spine to allow for one-handed opening. Select a folding knife that opens smoothly, without feeling loose or rattling. Stainless steel or high carbon steel blades can both be fine choices for an everyday carry knife.

2 BOWIE KNIFE The Bowie-style knife, popularized by the Western hero Colonel James "Jim" Bowie, is the quintessential blade to use for hunting, fighting, and survival tasks. Modern incarnations abound; buy one that has a full tang (the blade metal extends all the way through the handle). Pick one that has some weight to it for chopping but isn't so heavy that you don't want to carry it. Many different steel types are (and have been) used for Bowies.

3 FILLET KNIFE Skinning and butchering turn from a chore into a pleasure with a sharp fillet knife in your hand. You may have special

ones for fish, fowl, and red meat—or you can just use one knife for all. Plastic handles are common to help facilitate cleaning the knives when the chores are done. Select a thin blade made from stainless steel for years of trusty service.

4 CHEF'S KNIFE Cooking and food processing can get a lot easier if you add a chef's knife to your chuck wagon. This versatile blade slices, dices, and preps food with the greatest of ease. Stainless steel is a great choice. Avoid high carbon steel for your chef's knife, as this steel is prone to rust with such watery workloads.

5 TACTICAL KNIFE This knife is all business, and that business is self-defense. These blades are often used as backup for firearms in military and law enforcement. They should be rugged and large like a Bowie. They should also be razor sharp, with a penetrating blade tip. The tanto style of blade tip is ideal for some serious "punch through" capability.

6 RESCUE KNIFE Also known as an EMT knife, this versatile survival tool is commonly carried by various emergency services personnel, from firefighters to police to paramedics. It's a folding knife with an edge that's at least partly serrated, and bears two important accessories: a seat-belt cutter, and window breaker. A belt clip on the handle allows it to be carried within easy reach to use at a moment's notice.

7 COMBAT KNIFE As the name indicates, these blades are made primarily with hand-to-hand fighting in mind, with secondary use as a utility knife. A single-edged, high-carbon steel straight blade with a clip point allows the wielder to both thrust and slash. Other occasional innovations for utility include a serrated spine, or a hollow handle for survival gear storage. The models made famous by the United States Marine Corps (see above) are popular for their design and proven, field-tested effectiveness.

8 MULTITOOL More than just a blade, the multitool got its start as the venerable Swiss Army knife, although the more robust Gerber-type tools are a modern stereotype. Its folding mechanism holds things like pliers, screwdrivers, saws, and at least one knife blade. While not as effective as a set of purpose-built tools, this is still a versatile mini-toolbox that fits right in the palm of your hand.

Tie 7
Simple Knots

Knot tying has always been one of those key outdoor skills that the inexperienced take for granted. The experienced outdoorsman, however, has had enough success and failure to know that there are right and wrong knots for certain jobs.

A good knot can save lives when you're dealing with a survival situation, performing first-aid tasks, or working over heights or water. But you have to know how to tie it. So make sure you know what to do with your rope the next time you head into the wild by learning these simple yet essential knots. Want more? See items 191 and 315.

SQUARE KNOT

This is a classic for connecting lines. Whether you are tying two ropes together to make a longer rope, or you are tying up a bundle of firewood to carry, the square knot is a winner. It's much more secure and stable than its cousin, the granny knot.

HOW TO TIE You can tie a solid square knot by lapping right over left, and then tying again in the reverse direction—left over right.

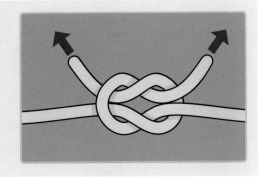

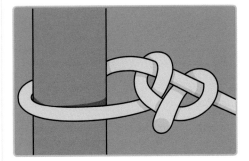

TWO HALF HITCHES

Here's a handy way to secures a line to trees or poles (or to itself, in the case of the trucker's hitch—see item 315).

HOW TO TIE This knot is pretty easy and can be used to secure tarps for shelters and hang up hammocks. Once you have wrapped the free end around the standing end to make the first half hitch, wrap it around the line in the same direction again to make the second half hitch. Pull it tight and you have two half hitches. An overhand knot in the free end will keep them from slipping.

CLOVE HITCH

This easy-to-tie knot secures a line to a tree or post quickly, but it does slip when used alone, without any other knots as a backup.

HOW TO TIE Make a loop of rope around a tree, branch, post, or stake (or form a loop in the rope and slip it down over the object in question). Make another loop, and then pass the free end of the rope under the second loop before tightening.

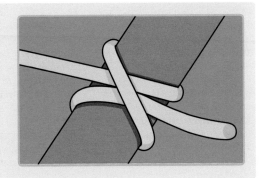

FIGURE 8

Use this handy option (also called the Flemish knot) as a stopper knot at the end of a line. Spoiler alert: It's also the basis for some of the complex knots we'll cover later in the book.

HOW TO TIE Simply pass the free end of a line over itself to form a loop. Continue under and around the line's end, and finish the knot by passing the free end down through the loop.

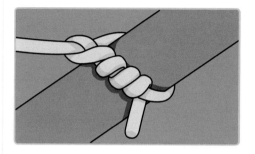

TIMBER HITCH

Here's a useful knot for securing a rope to a cylindrical object for hauling or as a support.

HOW TO TIE All you need to do is to run the free end of the rope around the log you intend to pull. Then wrap the free end of the rope around the standing end of the rope. Wrap the free end around itself three or four times. Finally, tighten so that your three or four wraps are tight against the log.

WATER KNOT

When you need to safely join webbing, belts, and straps together, this knot is your friend.

HOW TO TIE Start with a loose overhand knot in the end of one strap. Pass the other strap in the opposite direction, mirroring the route of the first overhand knot. Take the ends of two straps and pull the knot tight.

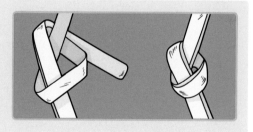

BOWLINE

Here's a way to create a loop at the end of a rope that cannot shrink or expand. This knot is often taught as a rabbit coming out of a hole, hopping in front of a tree, then behind the tree, and back down the hole.

HOW TO TIE Form a loop on top of the long end of the line. Pass the free end through the loop and around behind the line. Bring the free end through the original loop, and maintain the secondary loop, which becomes your Bowline loop. Once the "rabbit" is back down his hole, pull the "tree" up and the Bowline is tightened.

66 Have a Financial Plan

Whether the economy gets a little shaky or society totally collapses in the wake of a local (or larger-scale) disaster, you should have a plan for your finances as well as your health and safety. At the least, learning to closely manage your money and funds will help your day-to-day expenses and let you afford the cost of other disaster preparedness or financial hardship. Handling your finances means being able to control and plan for other events, such as disability, retirement, home renovation, and more.

SPEND LESS Live below your means, and you'll have more to spend or save elsewhere. Take a look at your finances and reduce your spending in unnecessary areas, from dining out to entertainment. There's also no shame in buying used instead of new, finding good deals, collecting coupons, or going for bulk discounts.

SAVE UP If you suddenly find yourself without a job, whether due to economic trouble or disaster, you'll still need a way to pay for things. Save a minimum of 10 percent of your gross income, and plan and save for a buffer of at least three months of funds. If you can, look six months ahead. Start with your basics: mortgage or rent, utilities, and food, and go from there to personal supplies, transportation, medical care, more extensive disaster preparedness, and other expenses.

CASH & CARRY It's easier to manage finances if you have less debt. Pay off credit cards, starting with the one with the lowest balance, and renegotiate interest and payment rates if you have a good track record, until you're debt-free. Meanwhile, create a budget that lets you pay for everything with cash or debit, instead of further relying on credit.

67 Shelter Your Funds

Ready for something a bit more exciting than a savings plan at the local credit union? These options are higher risk but also give better coverage in case of certain potential disasters. Of course, if all the computers go down worldwide, and your money's in Bitcoins, you may have a lot of useless 1s and 0s.

GO OFFSHORE If you have some funds to spare, consider investing in foreign currencies in more economically stable regions of the world, or look into having a bank account outside the country. Just be sure that in the event of an emergency, you'll have a way to access those funds.

GO FOR THE GOLD Precious metals have been used as a medium of exchange for millennia, due to their rarity and beauty. Buying platinum, gold, or silver by the ounce is a little costly but may ultimately be worth it. Their value has stayed fairly consistent or risen over the years (though not so much, of late), and depending on how you buy them, their worth is measured in either intrinsic (the cost of the metal itself) or collectible value (if it is in the form of rare coins or memorabilia, either as a pure metal or mingled). Whatever metal you choose to invest in, don't just rely on certificates that can be cashed in for metal later; get hold of the stuff itself and store it securely where you can access it Just like any other currency, it'll be worthless if it's out of reach.

GET CRYPTIC The last few years have seen the rise of "cryptocurrencies"—created "moneys" used by people on the Internet (and sometimes offline), to buy everything from cupcakes to computers. Bitcoins, Litecoins, and the like are traded all the time by aficionados and can fluctuate in value, but in countries where the local economy and currency have been very unstable (such as Greece and Cyprus) some people have turned to this method of exchange for goods and services. It can be slightly tricky to get into the world of cryptocurrency, but it may be well worth the effort.

68 Stash Your Cash

Once you decide how much money to keep on hand for emergencies, you've got to figure out how and where to keep it. In an ideal world you'd have it all in smaller bills, since in an emergency, shopkeepers are probably going to be cranky about making change for those Benjamins. That said, two grand in twenties is a big wad. Use your best judgment, and store as much of it as is reasonable in smaller bills, then use big bills for the rest of the stash for convenience. And we beg of you, whatever you do, don't hide it under the mattress. That's the first place burglars will look (the second is taped to the back of paintings, in case you were wondering). So, where to put it?

BURY TREASURE Go all pirate-style and bury the booty in your yard. Be sure you use an airtight, waterproof container. A common mason jar is a great choice. And don't forget where you buried it!

FREEZE YOUR ASSETS If your freezer is packed with foil-wrapped leftovers, it's easy to make one of those packages actually contain money, not mom's meatloaf, as the label suggests. If you have a fairly empty freezer, this is a worse idea, as it may just stand out.

PICTURE THIS Taping cash to the back of pictures is a terrible idea. But if you want to get a little craftier, you can stash currency in between a framed photo or poster and the cardboard backing.

BOOK IT Ah, the old hollowed-out book trick. Corny as it sounds, if you have a bookcase full of hardcovers, it's not hard to hide your cash among them. Use a sharp blade to carve out a pocket in the midst of the pages. Choose a really boring book so no one pulls it off the shelf and accidentally discovers your stash.

69 Know the Right Amount

In most natural disasters and other emergencies, electrical power and computer lines go down for at least a little while. That means that not only are ATMs and card readers at your local supermarket down, even if you can get to your bank (assuming it's not flooded, destroyed by a quake, or shut down due to terrorist threats) they may not be able to call up your account information.

So once you've found the right place to squirrel it safely away from thieves and partying teenagers (not to mention yourself—always resist the urge to dip in "just this once" when you need a few bucks), how much is smart to save? It rarely takes more than a week for utilities to come back on after a storm, flood, or earthquake, so a week's worth of funds is the place to start.

Calculate what you'd spend on groceries and emergency supplies (also factor in the fact that price-gouging is more than likely, unfortunately). If authorities order an evacuation, gas and motel costs will come into play, as well. Your specific needs will vary based on the size of your family, where you live, where you're going, and so forth, but experts estimate that a rough amount of two thousand dollars should cover those costs, with a little extra on top—just in case.

Understand Your Fuel Types

You'll probably want to have a range of fuel options on hand, depending on your needs and what sort of emergency you feel is most likely to happen in your region. This chart gives you a starting point for considering your needs and making decisions.

FUEL	SOLIDS			LIQUIDS				GASES
	WOOD	COAL	CHARCOAL	PETROL	DIESEL	KEROSENE	OIL	NATURAL GAS/ PROPANE/BUTANE
USES								
Cooking	○	○	○			○		○
Heating	●	●	●			●	●	●
Lighting	○					○	○	○
Electricity (Generators)				●	●			●
Vehicles				○	○			
STORAGE	Dry storage (bins, bags)			Plastic or metal canisters/jugs				Pressurized bottles/ tanks
PROS	• Durable (if kept dry) • Usable in- and outdoors (campfires, stoves, fireplaces, etc.)			• Portable • Versatile (some stoves, lamps, generators, etc. will accept multiple liquid fuels)				• Most versatile fuel type
CONS	• Charcoal can only be used to cook outdoors • Can be heavy • Bulky, requires a lot of storage space • Will not burn if wet • Wood can rot			• Some liquid fuels can degrade over time (unusable for vehicles) or evaporate/leak • Vapors are flammable				• Sealed bottles or tanks require refills • Can be punctured • Portable only in small to moderate amounts

71 Know Your Color Codes

There are many different types of fuel containers, but for gas the most common style is red plastic with a built-in spout of some form. It's standard that kerosene containers are blue and diesel ones are yellow. It's important for you to know and follow this convention so you don't end up pouring diesel into your car and ruining it, or putting gasoline into your camping lantern and frying your eyebrows (at the very least).

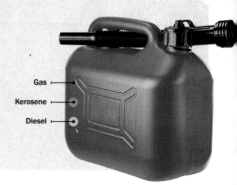

Gas ⊢

Kerosene ⊢

Diesel ⊢

 **Make It Last Longer**

All liquid fuels lose potency over time. For example, diesel will last about a year if you're storing it in a sealed container at temperatures below 70°F (21°C). If storing at much higher temperatures, that time drops down to six months. Fuels can also develop deposits that block filters and affect efficiency—or even damage your engine.

So, what to do? Luckily there are additives you can use to extend your stored fuel's life without affecting its eventual efficiency. Check your local home-improvement store for products, and follow instructions carefully. You should be able to extend the life of stored fuel for a few years, which could quite literally be a lifesaver.

You might also want to consider looking into storing pure gasoline, which is different than the stuff you pump out of your local station's pumps, in that it has no ethanol mixed in. Look on the Web to find stations.

73 Store Fuel Right

No matter how much liquid fuel you're planning to stockpile, certain considerations remain the same. You're dealing with a combustible, poisonous material, so you should apply a few extra measures of caution.

CONTAINERS Even the fumes are combustible, so liquid fuel should be stored in airtight containers that do not vent. You should be able to walk into the area where your fuel is stored and smell nothing. If that's not the case, either fumes or liquid is leaking, and you need to fix that fast. Store your fuel in approved plastic or metal containers, and check them frequently.

LOCATION Don't store fuel in your basement or even in your garage if you can help it. The ideal spot is a storage shed on your property located at least 30 feet (9 m) from your home (this is true for firewood as well). In the event of a house fire, you don't want to add any more combustibles to the mix. Some recommend underground tanks, but this is illegal in many places and a serious risk to the quality of your groundwater. Don't risk it. If you want to stockpile fuel in bulk, you can purchase above-ground storage drums.

TEMPERATURE As with food storage, you want your fuel kept somewhere clean, dark, and as cold as possible. Direct light and higher temperatures can degrade fuel's quality quickly and, in a worst-case scenario, pose a fire risk as well.

74 Determine How Much Fuel You Need

There's a school of thought that says you can never stockpile too much fuel. While there's something to that, your space and resources are limited, so you need to do a little figuring and make the right decision for your circumstances. Here are the rock-bottom basics.

BUGGING OUT If you need to leave fast, and gas stations are unlikely to be open (which will happen in just about any natural disaster), figure out how much gas or diesel you'll need to fill your tank and to refuel on your way to wherever you imagine will be your destination. That will vary wildly depending on where you are, how many cars your family has, and how far you reckon you'll need to drive. Do that math and then add a little extra just for safety.

STAYING PUT If you have a gas-powered generator, try and estimate how you'll use it and what that would burn. A rule of thumb is about 15 gallons (57 l) per week, assuming absolutely minimal usage. How many weeks do you think you'll need to prepare for? Do that math and stock up accordingly.

75 Burn This, Not That

Some fuels can be swapped, should you run out of one but have another. Others aren't so versatile or may even be explosive if substituted. If you do have fuel on hand in a crisis, be sure you use it safely.

DIESEL AND HEATING OIL These two fuels are good substitutes for each other. Diesel burns a little cleaner than home heating oil, but either of these can burn in a diesel vehicle or your home furnace.

LANTERN FUEL Anything other than kerosene or liquid paraffin in an old-fashioned, wick-based lantern is *not* an option. Diesel, white gas, alcohol, or other fuels can lead to an explosion. Pressurized lanterns should only be filled with white gas (naphtha).

ALCOHOL Pure alcohol in the form of high-proof (anhydrous) ethanol or methanol can be added to gasoline to stretch your vehicle fuel supply, but keep the alcohol percentage low—somewhere around 25 percent of the total fuel volume. If you use too much alcohol, the engine will run very poorly.

76 Live on Solar Power

In the event of a temporary or (hopefully not) permanent loss of public utility power, you can provide power on your own (see item 196) at a small scale, or make use of a fuel-powered generator. A longer-term solution is also available: A solar array on your home can easily provide a good measure of backup power.

Solar power systems are usually either grid-tied or off-grid. You can save money on your utilities and sell excess power in some areas if you're grid-tied, but if the power grid goes down your solar setup will also be compromised. Off-grid power systems can be totally independent but are a bit more costly, although they can also be supplemented by generators. Some setups can be hybridized: grid-tied solar with a battery backup and inverter, which will automatically switch over if there's an outage.

The biggest cost comes from installation (and the setup lasts for decades), but some areas of the United States and elsewhere often provide incentives for those who choose to get solar power systems. A professional vendor can provide more information on getting solar power for your home, but here are some questions for you to consider.

- Is your solar setup going to be grid-tied, off-grid, or battery-backup?
- What state or federal incentives or rebates are available for solar power?
- Will my local power authority pay me for electricity?
- How many panels will I need to account for my home's power needs? What battery setup will I need for off-grid or battery backup?

Do the basic research first, then find a professional to see what your best options are. As with any big investment, shop around. It's worth doing right.

77 Get the Most from a Propane Stove

Propane stoves are a great convenience for cooking when you're in the wilderness, off the grid, or making do while waiting for power to come back. But they are designed for small tanks, which run out quickly, are annoying to store, and are costly. Luckily, you can buy an adapter from camping stores or often directly from the stove's maker that will allow you to hook up a 5-gallon (19-l) tank instead. The adapters are cheap, and the bigger tanks are a great bargain and can last for months. (For those seven people in the world who have never been camping, you can cook just about anything on a propane stove that you'd cook on your regular indoor range.)

78

Make Recycled Briquettes

Making your own briquettes is a bit labor intensive—but with a little up-front effort, you can make burnable briquettes for almost nothing. They take a bit of effort to get alight, but will burn well in a wood stove, and you can stack them in storage areas much more efficiently than wood. Just be sure to keep them dry! There are lots of methods for making these briquettes—the main trick is to compact them as tightly as possible and squeeze out every drop of water that you can. Then stack them somewhere warm and dry and let them continue to dry and harden. (Wet briquettes will be smoky, even if you can get them to ignite.)

Your briquettes can be made with any combination of shredded paper or newspaper, sawdust, and mulch. The trick is to tear, clip, chop, or grind everything up as fine as possible, soak the stuff in very hot water until it's totally sodden, and then blend well. The longer you soak it, the better—it may take a few days for everything to really start breaking down. Adding a splash of bleach can help.

Once the mixture is the consistency of oatmeal, press as much water out of it as you can with your hands and/or using a big colander or sieve. Then use a mechanical press like the one pictured here to further shape, drain, and compact the briquettes. (You don't have to use a press—it's possible to just squeeze the briquettes by hand or press them under a board, but they'll take longer to dry and likely won't burn as cleanly or as long.)

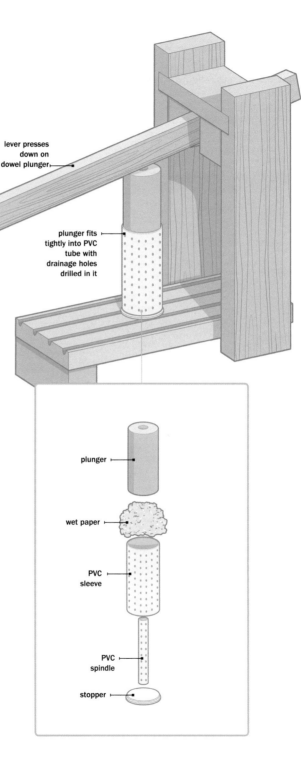

lever presses down on dowel plunger

plunger fits tightly into PVC tube with drainage holes drilled in it

plunger

wet paper

PVC sleeve

PVC spindle

stopper

Get Ready to Get Around

It's never too early to think about how you'll get around town and country in a serious emergency. Here are a set of options and why they might or might not be best for you. Shopping for new wheels? Keep in mind that many modern automobiles in the SUV and van (or at least minivan) categories—and some trucks—are built on the same chassis types as cars. This means that they're essentially the same vehicle's frame, so that light truck you're eyeing might actually be no better than your average four-door sedan equipped with two-wheel front drive. Be sure of your vehicle's actual specifications and what it can (and can't) do for you before you settle on making a purchase—even if you're not shopping with survival in mind.

MODE	PLUSES	MINUSES
WALKING	· No fuel needed · Most agile "vehicle"	· Slowest form of travel · Fatigue, possible injury can slow you down
BICYCLE	· No fuel needed · Lightweight, can be carried · Can go places cars can't	· Almost no cargo capacity · Limited mostly to roads or similar terrain · Exposed to elements
MOTORCYCLE	· Fast, agile · Variety of choices (on/off road) · Able to fit through places cars can't, handy in a pursuit	· Needs fuel · Rider is exposed to elements · Steeper learning curve for use than a car

MODE	PLUSES	MINUSES
CAR	• Variety of choices for cargo space and passenger capacity (car, station wagon, minivan, SUV)	• Needs fuel • Lower fuel efficiency than motorcycles • Hard to take off road • Usually two-wheel drive only
TRUCK (4X4)	• Easily manages rough terrain • Can carry lots of gear • Tows other vehicles or trailers	• Needs fuel • Lower fuel efficiency than cars • Large size, less maneuverable
BUS/RV	• Loads of cargo space • Loads of passenger space too • Mobile living space (RV especially)	• Slow • Not very agile • Almost entirely roadbound • Very low fuel efficiency • Expensive
WATERCRAFT	• Can double as living space • Goes anywhere there's water • No fuel needed in some cases • Various sizes and types to choose from	• Can only go where there's water (or be towed on land) • Needs fuel (motorboats) • Need skill to sail and navigate • Vulnerable to inclement weather; can sink • Very expensive
AIRCRAFT	• Can go almost anywhere • Various sizes and types (from hot-air balloon to blimp to helicopter to airplane) • Some are amphibious • Varying cargo and passenger capacity	• Needs fuel (even the balloon) • Needs special training to pilot and navigate, and fix/repair • Subject to inclement weather • Can crash • Very, very expensive
MILITARY/ POLICE VEHICLES	• Robust construction • Made to survive combat and harsh elements • Made to go almost anywhere • Some come equipped with weapons	• Needs fuel (tanks use hard-to-find jet fuel for turbine engines) • Specialized needs/repairs • Insanely expensive • Just where are you going to get one of these, anyway?

80 Buy the Best Vehicle

The next time you're in the market for a new vehicle, you may want to give some thought to the worst conditions you may face behind the wheel of your new ride. Consider some emergency extras and a few nice upgrades to turn your mild-mannered auto into a mayhem-proof battle wagon.

SUV

These vehicles have lots of features that allow you to drive far off the blacktop. Find a full-size, full-frame model with four-wheel drive; avoid small/medium SUVs. Get one with a two-speed transfer case, which allows you to run in two high-, four high-, and four low-gear options, to enhance traction depending on weather/terrain.

HEAVY TRUCK

The horsepower, high ground clearance, and tow capacity of a heavy truck make it a top choice for driving in bad conditions and off road. This truck can tow twice the weight that a full SUV can pull (20,000 lbs/9 metric tons). Four-wheel-drive heavy trucks also come standard with a two-speed transfer case for many driving conditions.

VAN

It's very hard to beat the covered cargo room and passenger numbers you can carry in a van. You can carry the whole family and a good amount of gear in a standard minivan while getting reasonable gas mileage. If you have a lot of gear and people to haul through bad weather or crowded streets, the van could be your best option.

81 Upgrade Your Ride

Some vehicle upgrades serve a variety of situations; others are very specific. Here are a few to consider.

BRUSH BAR These bars are mounted to the vehicle's frame and protect the vehicle in a front collision. The brush bar can also push vegetation and debris out of the way for off-road driving.

SNORKEL AIR INTAKE Driving through flood waters and rivers is incredibly dangerous, but it's possible with a raised air intake for your engine. Ideally, many vehicle systems should be waterproofed, but the mandatory item for driving through water is the snorkel.

ELECTRIC WINCH Pull yourself out of a jam with a sturdy electric winch. These are typically mounted on front brush bars and allow you to pull yourself (or another vehicle/object) out of a hole.

HIGH-FLOTATION TIRES Wider, higher-flotation tires make a big difference in off-road driving. These offer enhanced traction in loose sand, deep mud, and snow.

TOW HOOKS These hooks are attached to the vehicle frame and are a big help—whether you're the one towing or the one getting towed.

HIGH-CAPACITY FUEL TANK This option may only be available as an aftermarket part, but larger fuel tanks can certainly be an option in many vehicles. Upsize your 15-gallon (57-l) gas tank with a generous 20-gallon (76-l) tank, or even a beefy 25-gallon (95-l).

82 Charge It Yourself

To be as self-reliant as possible, consider carrying a portable battery jump-starter in your vehicle. These battery packs can deliver 400 to 1,700 amps of engine-cranking power and have integrated jumper cables to connect directly to your failed vehicle battery, with no friendly neighbor necessary. Some models include additional features, such as air compressors, battery-power-level gauges, built-in lights to illuminate your work area, and 12-volt DC charging sockets that can power and recharge important electronic devices, such as cell phones.

83 Provide All the Air

A portable air compressor is a very handy piece of machinery that lets you properly refill a flat tire during emergencies. This easy-to-use device plugs into your car's cigarette lighter or 12-volt power outlet and is capable of inflating the tires of cars, SUVs, and light trucks. A 12-volt motor provides good air compressing power, but they may take several minutes to fully inflate larger tires. Depending on the device, extras can include an in-line tire pressure gauge, long air hoses, and various nozzles to inflate rafts, air mattresses, and other items.

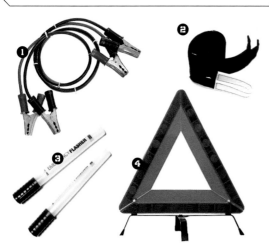

84 Get the Tools for Your Car

You can't do the job if you don't have the right tools. Stock up your vehicle like a rolling warehouse by carrying these tools and supplies to help you tackle an unexpected roadside emergency.

① JUMPER CABLES A heavy-gauge set of good jumper cables and a second vehicle can get your car running in the event that your battery has lost its charge or it needs a little boost in cold weather.

② TOW STRAP A nylon tow strap can get your car or truck out of a ditch, snow bank, or swamp, if there is another vehicle to pull you out. Select a heavy strap with *no metal parts*. A tow chain or a strap with metal hooks on the end can kill someone if it breaks while under tension.

③ ROAD FLARES Let the other drivers know you're there by signaling with road flares. Some will burn for up to 30 minutes. The old-fashioned kind also make great fire starters in severe weather conditions.

④ REFLECTIVE SIGN The flares will only last so long, which is the reason for having a back-up distress signal such as a reflective sign. Get one that is freestanding and heavy, so that the wind or vehicles won't blow it over.

⑤ WATER For your drinking water and for radiator fill-ups, keep several gallons of water in your ride. Keep more than that if you live in or travel through a dry climate.

⑥ FIX-A-FLAT This can of tire-mending spray is able to seal up small holes in a flat tire, and reinflate the tire enough to get you to a repair shop. For large holes, use this product in tandem with a tire plug kit.

⑦ TIRE PLUG KIT A tire plug kit consists of glue, a few tools, and some rubber/fiber strips that can be glued in place if there is a hole in your tire's tread. Use one rubber strip for little holes, use the whole bundle if there is a gaping hole.

⑧ SOCKET SET Simple repairs, as well as the more complex ones, will require a socket set. If you're going this far, go all the way and buy a set that has both standard (imperial) sockets and metric sockets.

⑨ HAMMER Possibly the greatest simple tool ever devised, a hammer can be useful for many car repairs and related work. It can also pass for a weapon, in the event that you need one.

⑩ DUCT TAPE Purchase automotive duct tape for your car tool kit, as it is more resistant to heat and UV light. You can use it to fix or secure almost anything in your ailing vehicle.

11 WRENCHES & PLIERS Adjustable wrenches can be lifesavers when you're working on a vehicle. Keep a few different sizes of pliers in your vehicle, in case you have to pull a nail out of a tire, fix battery terminals, or mend a major breakdown (assuming you know what you're doing).

12 NONPERISHABLE FOOD If you get stranded for a long time, a food supply can provide you with energy and a morale boost. Rotate this food often, and plan according to the seasons and weather. Pass on any items that will go bad in the heat or that will be too hard to eat if frozen.

13 FULL-SIZE SPARE Don't just settle for one of those dinky little emergency tires. Get a full-size spare for your vehicle, and include it when you're rotating your tires for better wear.

14 FLASHLIGHT WITH SPARE BATTERIES It gets dark underneath your vehicle, and even darker at night. Give yourself every advantage you can by keeping a flashlight or two, and some extra batteries, in the vehicle at all times. Rotate the batteries every season, so you know you'll always have them in case of trouble.

15 BLANKETS OR SLEEPING BAGS Ideally, you should have one of these items for each seat in your vehicle. This will cover every passenger and the driver, in the event of a cold-weather car breakdown.

16 TIRE IRON & JACK The tire iron will be needed to break loose the nuts that hold a tire in place. The jack will be needed to raise and lower the vehicle to complete a tire change or other repairs.

17 MAPS Good, old-fashioned paper maps can be a lifesaver when you are lost. Keep a set of maps for your home state and other areas that you may travel through frequently. Add to this treasure trove of information with every long car trip.

18 FIRST AID Sometimes the vehicle needs repairs; sometimes a person needs to be patched up too. A good first aid kit will serve you (or any other injured person) well, especially during an emergency.

19 FIRE EXTINGUISHER Small fires in a vehicle can be put out by unloading a fire extinguisher at their base, but if you think that gasoline is involved in the fire, don't stay that close to danger. Run away!

Don't Get Caught Without:
PARACORD

This incredibly versatile braided cord was first used in parachutes in World War II (hence the name). Once in the field, paratroopers found that this cord was incredibly useful for everything from pitching tents to sawing logs. Astronauts have even used it to repair the Hubble telescope. Never be without a reel of this stuff somewhere nearby. You can use cord as bootlaces to ensure it's always right there when you need it, or weave a snazzy bracelet or belt that just happens to unravel into a nylon multitool.

❶ SLING
Weave a sling and take down prey David & Goliath–style! Yes, it's strong enough. You'd be surprised.

❸ DENTAL FLOSS
Pull off the outer covering of your paracord—it's woven from many smaller filaments. These fine but sturdy threads serve as excellent dental floss. Not so worried about hygiene? They also make great fishing line or even sutures.

❹ BOW DRILL
Making a bow drill to start a fire? Paracord's a great choice for the string on that bow.

❷ FIELD WRENCH
Can't loosen a rusty nut? Wrap paracord around it counterclockwise, and give a good yank.

8 BOLA
Weave paracord around a lead weight, large ball bearing, or even a nice round rock. Braid a handle and you've got a throwing weapon that can take down a rabbit for dinner—or a pesky intruder.

9 SURVIVAL BRACELET
Get in the habit of wearing a woven paracord bracelet at all times. It goes with everything and means you're never without a good amount of lifesaving rope.

6 BORE SNAKE
Braid to the right thickness and use to clean your gun.

7 EMERGENCY KNIFE
Just about any soft-to-medium-consistency food can be sliced with paracord. In case you forgot the cheese knife.

10 SHOELACES
Lace your boots with paracord and you'll never be without this essential item!

5 TOURNIQUET
Wrapping cord around a stick allows you to easily tighten or loosen a tourniquet to avoid damaging healthy tissue.

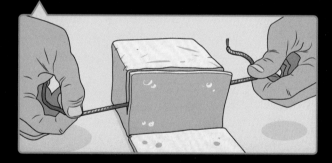

SKILLS

Having skills and experience in a wide range of survival techniques can take a person much further than gear alone. When supplies run low, a well-rounded survival skill set can keep providing for you and for those in your care.

In this second chapter, we will have a look at a diverse assortment of survival and self-sufficiency skills. These pages will help you in every aspect of survival, from shelter and water to food, medicine, and self-defense. But this book is of little use if you don't pay attention to one particular cornerstone of survival—practice. A mind full of facts and data is better than a mind full of trivial nonsense, but knowing the information and performing the skills are two very different things. You need practical, hands-on learning before an emergency hits in order to make a useful difference—and you must learn these things for yourself because, ultimately, you are the only one truly responsible for yourself.

It's high time more people decided to take responsibility for themselves. We live in an era when a professional is always available to solve your problems and there's a 24-hour store stocked with food and supplies around every corner. People have become dependent on these support systems to the point of being slaves to them. Generations are growing up without the skills to provide for themselves, the knowledge to repair the things around them, or the ability to either improvise the tools they need or simply do without.

I have always been a big believer in practical skills. Even if your materials or supplies are lacking, a little creativity and some solid self-reliance can make all the difference in any situation, especially in an emergency. And once you've learned a skill, it's with you forever. For example, you may run out of fishing gear, but you'll never run out of fishing techniques. Your food supplies may dwindle, but once you learn to garden, you'll never forget how you grew your own vegetables. A set of skills is the one thing that can't be lost, broken, used up, destroyed, or taken from you during a survival situation. Skills are weightless, easy to carry, and they will last a lifetime.

86 Know Basic Life Skills

Somehow, millions of people make it through life without learning these basic skills. They may not seem related to survival—but you just never know when you'll be confronted with an outside-the-norm situation, such as having only one working car available for a getaway and a group of people who have never driven a stick shift. Here are a few of those things that you should already know—and if you're missing any, you should learn and teach others, pronto.

PERFORM ARITHMETIC You don't need to be able to perform vector calculus in your head at the drop of a hat, but you should know more than just 2+2=4. When you're trying to determine measurements for building, or doing a little bartering, you may not have a calculator available.

LEARN BASIC AUTO CARE This is one of those skill sets you might think you have a good handle on—but it pays to be sure. At the least, you should know how to change a tire, as well as your oil and filters.

OPERATE A MANUAL TRANSMISSION Whether your creaky old uncle scared you off his truck when you were 16 or you simply never had any other car besides automatic put in front of you, go find a friend who's into cars and get driving.

HANDLE BASIC TOOLS You don't need to master a router, drill press, table saw, or belt sander for every possible need, but you should know how to handle tools. We'll assume you can probably use a hammer or screwdriver without help, but make sure you're good with the rest of the toolbox as well. A handsaw or axe can be trickier than you might think.

RIDE A BIKE You never know when having to get somewhere in a pinch may come down to a set of wheels powered by your own two legs—and the cliché that you never forget how to ride a bike isn't really true. You should definitely consider learning to ride a motorcycle as well.

87 Revisit Home Ec

Think sewing's got nothing to do with survival? Wait until that first cold winter when your old coat is falling apart and the nearest settlement is a day's walk through the snow. A lot of the skills seen today as mundane tasks or outdated pastimes were vital to our forebears' subsistence—and might be again.

COOK THE BASICS This doesn't mean pouring boiling water over a cup of noodles. Basic cooking knowledge encompasses how to stay healthy, what wild foods are edible, and how to safely prepare the food you've stored and that you hunt or gather—as well as avoiding kitchen injuries and foodborne illness.

SEW It's not just a skill for little old-fashioned grandmas. Learning to sew means you can patch up a damaged piece of clothing or make a new one. It's a skill that's transferable to fixing other items and, to a degree, even to medical care.

PLANT A GARDEN In this day and age, not very many people know how to keep a plant alive—much less grow a garden. Learning to properly cultivate plants isn't just about having pretty flowers or a pot of herbs at your window; it's another of our oldest skills—and one that you could potentially use to grow your own food.

Build Your Survival Skills

Everything that's in these pages can be considered a survival skill, but some situations are a little bit more immediate than others. After all, if you need to learn to garden, there's probably time for someone to teach you. If you need to learn how to win in a fistfight, that's a good thing to know before the brawl breaks out. The skills below will help keep you alive and unharmed when the chips are down.

READ A MAP Don't just rely on a GPS or smartphone's navigation software. Know your way around a real map, on paper. Learn how to find where you are and how to get where you're going—and you should know how a compass works, too.

BUILD A FIRE This is one of humanity's oldest and most important skills. Even if you have matches or a lighter, you should learn how to start a fire without them; it's a skill that might save your life. (See items 101–104 for more detail.)

SWIM You'd be surprised how many people don't know how to swim (or aren't confident in their abilities), and considering that more than 70 percent of the Earth's surface is covered by water, it's a lifesaving skill. If all else fails, you should at least know how to tread water and how to float on your back.

RIDE A HORSE You don't have to make like the Lone Ranger, but in a hard-core survival situation, horses might be your best or only form of transport. Knowing how to saddle up and ride with some skill will keep you from being sore, laughed at, or left behind. Extra points for mastering the art of mounting and riding bareback.

KNOW BASIC FIRST AID Even knowing how to take care of minor injuries can make a big difference in a difficult situation. Add in some CPR training and the Heimlich maneuver, and you're well on your way to the foundations of medical care. (See items 89–100.)

TAKE AND THROW A PUNCH You might hope never to get into a fight, but if push comes to shove (or jab, or hook, or uppercut), you should learn how to defend yourself and others with your bare hands. (More about this in items 211–214.)

HANDLE A GUN Firearms are both a tool and a weapon, and, as such, owning one involves great responsibility. Plenty of people are unreasonably afraid of guns simply because they don't know very much about them. Even if you've never hunted or don't expect to have to defend yourself, take a basic firearms course at a local shooting range. You'll learn how to safely handle and use a gun, should the need ever arise. (Also see items 225–228.)

89 Build Your First Aid Kit

If you're the type of person who's always asking for a bandage or aspirin, it's time to get it together. Create a kit that includes the following items.

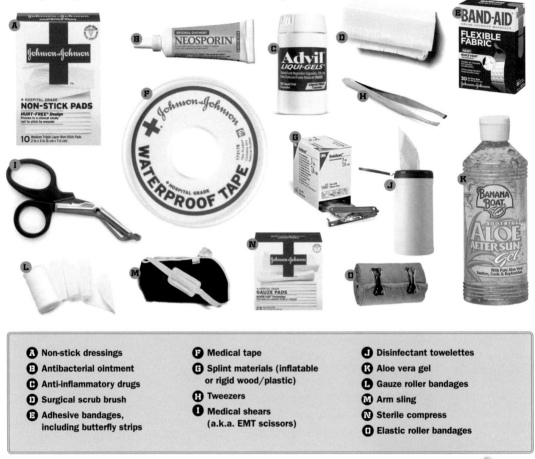

- **Ⓐ Non-stick dressings**
- **Ⓑ Antibacterial ointment**
- **Ⓒ Anti-inflammatory drugs**
- **Ⓓ Surgical scrub brush**
- **Ⓔ Adhesive bandages, including butterfly strips**
- **Ⓕ Medical tape**
- **Ⓖ Splint materials (inflatable or rigid wood/plastic)**
- **Ⓗ Tweezers**
- **Ⓘ Medical shears (a.k.a. EMT scissors)**
- **Ⓙ Disinfectant towelettes**
- **Ⓚ Aloe vera gel**
- **Ⓛ Gauze roller bandages**
- **Ⓜ Arm sling**
- **Ⓝ Sterile compress**
- **Ⓞ Elastic roller bandages**

If you've got the know-how (perhaps with EMS or some other medical training) you might add these to your medical supplies. Some "jump bags" are even prepacked with these items—and many more.

- Trauma pads (some even help speed blood clotting)
- CPR mask
- Chemical hot and cold packs
- Normal saline (for rinsing injuries)

- EpiPens (for anaphylactic allergic reactions)
- Oral glucose tubes (for diabetic emergencies)
- Activated charcoal (for ingested poisons)
- Tourniquet rubber strips

- Wilderness/travel medicine guidebook
- Nitrile or latex gloves
- Penlight
- Stethoscope
- Blood pressure cuff

90 Improvise Medical Supplies

In an emergency, having the medical gear you need can be a godsend. But what if you're forced to make do with the materials at hand? There are plenty of DIY options.

BUTTERFLY STRIPS Small pieces of duct tape can be snipped with scissors to create butterfly dressings to hold cuts closed. Snip them twice on each of the long sides, and fold the middle under to create a non-stick section that would float over the laceration.

DRESSINGS Although they are not sterile, feminine hygiene pads can provide you with a decent wound dressing. Tampons are a bit more sterile, and they can be laid sideways on a wound. Strap down any of these dressings with clean cloth strips, tape, or any other binding you have at hand.

INSECT STING RELIEF Meat tenderizer is made of enzymes that break down tough steak proteins—and those found in bug venom! Mix the tenderizer and a drop or two of water into a paste and apply it directly to the sting or bite. It won't help a rattlesnake bite, but this mixture can somewhat relieve the pain from hornet, wasp, scorpion, and ant stings.

SPLINTS Splints are one of the easier bits of medical gear to improvise. Your goal is immobilization, which can be achieved with any number of rigid items and binding materials, such as a board and some duct tape. Make sure you stuff adequate padding inside the splint to properly stabilize the limb and ease your patient's pain—use crumpled toilet paper or newspaper, spare clothing, or anything else that works.

BURN GEL Smear a light coating of toothpaste onto the dressing for a burn wound and then apply. It's simple and surprisingly effective, too.

DISINFECTANT Keep infections at bay by putting hand sanitizer or straight liquor onto topical wounds. Yes, it will hurt, but it's better to hurt now and heal than to let a wound become infected, which will result in a lot more pain later.

91 Level Up

Remember, the first step in taking care of injuries is knowing what supplies to use and how to use them properly. This is the baseline level of what any well-prepared person should know. To take your knowledge to the next level, there are no shortage of first-responder and first-aid courses and books available. You can also inquire with your local Red Cross for information on classes.

First-aid and first-responder courses are just the beginning when learning about emergency medical treatment. Your local college or other educational institution may offer EMS classes lasting from a few weeks of accelerated training to a few months of intermittent sessions that you can fit into your schedule. These classes will not only give you training but also prepare you to acquire an EMT license.

92 Check Vital Signs

The two most important aspects of a person's vitals are their respiration and circulation—breathing and heartbeat. To count someone's breaths, either watch for the rise and fall of his chest or listen to his breathing (with or without a stethoscope) for 15 seconds, then multiply by four (normal is 12–20 breaths per minute).

The easiest places to take someone's pulse are the wrist and the throat. For the wrist, press two fingers against the inside of the forearm, on the thumb side. Count the number of beats in 15 seconds, and multiply that by four (60 to 100 is normal). For the throat, find the Adam's apple, then move your fingers to the side just under the jaw. Press gently with two fingers, and measure the beats using the same method.

93 Assess and Control Bleeding

Diagnosing the type of blood flow coming from a wounded person will help you determine the severity of his or her injuries and how to treat them. Always handle the most serious injuries first.

OOZING BLOOD Scrapes, scratches, or abrasions that open capillaries result in oozing blood. Infection is the biggest worry here, since the skin, which is the body's first layer of defense, is damaged. Clean and disinfect the wound, then apply antibiotic ointment and dressings, and change the dressings daily. Look for infection, which may need skilled treatment.

FLOWING BLOOD If blood flows, it's the result of damage to a vein. Elevate the injury above the heart, clean any debris from the wound if possible, and apply direct pressure. Add more bandages as needed and, once the bleeding stops, secure dressings to the wound. You may need to find more skilled medical care for further treatment.

SPURTING BLOOD If blood is bright red and spurts, it comes from an arterial injury and is immediately life-threatening. Elevate the injury, apply direct pressure, and add more bandages if they soak through. If needed, locate and apply pressure to the nearest arterial pressure point (see item 335). If the bleeding won't stop, use a tourniquet to cut off blood flow (but be aware that this increases the risk that an amputation will be necessary, and should therefore be an option only in cases of arterial bleeding). Seek medical care immediately.

INTERNAL BLEEDING When an organ or vessel inside the body has been injured, blood can fill the spaces inside the body. The injured person may go into shock, become confused due to low blood flow, or have decreased fluid (urine and sweat) output. Incline the victim with the injured area raised to restrict blood flow, and he or she should be treated for shock. Again, seek medical care immediately.

95 Disinfect a Wound

Knowing how to disinfect wounds can be vital—even small cuts can get infected. And if your body's fighting off an infection, it has fewer resources to provide for your overall health.

STEP 1 Stop the bleeding and assess the injury. If it won't stop bleeding or it's deep and needs stitches, get professional medical help.

STEP 2 Flush the wound with clean water or saline. Avoid peroxide or alcohol, which can actually damage healthy tissues.

STEP 3 Cover the wound with antibiotic ointment and apply dressings to keep out dirt and debris.

94 Bandage a Wound

Skin takes up to 72 hours to seal after an injury. Small cuts and scrapes just need to be kept clean, but larger cuts will need more care.

Unless you have proper sutures and surgical needle, don't stitch the wound. Line up the edges of the cut and place adhesive butterfly strips in a criss-cross pattern down the length of the wound. Dress with sterile wrappings.

In a pinch you can also use superglue (which was first tested as a wound sealant in the Vietnam war). Coat only the outside of the cut's edges, not inside the cut itself.

96 Know CPR

If you're getting ready for emergencies, you should get trained in CPR—but even without it, you can still help.

STEP 1 Call 911 or some other medical help ASAP.

STEP 2 Place the heel of your hand on the victim's sternum, in the center of his chest, with your other hand on top.

STEP 3 Lock your elbows and use your body weight to compress the chest, pushing down about 2 inches (5 cm)—lighter for children. Aim for 100 compressions a minute.

STEP 4 If you're trained in CPR: After 30 compressions, gently tip the victim's head back to open the airway, and pinch his nose shut before applying two deep breaths. Repeat steps 2–4 until help arrives or the victim recovers.

97 Treat for Shock

Trauma will cause the body to divert blood to vital internal organs, leading to shock—which can be fatal if not treated properly. Signs include paleness, rapid pulse, and cold, clammy skin. Other signs like vomiting or gasping for air occur as shock worsens.

Lay the victim down, elevate her legs, and keep her head low. Treat any visible injuries, and loosen restrictive clothing. Keep her warm with blankets or coats, and keep her talking to focus her mind. Reassure her that everything will be okay.

98 Set Broken Bones

If a fracture is misaligned, blood circulation is reduced, healing time is extended, and worse, the limb may be lost if the break is bad enough.

First, assess the break. Many won't need to be set, but if the bone is displaced you might have to. If the bone is protruding, don't move it. Cover it with a moist saline dressing, immobilize it, and get medical help.

Check for blood flow by gently compressing the skin below the fracture. If the skin does not quickly restore to normal color, you should set the bone to restore circulation. Pull slowly but firmly along the long axis of the bone to reset the break.

Apply a splint and wrap with bandages. The splint can be an air cast or a rigid cardboard, plastic, aluminum, or wood panel with padding for stability and comfort. Secure the cast above and below neighboring limb joints, or immobilize with a sling.

99 Identify and Treat Burns

The skin is the body's largest organ and its primary defense system. A burn's severity (and its course of treatment) depends on how deep it penetrates the layers of tissues.

1ST DEGREE These types of burns are superficial and are caused by anything from sun exposure to hot fluids. They heal on their own but you can apply cool compresses or aloe vera gel, and speed along the healing process with anti-inflammatories.

2ND DEGREE Partial-thickness burns, a.k.a. second-degree burns, penetrate the dermis and can raise blisters. Flood the area with cool water and trim loose skin (but leave blisters alone to avoid infection). Aloe vera and bandages are recommended, but if the injury is to the face, hands, feet, or groin, seek skilled medical attention.

3RD DEGREE These are also called full-thickness burns, having penetrated all layers of the skin. Tissues are often dry, stiff, leathery, and painless (due to nerve damage). Cover with a dry dressing and immediately get help.

4TH DEGREE These burns penetrate through skin and into muscle, fat, and bone. These are the most severe and require extensive, skilled medical care.

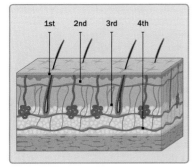

100 Perform the Heimlich Maneuver

Someone who's truly choking cannot breathe or tell you what's happening. He'll often grab at his throat, but it's up to you to recognize the situation and act quickly.

Stand behind the victim and put your arms around his waist, with one fist below the ribs and above the navel, and your other hand covering your fist. Pull your fist upward and into the abdomen, pressing firmly with both hands. Repeat the motion until the airway is cleared.

If you can't reach around the person or he passes out, lay him on his back and then perform the maneuver while straddling his legs or hips.

If you're dealing with a very small child or infant who is choking, cradle her in one arm and compress her chest with your fingertips five times, alternating this with turning her over and applying five firm slaps to her midback until the airway is cleared.

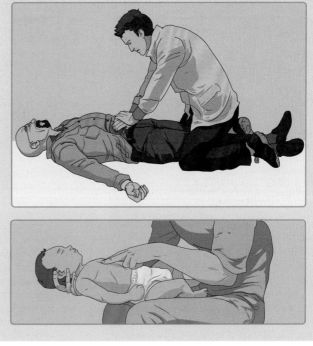

101 Build a Fire in the Rain

Your main issue here is going to be finding dry tinder. If rain looks to be falling soon, gather dry tinder as you hike through the woods, stashing it in your pack or jacket. Once things are already wet, check underneath rocks, ledges, and logs and in tree hollows for moss or dry grass that may be covered. In a worst-case scenario, choose big dead branches and use your knife to scrape away the wet exterior.

Know that building your fire is going to take much longer than it would in dry conditions. Once you have a decent fire going, stack wet wood around and over it in a sort of log cabin. This will protect the fire from rain and dry the wood for later.

102 Get the Best Materials You Can Find

Whether your ignition source is a match, a lighter, a road flare, or a friction fire, you'll need the same type of materials to get the fire started and keep it burning. The first material is tinder. These slight materials have a lot of surface area and little mass, so they release their flammable gases more quickly than stouter materials. Tinder should always be fine, fluffy, dead, and dry, and it should come from the plant kingdom. Hair, fur, and feathers do not make good tinder. Instead, try dead pine needles, crunchy leaves, crumbly dead grasses, and the fibrous inner bark from dead tree branches.

Next you'll need an assortment of very slender dead twigs, wood shavings, and/or split wood splinters for kindling. These work best formed into a cone shape around a core of tinder. Add a few finger-thick sticks on the exterior of the cone and it's ready to light near the bottom. Insert a lit match, or light several spots with a lighter—and watch your hard work pay off with flames.

103 Make Char Cloth

Char cloth uses a process called pyrolysis (burning without oxygen) to turn ordinary cloth into a fire starter that's great to use with flint and steel, since it only takes a single spark to ignite. Here's how.

STEP 1 Make a small hole in the top of a tin that closes tightly.

STEP 2 Fill the tin with scraps of cotton cloth (it needs to be all-natural; no synthetic fibers).

STEP 3 Place your container in the coals of a fire. Smoke should start streaming steadily out of the box's vent hole.

STEP 4 After 5 minutes, pull the tin off of the coals. The resulting cloth should be solid black and have a silky texture but not fall apart. Now you have tinder that you can carry with you until you need it for firestarting in almost any situation.

STEP 5 When you need tinder, pull the char cloth out and strike a single spark onto it. It should burn slowly and steadily.

STEP 6 Use the cloth to ignite your larger bundle of tinder.

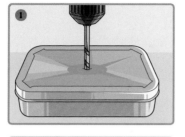

104 Learn the Tricks to Tinder

You can become a fire-building genius with a little know-how and some practice. Tinder is essential, and it's worthwhile to know what to burn.

Use only dead stuff, nothing green, and have extra on standby. The center of your fire lay should be loaded with tinder, and it's this you light—not the wood. Make sure to block the wind with your body when lighting.

Pine, firs, spruce, and most other needle-bearing trees have sap in their wood. This is pitch, which is usually very flammable. Select dead twigs from these trees to get your fire going quickly even in damp weather. And pine needles make a good addition to tinder at any time, because they light easily even when wet. Another tip? Douse your tinder with bug spray before lighting—it will add some serious flammability. Stand back.

wind

Don't Get Caught Without: SARDINES

Maybe you're sitting on a bunker full of these stinky little canned fish, or maybe you just have a can or two in the pantry. Believe it or not, sardines can be used for a variety of survival applications.

❺ EAT 'EM!

There's always their intended purpose: You can eat the fish, too. A few crackers and some hot sauce will work wonders to liven up those little guys.

❶ GREASE LAMP

To make a grease lamp from a tin of sardines, you should start with some sardines packed in oil. Eat the fish and place a string in the oil with just 1 inch (2.5 cm) sticking out for a wick.

❷ ANIMAL TRAP

Cut an X in the tin, secure the tin to a stake with a length of wire, and place it over a hole. If something slender-footed yet heavy (like a large fox) steps on the X, it'll punch through and get stuck (for a little while).

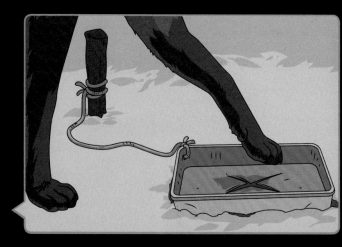

❸ SIGNAL MIRROR

A shiny can will pass for a signal mirror in a pinch, especially if you have a way to polish it, such as rubbing a little chocolate or toothpaste on the metal with a piece of paper or a rag.

❹ TRAP BAIT

Raccoons and other omnivores love fishy things, so use the sardine liquid or actual sardine pieces to bait your traps. That coon or bobcat will give you a beautiful pelt, and it could be a welcome change in menu if times are tough.

❻ SURVIVAL KIT

You've probably seen the sardine-can survival kits that are commercially available. While the can is a good idea, the contents are usually sub-par, so make your own. Fill an empty can with your survival gear, and use a generous amount of duct tape to seal it up. Now you have a water-resistant can, quality survival goodies, and duct tape (see item 224).

7 MINI FRYING PAN

A large-sized tin will make a fine little frying pan for a one-person cooking set. You could also boil water in it, but it would take a while to get any reasonable volume to drink.

8 CAMP STOVE

Pour a splash of high-proof alcohol in and light it up. Or coil a few cardboard strips and drizzle melted wax over them for a "fire can," which can be used for cooking or fire starting.

9 EMERGENCY PET FOOD

Cats and dogs could subsist for quite a while on sardines, if no other foods were available.

10 SHELTER SMOKER

If you have a bug-infested shack that you need to smoke out, place some red-hot coals in a large sardine can, crumble some dry rotten wood over the coals, and place the container in a fireproof spot inside the shelter. It will create tons of smoke and should resolve your bug troubles—at least for the time being.

106 Know Your Water

Safe drinking water can make or break an emergency situation. Contrary to what you see on many survival shows, it's never wise to drink raw water from sources in the wild. Numerous pathogens and contaminants can taint the water supply wherever you are and cause serious harm or death if consumed without the right treatment or disinfecting process. Consider these methods to deal with suspected problems.

PROBLEM	EFFECT	ZONE	METHOD
BACTERIA & VIRUSES	These can cause diarrhea, vomiting, dysentery, and death	Freshwater anywhere, especially in the tropics	Boiling, chemical disinfection, UV devices, and water filters
PROTOZOA	These can cause diarrhea, dysentery, and death	Freshwater anywhere	Boiling, chemical disinfection, and water filters
PARASITES	Fluke worms and other parasites can cause liver damage, lung ailments, and a host of odd symptoms that are potentially fatal	Freshwater anywhere	Boiling, chemical disinfection, and water filters
SALT	Even drinking a small amount of saltwater can lead to kidney damage and electrolyte imbalance, which can be fatal	Oceans and bays	Steam distillation and reverse osmosis filtering will remove salt from water
HEAVY METALS	Depending on the type of contamination and its severity, heavy metals like lead and mercury can cause organ damage and death	Rivers and oceans near industrial areas	Steam distillation will remove all heavy metals from water
RADIATION	A variety of cancers and tissue damage occurs from ingesting irradiated water, leading to a long and painful death	Freshwater and saltwater after a radiological event	Steam distillation is the most effective method to remove radiation, but it is not 100 percent effective

107 Disinfect with UV Light

One of the most recent innovations in water disinfection is the portable UV light purifier. This device doles out a lethal dose of ultraviolet light, which kills or wounds many different types of waterborne pathogens. There are two main types of UV purifiers to choose from.

UV PENS These little pocket-size UV purifiers typically run on two AA batteries and work with push-button ease. To use, stick the light element into a glass of water. Hit the button and a 45-second cycle of glowing blue light will begin. The lightbulb should be stirred through the water. In most cases, the water should be safe for immediate drinking. If the water was slightly cloudy, zap it a second time.

UV HAND-CRANK MODELS What if the power's out? There are hand-crank UV purifiers that provide disinfection with just a minute of manual labor. Fill the water bottle (in the kit) from your local source. Screw the bottle onto the device's housing and flip it. Crank the handle until the LED light turns green (about 90 seconds). Flip it again, unscrew the bottle, wipe the threads clean, and repeat.

109 Keep Clear

Any cloudiness or significant solids in water will create hiding places for bacteria and other tiny vermin to elude the burning light of a UV device. This can mean that multiple doses of UV light still cannot properly disinfect the water, so make sure you use only clear water with any UV method.

108 Disinfect with Boiling Water

Boiling your water before drinking it may seem like a labor-intensive and antiquated method of removing any biological contaminants from a questionable source. In many cases, however, this old-school trick is still the most effective option—killing 100 percent of the living organisms that would cause you to become ill—without having to use any chemicals or specialized equipment.

HEAT SOURCE Any form of fire will work to provide the necessary heat for boiling water. The heat can even be a byproduct of some other activity, such as a wood stove in your household, or the engine block of your running car.

BOILING CONTAINERS Metal and even some glass containers can handle the heat. Make sure that the container is a safe material and is set up in a sturdy way. You can boil water in pots, pans, cans, and other metal containers, but avoid galvanized metal, which imparts toxins into hot water. You can even use glass bottles if you place them on the edge of the fire or heat source.

BOIL TIME Ten minutes of actual boiling temperatures will give you a much safer window of disinfection than the often-recommended one or two. Start your count when the first big bubbles start to jump to the water's surface. Continue to boil, then let cool completely.

110 Use Your Canner to Distill Water

Radiation, lead, salt, heavy metals, and several other contaminants could taint your water supply after a disaster, and if you try to filter them out, you will ruin your expensive water filter. In a scenario where the only water available is dangerous water, there aren't many options to work with. The safest solution lies in water distillation. Water can be heated into steam, and the steam can then be captured to create pure water—removing many forms of contamination, including radioactive fallout. Distillation won't get out all possible contaminants, such as volatile oils and certain organic compounds, but it will work on most heavy particles.

A quick way to make a steam distiller is by using a pressure canner and a length of small-diameter copper tubing. The best part of this operation (aside from getting safe water) is that the canner stays intact. This allows you to shift gears from water distillation to food preservation very easily (assuming you are not dealing with radiation). The only tricky part is getting the copper line fitted to the steam vent on the canner's lid.

SET UP Locate a canner and about 4 feet (1.2 m) of ¼-inch (6-mm) copper line. Set your canner pot on your stove top, over a camping stove, or over an improvised cinderblock fireplace. Fill your canner pot two-thirds full with questionable water and screw on the canner lid. This can be saltwater or muddy water—any water except that tainted by fuels (which evaporate at low temps).

CREATE YOUR COIL. The coil, also known as the worm, is made from copper line coiled in a downward spiral. Use a stick or some other support for the coil to avoid stress on the joint at the canner's steam vent. Ream out one end of the copper tubing and force it down over the steam fitting on top of the canner lid if it's smaller than the steam vent. Compress the line if it's bigger than the vent. Tie this joint with rags or dope it with a paste of flour and water once everything is in position.

LIGHT IT UP Whether a stove or a campfire powers your still, you'll have to play with the size of the fire for best results. If you run it too hot, you'll just blow steam out of the coil. If you run it too cool, nothing will happen. Start out with a small amount of heat, and work your way up if needed. Once the pot gets close to boiling, water should start to pour out of the coil. The surrounding air will naturally cool the copper, and the steam will condense into distilled, drinkable water.

111 Build a Solar Still

The solar still is a simple invention that collects water and distills through a greenhouse effect. It's not perfect, nor does it collect massive quantities of water, but it does provide fresh water in arid climates and it can effectively desalinate saltwater.

In the original method developed in the 1970s, a square of clear or milky plastic is draped over a pit with a clean cup in the bottom. The plastic at the edge of the pit is sealed with a rim of dirt or stones to keep any of the steam from escaping. The plastic sheet is weighed down in the middle with a small rock, pushed down to shape the plastic into a cone shape. The sun will create a steamy environment under the plastic, and the steam will condense on the underside, running down into the cup below. Each site works for days, and you may get a up to a liter of water per still per day.

STEP 1 Set up the still in a sunny area with the dampest dirt or sand available.

STEP 2 Make certain that the point of the cone of plastic is directly over the container inside the still.

STEP 3 Add vegetation inside to increase production.

STEP 4 Urine can be recycled by peeing down a hole dug next to the still so the liquid can soak through the ground and vaporize into the still.

STEP 5 A rubber, plastic, or vinyl drinking tube can be placed in the cup and lead outside the still. This way, water can be sipped as it collects without having to take the whole still apart to get the water out.

112 Double Up

When it comes to the procurement of water in an emergency, we all want to be choosers, not beggars, but you'll rarely see crystal-clear streams in the places where water is scarce. If the only available water looks awful, a little bit of overkill is certainly justified. All you'll need for double-duty disinfection is a water filter, a cloth, and a little bleach to give your water the old double-tap. Follow these easy steps and you'll be killing all of the disease-causing pathogens and keeping new ones from growing in storage.

STEP 1 "Rough filter" chunky, slimy, or particle-laden water by pouring it through a piece of cloth. This will help extend the life of your filter.

STEP 2 Use a reputable filter with some capacity for microbe destruction. A ceramic filter will screen out big pathogens, while a silver or iodine element will kill the more diminutive bacteria and viruses.

STEP 3 Now the real doubling occurs. Add 2–4 drops of household bleach per quart or liter of water, shake aggressively, and let the water sit for 1 hour.

STEP 4 Store or drink your water—it's as safe as it's going to get. Any mini-microbes that slipped past the filter should be thoroughly fried by the chlorine. It can be stored or drunk as long as it retains a faint bleach odor. Use this technique with swamp water, an aging water filter, or any time you are feeling a little paranoid about your self-made water supply.

113 Dig Your Own Well

The art and trade of traditional well digging has almost been forgotten by modern people, but in its most basic form, digging a well requires that you simply dig a hole deep enough to hit the water table. This hole will fill with water from the surrounding soil and may be clean enough to drink as is, but you should boil it just to be safe.

SITE SELECTION & PREP Short of learning how to use a set of dowsing rods, your site selection will be mostly guesswork. If possible, place your well site close to your home and in a water-rich area. Digging near the base of a hill is usually productive, as the hill pulls the water table up toward the surface. Don't dig the well in a low-lying area that is prone to flooding. This location will compromise the soil in the walls of the well and end up introducing a lot of contamination from surface water.

Creating a solid surface, like a circle of flat rocks, can help to stabilize the mouth of the well.

DIG IT You won't need much more than a short-handled shovel, a bucket and rope to haul up dirt, a digging bar to break up rocks, and a ladder to get your brave well-digger out of the hole. Dig a round shaft 5 feet (1.5 m) wide, and dig straight down. Use rocks tied to strings for string lines to determine straight walls. Be aware that people died often in the well-digging trade, due to well collapse or deadly underground gases like methane. For these reasons and others, well digging and open wells are illegal now in many areas. If you have to dig more than 15 feet (4.5 m) down to hit water, make sure you taper the walls of the well as you go down and keep several people on standby to help in the event of a collapse.

114 Get the Water Up

The average household well is around 100 feet (30 m) deep, although some areas may require wells that are twice or three times that deep to hit the water table. The water is drawn up from these wells by an electric-powered pump located at the bottom of the well. In the event of a power failure, this pump won't run and your water will be stuck deep below the surface. This may seem like a hopeless scenario, but there are ways to pull the water to the surface.

WELL BUCKET A well bucket for modern wells is a slender plastic or metal sleeve that can be lowered down on a length of cord. This sleeve has a foot valve at the bottom, allowing it to fill up with water but not spill when lifted up. Make sure you have enough cord to reach the water level, and tie off the free end of the cord at the top of the well. This will keep you from losing your bucket and line. If you have to improvise a well bucket, use an arm's length of steel pipe with a cap at one end and a cord tied to the other. That much steel will weigh enough to submerge in the water, while other slender containers will probably just float on top of the water in the well.

EMERGENCY HAND PUMP This will require some advance planning on your part. You can purchase an old-fashioned hand pump to attach to your modern well head. Some styles of hand pump can be mounted on a well as a backup method, without disrupting your existing electric pump. Do your homework to find the right pump, as some pumps will only pull water up a few feet and others can pull water out of a 200-foot (60-m) well.

115 Make a Gypsy Well

Dig a "gypsy well" to clarify muddy or stagnant surface water. This technique doesn't filter out contaminants, but it can filter larger particles from the water to help with disinfection.

STEP 1 To make the well, dig a hole about a foot (0.3 m) away from the edge of the questionable water source. Dig the hole about 1 foot (0.3 m) down and at least that wide across to make the well's volume worth it. This well can also be dug in a dry creek beds, allowing any subsurface water to collect in the hole for emergencies.

STEP 2 Wait. The hole will fill with water as the fluid seeps through the soil. Allow the water to sit for a few hours or overnight to clear out some of the mud and particles. This type of well works best in sandy, silty, or loamy soils; substances like mud and clay don't percolate the water very effectively.

STEP 3 Collect and disinfect the water using the best method you have available. You can boil the water for 10 minutes, treat it with chemicals, or even run it through a proper filter if it is not too muddy.

116 Boil in a Bottle

Did you know that you can use your water bottle to boil water by the campfire? It's a great backup method for disinfecting your drinking water. Many water bottles developed for the outdoor-sports industry are made from impact-resistant and heat-resistant Lexan plastic. While you shouldn't try to put your Lexan bottle over a fire, you can put the heat of a fire inside the bottle using hot stones.

STEP 1 Collect about two dozen small stones from a dry location.

STEP 2 Heat the stones in your fire for 30 minutes, and use some wooden tongs to drop a hot stone in the bottle of water.

STEP 3 Replace each stone as it cools. The stones will emit heat into the water, bringing it to a boil. It will keep boiling if you keep replacing the stones. Keep one stone at a time in the water until 10 minutes have passed.

117 Maintain Your Perimeter

Your home is your castle, and while you may not be able to dig a moat, you can make sure that the exterior is as impenetrable as possible, whether the danger comes from humans or from Mother Nature. These seemingly mundane things can make a major difference in a survival situation. After all, when a hurricane strikes, your rain gutters suddenly become vitally important. And repairmen will be hard to come by.

ROOFS Be sure your roof is free of debris, fallen leaves, pine needles, or other plant material. This will help to maintain its structural integrity, keep any decomposing substances from affecting the roof materials, and to prevent any flammables from becoming a fire hazard, which is especially important in hot, dry weather or if your property has trees that shed. In addition, if you have a wooden-shingle roof, be sure to give it a proper coating of stain at least every five years, and replace any cracked or missing pieces.

GUTTERS Your gutters shed water from your roof, preventing water damage, but if they fill up with debris they'll be useless. Keep your gutters and downspouts clear of dust, dirt, leaves, and other foreign material.

SIDEWALKS & DRIVEWAYS Keep all of the concrete perimeters of your home in good working order by treating them with a sealant—one that protects them from the elements and also roughens them up, which helps avoid injuries from slips and falls. If you have any sprouting weeds, apply weed killer or uproot those pesky plants, and fill in any cracks.

WINDOWS & DOORS Check your doors and windows to ensure they're closing properly and that their locks function smoothly. (Deadbolts are a more sturdy lock than a simple slide chain, in terms of security.) Check your weather stripping around the bottoms of doors and windows and replace it if it's worn or cracked.

118 Be Your Own Chimney Sweep

Heating fires are responsible for more than a third of all U.S. house fires, and most of them occur due to creosote buildup in the chimney. This mixture of incompletely burned flammable substances, soot, and condensed gases forms an oily coating inside your chimney that can burst into flames.

You can reduce buildup by using only seasoned hardwoods (other flammables leave more deposits) and keeping your fireplace or woodstove clean. However, creosote will accumulate regardless, so you should clean out your chimney at least once a year. You'll also be able to clear out anything else

stuck in there that could be a fire hazard.

Set up a tarp around your fireplace to keep the inside of your house tidy when cleaning your chimney, and sweep or vacuum up any ash, soot, creosote, or other contaminants. The chimney itself can then be swept out with a long scrubbing brush, usually one with a spiraling head. You can also make do by lining a burlap sack with chicken wire, filling it with rocks or small weights, and lowering it down the chimney on a rope to scrape the sides. Various chimney-cleaning solvents are available, or you can use kerosene to help break up the stuff.

119 Keep Your Fortress in Good Shape

Keeping your residence in working order means more than just doing the dishes and vacuuming the carpet. Your home is a shelter from the elements and an environment meant to keep you healthy by managing heat, atmosphere, water, and waste. If you take care of your home, it'll take care of you in return.

☐ **PLUMBING** Know how to keep drains, sinks, and toilets open (or unclog them if they become blocked). A good wrench or two and some other tools will help you maintain everything from the bathroom sink to the kitchen U-bend. If you end up springing a leak, know how to shut off the flow to that fixture or, if necessary, the whole house.

☐ **HEATING VENTS** Air flow for heating and cooling is ducted through your house's vents. Keep your air filters clean to avoid buildup of dust, pollen, and other particles that can impair your home's ventilation, cause allergies, or in some extreme cases, increase the risk of fire due to dust and lint buildup.

☐ **ELECTRICITY** Home electrical repairs are not to be undertaken lightly, as the risk of death or serious injury are very real. That said, you should know the basics, like whether your home has a fuse box or (more likely in modern houses) a circuit breaker box, where it's located, and how to use it. In addition, keep an eye out for frayed wires or other hazards, and have them fixed promptly.

120 Stock Your Home Plumbing Toolbox

Whether you need to unclog a sink, replace a U-bend, or fix a leaky pipe, here's a short list of tools to help you become your own in-home plumber. (Mustache and overalls not included.)

- Crescent wrench, monkey wrench, and/or pipe wrench
- Basin wrench
- Channel-lock pliers
- Propane torch
- Hacksaw and/or pipe cutter
- Metal file and plumber's tape
- Plunger
- Plumber snake, or drain auger
- PVC cement
- Drain cleaner, lye, or baking soda and vinegar

121 Clean with the Basics

With your household properly stocked and maintained, you can potentially keep yourself, your family, and your home safe for years to come. But what about sanitation? Don't waste your valuable pantry and storage space on any chemical cleansers—they're really not that necessary. Here's a list of some far simpler substances that can do just as thorough a job if used properly. As a bonus, they're free of potentially toxic chemicals.

BAKING SODA This old standby does more than just help around the kitchen. It's a mild abrasive, which means you can use it to polish pans, metal, and ceramic fixtures. It's a known odor-fighter, and it can also help soak up spills like ink and oil. Plus, when mixed with vinegar (see below) it can clear drain clogs.

WHITE VINEGAR Aside from pickling foods, the mild acid in vinegar is a proven remover of stains, a de-tarnishing agent, weed killer, fabric softener, and mildew remover, among many other uses.

LEMON JUICE Another good stain remover like vinegar, the acid in lemon juice can also be used to brighten metals, and clean glass and toilets. It's also an insect repellant, a useful remedy for sore throats, and a treatment for the itch caused by plants like poison ivy.

OLIVE OIL Not just tasty on pasta, it's a useful polish for wood and a rust guard for steel. Olive oil can also help remove tar stains from clothing, lubricate squeaky hinges, and condition leather.

122 Start Outside, Then Bring It All Inside

When it comes to panic and safe rooms, you just need to focus on making an interior room of your house safer and more secure. It doesn't have to be high-tech and ugly. In fact, there's no reason to change the purpose of a bedroom or home office. All you need to do is make it safer, so start with the outside of your whole home and then move inward. A home security system with a loud alarm is a start. After that, consider these construction tips before you go crazy with the surveillance system.

GET THE RIGHT DOOR Most interior doors are hollow core with an emphasis on noise reduction and privacy. Get a solid exterior door instead. You'll still have the functionality of an interior door, but it will be tougher. Many exterior doors also are steel, for greater security.

REINFORCE THE FRAME A strong door is pointless with a weak frame. Make sure the frame around the door is equally sturdy. Today, most frames are sold with the doors, so ask how much force the frame is rated for. It should be sturdy enough to withstand a grown man repeatedly throwing himself against it.

LOCK IT DOWN Just as you lock your exterior door with multiple locks, including deadbolts, do the same with your interior door. Also consider a drop-bar lock for even more security, and add more locks at the top and bottom of the door and frame to make it even harder to leverage against a single point.

REPLACE THE WINDOWS It may seem like a pain, but it will be necessary to swap out entire windows, frame and all, with security windows—not just the panes. Cover the windows with heavy curtains, too. Even with the lights on, the right curtains will prevent an intruder from seeing exactly where you are inside your safe room.

123 Stock Your Safe Room

Once your room is fortified, make sure you have the necessities just in case you have to barricade yourself inside. Depending on the circumstances, you should prepare for hunkering down for a few minutes or a few days. As with everything else in this book, err on the side of overpreparing. Assuming you've fortified an existing room of the house, consider these steps:

MAKE IT A SAFE ROOM Add an actual safe; in this case, the room can double as your gun room. A solid safe can be bolted to the floor. If the rule of thumb is self-defense, then be sure that, no matter what the circumstances are, you'll be able to arm yourself. Store guns, ammunition, and cleaning supplies here, and include some basic tools.

DON'T FORGET WATER You can survive for quite a long time without food. But it's easy to find yourself dehydrated in a short time. The safe room also might be used during natural disasters, so plan as if you were preparing for an earthquake or hurricane. Have enough

water stored away to last you three days.

CALL FOR HELP
The most important tool is a phone. No help is ever going to come if you don't have a means of contacting the outside world. Hollywood does a great job of scaring us with mastermind criminals cutting phone lines and disabling security systems. But chances are, you won't have to worry about it in reality. Just in case, keep a cell phone and charger inside the safe room. As soon as you are inside, call emergency services and stay on the line.

REMEMBER THE NECESSITIES If you or a love one needs prescription medicines, be sure you have them stashed. And speaking of the medicine chest, ideally you've reinforced a master bedroom with bath as your safe spot. If not, make sure you also include a method for waste collection (see item 274), because you're going to need a bathroom of some sort.

124 Grab the Popcorn

One of the best things you can do to make your safe room even safer is to install a video monitoring system. They can be expensive, but can you really put a premium on your life?

If you are serious about reinforcing a room, then go the extra mile to allow yourself to monitor the situation fully. Once you're inside, you need to know what's going on outside. If you're being robbed, you can explain to police who is doing what. The level of detail you'll be able to relay in real time will be much appreciated by the authorities, who will know exactly what to expect.

For a really reasonable sum in most areas, you can purchase a four-camera, split-screen monitor system that can patch directly into your safe-room television or computer. You can also consider going with a security firm for installation. Remember, they make most of their money not on the equipment they sell you, but from services like contacting authorities on your behalf.

You can contract them just to purchase your

equipment and install it, and handle contacting the authorities on your own. If you're the type to travel often, however, there's nothing wrong with having a security firm watch out for your home.

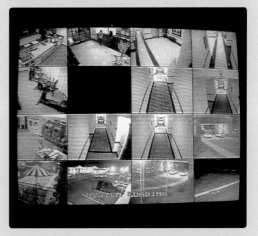

125 Don't Forget Your Pets

During times of crisis, pets often become separated from their owners. Some of the most heartwarming reunion tales in post-disaster areas are the unexpected, less-than-likely ones between pets and their long-lost owners. Unfortunately, there's a reason these are so touching—because they're surprising. More often than not, upheaval will separate you from a furry friend for good—but here are a few ways to make sure that you can find your way back to your little survivor.

MICROCHIPPING Microchip implants are permanent, inexpensive, and very common, so shelters and veterinarians know to check for them. You can change the associated information if you move or your phone number changes—just call up the company to make sure it's up to date.

DIGITAL ID TAGS Sure, Fido can have the regular kind on his collar—but a digital QR code can be updated more easily than an engraving. There are also special collars with USB clips, so your pet is always carrying around a handy emergency flash drive with your info.

DUCT TAPE Yet another use for our favorite supply-kit item: If your pet has the old-fashioned tags, write your new information and where you are traveling on a strip of duct tape and attach it to the back of the tag.

126 Alert the Authorities

Fire safety is important, especially for pets kept inside at all times. Place home pet alert stickers in an obvious location to help notify firefighters of the number and type of pets in the building. If a fire occurs when you and your family are not at home, the sticker will indicate that your home is not as empty as it seems. And for the love of Pete, leave it to the pros. Do not enter a burning building to rescue a pet—they are very resourceful creatures, and may have already escaped. It should go without saying that as much as we love our pets, your life and the lives of your family members are more valuable.

PET ALERT

FIRE RESCUE

PLEASE SAVE OUR PET(S)

☐ DOG(S) ☐ CAT(S) ☐ BIRD(S)

OTHER:

127 Board Up

In case of evacuation, consider places to go that will be open to your pets, like the homes of friends, pet-friendly motels, and kennels—and keep in mind that publicly run shelters might not be equipped to accept pets (aside from service animals). Ask questions if you do find a shelter that accepts pets—they may have breed restrictions or a cap on total number. In times of emergency, some non-pet-friendly hotels will make exceptions, so be sure to ask. If you're hunkered in a bunker, make sure you have pet supplies stored alongside your own—and remember that there's a big difference between omnivores (dogs) and carnivores (cats). Dogs can go vegetarian if need be, but cats need meat to sustain their health.

128 Stock a P.B.O.B.

Your pet's BOB isn't all that different from your own. Here are the essentials.

- ☐ Pet food in airtight containers
- ☐ Registration, rabies, and vaccination records (very important for shelters)
- ☐ Necessary pet meds
- ☐ Water
- ☐ Collar with ID tags
- ☐ Sturdy leash or harness
- ☐ Travel carrier or crate
- ☐ Cat litter and box, doggy clean-up baggies
- ☐ Cleaning and deodorizing materials
- ☐ Photo IDs of you and your pet
- ☐ Familiar items (toys, blankets)
- ☐ First-aid supplies (an eyedropper and syringe is useful for administering meds or flushing wounds, and hydrogen peroxide will disinfect as well as induce vomiting in case of poison ingestion)

129 Prepare to Leave Them Behind

If you absolutely have to leave your pet behind, and there is even the smallest chance you might not be able to make it back, there are some important steps to take. Place your pet inside an interior room (or rooms, with interior doors propped open so they can't shut themselves in one area) for safety, and consider leaving a TV or radio on to distract from outside sounds. Leave plenty of food and water in nonspillable bowls. You can also remove the toilet seats and fill the bathtubs with water for them to drink. Last, place signs on exterior doors to alert rescuers, and write your contact info on your pet's crate, then leave it just inside the door.

130 Train for Disaster

Training your pet is a very important part of an easy getaway and for keeping it out of harm's way. It's unsafe to let your pet roam loose when there may be hazards or disorienting scents or other stimuli nearby, so keep it leashed (even if it normally comes when called), and do some crate training.

- Use an airline-approved crate, which most pet-friendly hotels also accept as standard.
- It should be large enough that your pet has 2–3 inches (5–8 cm) of clearance when standing up completely and enough room to turn around.
- When training, introduce the crate gradually. Position it somewhere your pet likes to be, and put a favorite toy inside.
- If your pet is hesitant, take apart the crate and remove the top and door. Allow your pet to go freely in and out of the open half until putting the top back on doesn't cause alarm.

I WAS TENDING TO MY ROOF GARDEN ON A BLISTERING-HOT DAY WHEN A MASSIVE FIRE BROKE OUT IN MY BUILDING!

. . . A JUMP! I SPRANG OFF THE TAKEOFF FOOT, KEPT MY LEG STRAIGHT, TUCKED THE TRAILING LEG, AND PRAYED.

I SLID OFF AN AWNING TO SLOW DOWN . . .

132 Do Your Research

You can read all the gardening books and green-colored websites you like, but there's no substitute for real-life experience. After a catastrophic event, folks may be suspicious of strangers, or wary that you're out to steal their good stuff. So, start gardening now, and get all the local advice you can. What grows best in your local soil? What pests should you look out for? Local farmers and longtime gardeners will know, so seek them out and learn from their mistakes and successes.

133 Pick the Right Spot

The site you pick for your garden is critical and should take into account soil composition and light exposure. Visit your county's agricultural extension office—with a little help, you can learn which parts of your property are best suited for gardening and farming. Then pick a spot in the best soil area with at least 10 hours of direct sunlight each day.

Orient all rectangular beds or rows on a north-south axis for equal light exposure. Plant the tallest plants at the north end so they don't shade smaller plants. If you have containers, avoid placing them too close to metal siding or similar reflective surfaces during the hottest times of the year, as that will cause the plants to cook or dry out.

134 Get the Dirt

You can't just throw some seeds out on the lawn and expect anything productive to happen. Vegetables need to grow in loose, rich soil—without competition. Your garden should have the sod removed, and then be dug and chopped with a shovel, or tilled with a rototiller machine, at least 1 foot (30 cm) deep—but twice that is better. This is hard work, but the payoff is huge, as deep root growth pulls in more nutrients and provides a better water supply.

Before you pile on a bunch of fertilizer willy-nilly, purchase a soil test kit to get a rough idea of the nutrient levels. This testing can help determine the deficiencies of your garden soil and allow you to make the right amendments. No matter your test results, well-decomposed compost is always welcome. The good stuff will be aged, very dark in color, and will have gone through a high-heat stage of decomposition to kill diseases and weed seeds. Add as much as you can to your garden, blending it with the soil or just applying on the surface. For clay-filled soil, add sand; likewise, add clay to sandy soil, and you can add aged manure to any variety.

135 Place Your Plants

You can sow seeds directly into the dirt, or you can plant seedlings from their small containers. Either way, water liberally to settle the soil around them. Seedlings can suffer from transplant shock if planted in hot, dry soil—plant in the evening so they can adjust to their new home.

Certain plants grow better or repel pests if planted as companions to one another. One of the best-known plant companion sets is corn, beans, and squash (the Native American "Three Sisters"), which provide each other with needed shade and structure. Onions, garlic, chives, marigolds, and nasturtiums all offer you some degree of pest repellent. And never plant anything near black walnut trees, as they release vegetable-killing chemicals into the soil.

Unless it rains all the time in your area, you'll need to water all those plants. This can be done with collected rainwater (a great choice) or with a garden hose. Water deeply and thoroughly every other day. Water in the morning, if possible. Watering in the heat of a sunny afternoon will cause the droplets of water to burn the plant leaves like little magnifying lenses, and watering in the evening or at night can encourage fungal diseases. Here are a few factors to keep in mind.

- ☐ Divide plot into 12-inch- (30-cm-) square sections and plant a different vegetable in each.
- ☐ Put shallow-rooted plants next to deep-rooted ones so they don't compete for resources.
- ☐ Choose vegetable varieties that grow vertically to increase each square's yield.
- ☐ Plant tall plants at the plot's edge to keep their shadows off adjacent plants.
- ☐ Replant as soon as you harvest.
- ☐ Fertilize soil year-round.
- ☐ Variety is the spice of life! Plant and enjoy a wide range of nutritious crops year-round.

136 Go Urban

Living in the city doesn't mean you can't grow a garden. There's always a way to make the room that you need to develop a supplemental food supply. You may not get to produce the volume of food that your rural friends can grow in their wide-open spaces, but you can still grow a respectable amount of nutritious and tasty vegetables—and add to your growing sense of food security by becoming an urban gardener.

SEEK THE SUN Unless you live in a tiny basement apartment, chances are good that you have some direct natural sunlight coming through the windows of your home. A few lucky city dwellers may have a backyard or rooftop access, but for most folks, you only get what your windows and balconies provide. If you have a southern exposure to your dwelling, use these south-facing balconies and rooms for your urban garden. These get the most direct sunlight each day, regardless of season. North-facing areas will be the worst garden spot, as they remain fully shaded most of the day.

GROW UP Like cities themselves, if you cannot grow outward, then you must grow up. There are numerous styles of hanging containers, vegetable-growing towers, and even wall installations which allow you to grow food when floor space is at a premium. The inverted tomato-growing buckets do reasonably well, but using something with a larger volume of soil is much better

for your plants. Vine vegetables like cucumber and pole beans can be trained to grow upward or laterally by gently tying them to string, rope, railings, or latticework.

LIGHT 'EM UP Grow lights are often employed by indoor gardeners to supplement or replace the rays of the sun. But these are not the only options for plant lighting. Mirrors can also be very helpful, by bouncing direct sunlight toward your plants. You'll see the plants respond to the mirror's extra light within days. The phenomenon known as phototropism can be seen as plants grow toward the light and the leaves orient themselves perpendicular to the light streaming in. Use any size mirrors to redirect the sun to your plants, but bigger is better. You can even do a downsized version of this mirror trick by placing aluminum foil under your plants to bounce light up under the leaves.

WATER WISELY City water is treated with chlorine and other chemicals to make it safe for people to drink, but it's not all that good for your plants. Although small amounts of these chemicals seem to be tolerated by most plants and vegetables, the best way to water is to collect as much rainwater as possible (if it's legal in your area) and use that to water your plants. If you must use chlorinated tap water for your vegetables, let the water sit out in an open container for a day or two, to let a significant part of the chlorine evaporate.

137 Take It Easy

Since limiting factors like light and soil depth have such an important impact on urban gardening, you'll want to select the easiest plants to grow. In general, skip tall-growing vegetables, like corn, and ones with trailing vines, like pumpkin. Focus on herbs, tough perennials, root crops, and salad plants for the best results in your urban Eden. Here are a few ideas:

- Cilantro, chives, basil, and parsley (need to be replanted each year)
- Rosemary, mint, thyme, and sage (perennials that last years in the same pot)
- Potatoes, beets, and radishes (these do better in cool conditions)
- Sweet potatoes (these are ideal for very warm areas)
- Lettuce and spinach (can handle short day length or low light)
- Cucumbers and cherry tomatoes (do well if they have enough space and light)
- Green beans and peppers (can handle heat and dry conditions)
- Peas and kale (can handle very cold weather)

138 Build a Food Wall

If your space to grow is limited, or you just want to maximize your production, a shoe organizer and some potting soil can be used as an improvised growing wall for crops like herbs, lettuce, spinach, and small root vegetables like radishes.

STEP 1 Securely attach a plastic or nylon shoe organizer to a strip of wood or wood frame, using screws or nails depending on the surface behind the growing wall. Mount this to the sunny wall of a patio or balcony. Other outdoor installation sites can include an exterior wall of your home or a fence. Indoor installations can work as well, but protect your floors—you'll need a container underneath the grow wall to catch any water that drips through.

STEP 2 Fill each pocket of the shoe organizer with potting soil. This can include time-release fertilizer or you can mix in your own blend. If you may not be able to water the growing wall daily, you can add water-absorbing crystals to the potting mix. These soak up water and then release it slowly, keeping the plants healthier if you miss a day of watering.

STEP 3 Plant your seeds or seedlings in each pocket and water thoroughly. If the pockets are clear plastic or vinyl, the dark soil may heat up too much in strong sunlight or hot summer months. Hang a bit of light-colored cloth on each row to prevent overheating. In cool weather, however, this solar heat gain will help your plants grow.

STEP 4 Fertilize, harvest, and replant as needed. The potting soil, if fertilized every other month, should last for several growing seasons. Loose leaf lettuce and spinach could be ready to harvest within 30 days of planting seedlings or 45 days from planting seeds. Cut the fully grown crops and replant the shoe pockets immediately for the fastest turnaround.

139 Grow the Right Veggies

When you have limited space for your survival garden, you want to get the most nutritional bang for your buck. The numbers next to each vegetable reflect a ranking system created by the Center for Science in the Public Interest. This ranks different vegetables (with kale at the top) according to multiple nutritional ratings as well as their vitamins, minerals, and nutrients. The labels also note which plants do well in containers vs. raised beds, which are particularly cold or heat resistant, and which are the easiest to grow for beginners.

931 SPINACH

NUTRITIONAL **RANKING NUMBER**

464 RADICCHIO

570 PUMPKINS

700 SWISS CHARD

CHOOSE YOUR VEGGIES

- Very easy to grow
- Great for containers
- Great for raised beds
- Good in cold temps
- Good in hot temps

152 BOK CHOY

420 BROCCOLI

197 ACORN SQUASH ●●●○○

223 SWEET PEPPERS ●●●●○

394 ROMAINE LETTUCE ●●●●○

166 PEAS ●●●○○

1,389 KALE ●●●○○

397 CARROTS ●●○○○

547 MUSTARD GREENS ●●●○○

733 COLLARD GREENS ●●●○○

214 TOMATOES ●●●●○

140) Build a Raised Bed Garden

A raised bed garden can provide you with a surprising amount of food from a very small space, and it works in a variety of climates. This type of versatile garden bed can tackle a number of common problems in gardening, as it can make for good drainage in rainy climates and warmer roots in cold climates. Here's how you can set up a 32-square-foot (10-square-m) raised bed garden.

GO SHOPPING Your local home-improvement store should have everything you need, but you may already have some of these things at home, too. Grab a deer fence and assemble the following supplies:

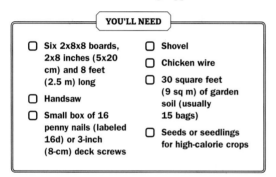

YOU'LL NEED

- ☐ Six 2x8x8 boards, 2x8 inches (5x20 cm) and 8 feet (2.5 m) long
- ☐ Handsaw
- ☐ Small box of 16 penny nails (labeled 16d) or 3-inch (8-cm) deck screws
- ☐ Shovel
- ☐ Chicken wire
- ☐ 30 square feet (9 sq m) of garden soil (usually 15 bags)
- ☐ Seeds or seedlings for high-calorie crops

PICK A SPOT TO BUILD Pick a site with at least eight hours of uninterrupted direct sunlight per day. Less than that will greatly reduce your production. To build your frames, cut one of your boards in half lengthwise. Nail or screw the ends of your short pieces to two long boards to create a rectangle. Repeat with the second set of boards and stack them for height. Align the long axis on a north-south line so that sunlight hits both sides.

DIG THE SOD Make marks on the ground that match the dimensions of your frame, and remove any grass, weeds, and roots by digging. You'll need to dig 3–4 inches (8–10 cm) down to get most of the roots, and be diligent. Use the debris in your compost pile.

FILL IN YOUR GARDEN BED Place your wooden frame over some chicken wire (to keep pests from burrowing up) on the ground you have prepared. Fill the frame with your garden soil and plant your seedlings or seeds. Water the bed deeply every couple of days.

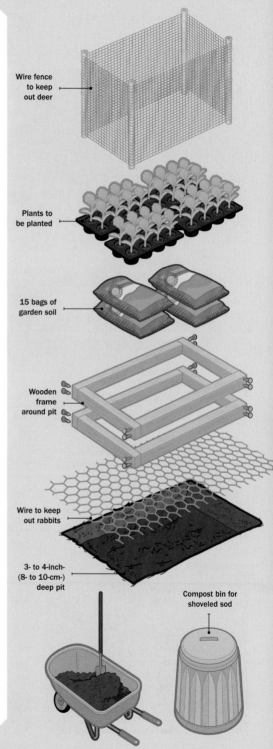

Wire fence to keep out deer

Plants to be planted

15 bags of garden soil

Wooden frame around pit

Wire to keep out rabbits

3- to 4-inch- (8- to 10-cm-) deep pit

Compost bin for shoveled sod

141 Feed a Family of Four

Exactly what to grow, and how much of it you want, depends on a wide range of factors, including how much space you have for gardening, what grows well in your region, and of course what your family likes (sure, you could force your kids to live on nothing but cabbage for the next few years, but is the convenience worth the whining?). There are computer programs out there to help with garden planning, but a pencil and a piece of graph paper work just as well. Grid out your gardening space and plan what to plant based on how much space is needed for each type. Then follow these rough guidelines for quantity, which is based on feeding a family of four. Adjust as necessary for your family's needs and cabbage-free desires.

142 Scare Off Critters

There are a number of ways to keep thieving animals and burrowing rodents from ruining all your hard work. One homegrown tactic is to pee (that's right, pee) around the garden bed perimeter. The scent will scare off those pesky critters.

VEGETABLE	# OF PLANTS TO GROW	SPACE NEEDED
BEETS	40	2.5 feet (0.8 m) apart
BROCCOLI	10	1.5 feet (0.5 m) apart
BEANS, POLE	6	*
BRUSSELS SPROUTS	10	2 feet (0.6 m) apart
CABBAGE	10	2.5 feet (0.8 m) apart
CARROTS	40	1 inch (2.5 cm) apart
CAULIFLOWER	10	2 feet (0.6 m) apart
CHARD, SWISS	10	8 inches (20 cm) apart
CORN	20	1 foot (0.3 m) apart
CUCUMBERS	4	1.5 feet (0.5 m) apart
KALE	10	1.5 feet (0.5 m) apart
LETTUCE	20	8 inches (20 cm) apart
ONIONS	40	4 inches (10 cm) apart
PEAS	40	*
PEPPERS	8	1.5 feet (0.5 m) apart
POTATOES	20	1 foot (0.3 m) apart
RADISHES	40	2 inches (5 cm) apart
TOMATOES	8	3.5 feet (1 m) apart
ZUCCHINI	4	2.5 feet (0.8 m) apart

* Good for tight spaces since they can grow on (or, in the case of peas, prefer to grow on) poles or trellises.

143 Grow Your Own Medicine Chest

Even with limited space, you can grow your own herbal remedies—and in a disaster scenario, this is valuable knowledge. These won't replace proper medical care, but they're nice to have on hand in a pinch—or a bruise.

A ALOE VERA Very soothing to burns and scalds, this tender plant is best grown in a container so that it can be brought inside for the winter (unless you live in a tropical climate).

B BORAGE The flowers can be soaked in alcohol to make a mood-boosting tonic.

C PEPPERMINT Similar to pennyroyal, peppermint can be a great tonic for digestion. Fresh peppermint, though, along with pennyroyal and other strong mints, should not be consumed by women who are (or may be) pregnant, as food and drink that contain fresh strong mint leaf can be dangerous to the baby.

D COMFREY The cooked mashed roots of comfrey are used for a topical treatment for arthritis, bruises, burns, and sprains. Just don't eat it. Recent research shows that it is damaging to the liver if eaten in quantity.

E YARROW Crushed yarrow leaves and flowers can be placed on cuts and scratches in order to stop bleeding and reduce the chance of infection.

F LEMON BALM Make the best lemonade of your life by adding bruised lemon balm leaves to the drink. This plant also makes an outstanding topical agent for cold sores, and it is often used as a calming "nightcap" tea to fight insomnia.

G ECHINACEA Echinacea, also known as the purple coneflower, is an American perennial wildflower best known for stimulating the immune system. Echinacea preparations are used to protect against colds and flu, minor infections, and a host of other ailments.

H PENNYROYAL This great-smelling mint relative can be crushed and applied to the skin as a very effective bug repellent. The leaves can also be crushed and then applied to wounds as an antiseptic, or brewed as a tea to settle upset stomachs.

I LAVENDER Typically used as a fragrance today, lavender has been used since ancient times to treat bug bites, burns, and skin disorders, and to relieve itching and rashes and reduce swelling. It should not be used by pregnant or nursing women, or small children.

144 Make a Self-Watering Container Garden

Containers are a great way to grow food in small spaces or to add extra growing space in and around your home and property. Many vegetables grow well in containers (see item 139 for a few ideas). It's best to use a self-watering container—this reduces your labor and also allows plants to suck up the water they need through their roots, which can help to eliminate any over- or underwatering. Daily watering can be annoying, and commercial self-watering containers can be pricey. Here's how to make your own, with some simple-to-obtain supplies. You'll need two 5-gallon (19-l) food containers, an 8-ounce (225-g) plastic deli container of the sort you'd buy potato salad in, a length of plastic pipe, and a power drill.

STEP 1 Drill some small holes all the way around the deli container, spaced about an inch (2.5 cm) apart.

STEP 2 Using a 3-inch (8-cm) hole saw, make a hole in the bottom of one of your large containers, and then follow up with smaller drainage holes all around the central hole. Then, using a $1^1/4$-inch (3-cm) hole saw, drill a water hole for the pipe to run through.

STEP 3 Assemble the container, placing the plastic deli container in the bottom tub (the one without the holes) and the drilled-out tub on top of it.

STEP 4 Determine where the inner container's bottom is (holding the whole container up to a strong light should make this apparent). Drill a small overflow hole about $1/4$ inch (0.6 cm) below the inner tub's bottom.

STEP 5 Run the watering pipe down through the $1^1/4$-inch (3-cm) hole.

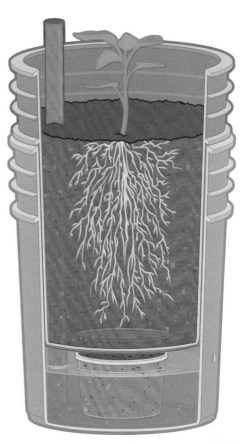

STEP 6 Fill the container with potting soil (it will fill the deli container as well) and plant your produce.

STEP 7 Pour water down the pipe until it flows out the drainage hole. This will now water your plants through their roots. Every week or so, pour a little water down the pipe and see how your reservoir is doing.

145 Know Fido's Risks

There are a whole host of things you should take into consideration when planning a survival garden. First and foremost are ease of planting, yield of crops, and nutritional density. You want to grow as much as you can as easily as possible. And you want those crops to be nutritious. You also want them to be safe for all members of your household—including Fido and Fluffy. Stay informed about which plants to keep out of reach of your pets. Aloe, garlic, leeks, rhubarb, and certain kinds of holly can be toxic to both dogs and cats if ingested. Effects can range from nausea (indicated by drooling) to tremors and death. Check with your veterinarian if you have any questions.

Rod Morey is a man of many talents: knife maker, mountain man, and herbalist. His uncommon story is enough to convince anyone of the power of natural remedies, wild medicine, and herbal wisdom.

146 Take Charge of Your Own Wellness

Some years ago, I was diagnosed with terminal, stage 4 squamous cell cancer of the larynx and trachea, and my prognosis was not good. My physician told me that my chance for survival—to live for more than a year—was less than 1 percent. I had been an EMT for more than two decades, and it felt like the medical system I had served for so long was failing me; I was being instructed to prepare for the end. I knew I would only survive if I took charge of my own wellness.

So I did.

I studied herbal and alternative treatments. I juiced fresh vegetables to give me strength and stamina, and I designed a daily herbal regimen to strengthen, nourish, and support my depleted immune system and to combat my disease.

My quest for survival led me to a passion for herbal medicine that I still share today—25 years later. Take charge of your own wellness—not just to survive, but to thrive.

147 Brew Rod's Favorite Remedies

WHITE PINE COUGH SYRUP This decoction/reduction of white pine bark and other herbs can quell a persistent, dry cough. It will feel soothing and is an excellent healing agent for the mucosa lining of the mouth and throat.

BLEND TOGETHER

- ☐ 3 parts white pine bark
- ☐ 1 part licorice root
- ☐ 1 part thyme leaf
- ☐ $1/2$ part slippery elm bark

Blend roots and bark in a heavy pan. Add 16 ounces (470 ml) cold water. Bring to a slow boil. Simmer for 30 minutes. Strain mixture through a sieve, return liquid to heat. Continue heating to reduce volume by half.

While still hot, add 2–3 well-rounded tablespoons of honey or molasses.

Optional:
- *Add 1 ounce (30 ml) or more of brandy to preserve up to one year (and give it a kick).*
- *Pine needles, red cedar needles, or balsam fir needles can add vitamins and a rich flavor.*

HARMONIC TEA Cook up some Harmonic Tea for harmony, balance, and nutritional support for the neuromuscular system. This tea is very high in vitamins, protein, and trace minerals, especially calcium, magnesium, and vitamin C. I drink a cup of this wonderful tea nightly; it helps maintain my blood pressure and I get a restful sleep.

BLEND TOGETHER

- ☐ 2 parts oat straw (a.k.a. *Avena sativa*)
- ☐ 1 part nettles leaf
- ☐ 1 part red clover, herb and flower
- ☐ 1 part comfrey leaf
- ☐ 2 parts red raspberry leaf
- ☐ $1/4$ part hibiscus flowers

Use 1 tablespoon of this mixture per 1 cup (0.2 l) of hot water. Let it steep, and sweeten as desired.

148 Know Three Essential Herbs

If you're new to the herbal world, some of these may not ring a bell—but you might be surprised how easy they are to find at your local health food store.

PLANTAIN (*Plantago major*) This healing herb has been studied and written about since the days of Chaucer in medieval Britain. Historically, it has been put to use both topically and internally for wounds and bleeding, insect stings and bites, swelling, fractures, as an antihistamine, and to treat diarrhea (using the seeds). Use it as a tea and in topical salves and balms.

ST. JOHN'S WORT (*Hypericum perforatum*) This plant is used internally and topically for pain, swelling, inflammation, burns, bruises, muscle damage, nerve damage/neuralgia, and as an antiviral and antidepressant.

MULLEIN (*Verbascum thapsus*) Mullein is an unparalleled herb for respiratory congestion, clearing lung and bronchial air passages, cough, and bronchitis. It's also used for pain with infused oils for earaches or ear mites, and as an antibacterial and antifungal.

149 Build a Backyard Chicken Farm

Raising chickens in your backyard is turning into an increasingly popular option these days for a whole range of reasons. Suburban dwellers (and even lucky urbanites with some serious backyard space) are being turned on to the benefits of fresh eggs. Chickens also provide great fertilizer in the form of their manure, insect control for the garden, and a tasty chicken dinner every once in a while (though many chicken-keepers rely only on eggs and don't use their chickens for meat). In a post-disaster world where you can't run down to the supermarket, a backyard chicken coop would be invaluable. Here are the basics you'll need to consider.

YOUR FLOCK You can buy chicks from farm-supply stores that will start laying in six months, but you won't know if they're all girls. Easiest is to buy "ready to lay pullets," which are older and guaranteed to be female.

THE COOP There are many possible ways to set up your chickens' home; the drawing below gives the basics.

CHICKEN FEED Commercial chicken feed can be purchased in bulk; you can also grow your own using the hints in item 152.

EGG COLLECTING You'll want to collect eggs on a daily basis, unless you're intentionally planning to hatch some young'uns. Hens will lay much of the year—anytime there's 12 to 14 hours of daylight.

GIRL TIME Chickens are sociable creatures; they'll be happiest and healthiest if you keep at least four to six together. If you want to breed them, you need no more than one rooster per 10 to 12 hens. Any more, and things are likely to get hectic—as in unintentional cockfights.

THE RANGE You'll want to let your chickens roam around a fenced yard, or at least provide them with a fenced chicken run. Chickens are a favorite prey for many predators, so be sure any area you set them loose in is well fenced.

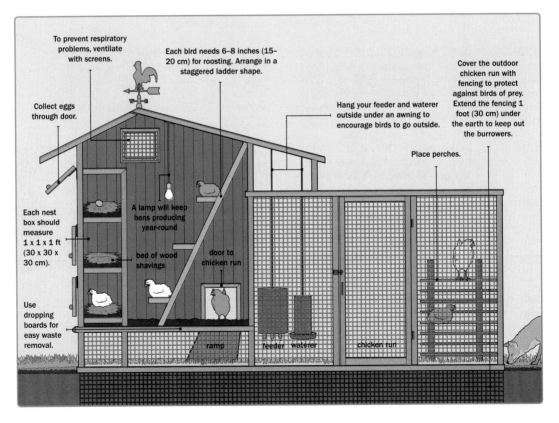

To prevent respiratory problems, ventilate with screens.

Each bird needs 6–8 inches (15–20 cm) for roosting. Arrange in a staggered ladder shape.

Cover the outdoor chicken run with fencing to protect against birds of prey. Extend the fencing 1 foot (30 cm) under the earth to keep out the burrowers.

Collect eggs through door.

Hang your feeder and waterer outside under an awning to encourage birds to go outside.

Place perches.

Each nest box should measure 1 x 1 x 1 ft (30 x 30 x 30 cm).

A lamp will keep hens producing year-round

bed of wood shavings

door to chicken run

Use dropping boards for easy waste removal.

ramp   feeder   waterer   chicken run

You can buy baby chicks newly hatched or "grow your own." To breed your own chicks, of course, you'll need a rooster, but you'll also want to be sure that you have a broody hen. That is, one that will actually tend to the eggs (not many modern chickens possess that maternal instinct). If one of your chickens pecks at you when you come to collect the eggs, or otherwise protects her nest, she's your girl. Bantams are known to be broody.

To raise your chicks in the absence of a mother, you'll want to keep them in a safe, warm "brooder pen." This doesn't have to be anything fancy; here are some basic guidelines.

STEP 1 You'll need to keep your chicks safely contained, and you'll want about 2 square feet (0.6 m) per baby. If the pen is more than 12 inches (30 cm) deep, you don't need to worry about a cover, as they won't be able to escape. You can use a kiddie pool, fish tank, storage tub, or even a big cardboard box.

STEP 2 Set up your heat lamp. This will take a little bit of experimentation. Start with a 250-watt heat lamp with a good clamp and reflector. Don't get excessively MacGuyver-y here, as this can be a fire hazard. Use a red bulb with a screen over it (the screen helps prevent fires if the lamp falls into your shavings). You'll need to move the lamp up and down and check the temperature before committing your delicate little chicks to this environment. The temperature should measure at 92°F (33°C) about 2 inches (5 cm) above the pen's floor.

STEP 3 Add bedding. This can be paper towels or pine shavings. Don't use cedar shavings or newspaper, as they can be toxic to chicks.

STEP 4 Be sure they have food (use commercial chick-starter feed for greatest ease) and clean water.

STEP 5 After a couple of weeks, they'll start developing feathers. At that point, they don't need so much heat. Reduce the temperature in the brooder by 5°F (3°C) per week for six weeks.

STEP 6 Move the new kids to the coop. They're all grown up!

151 Get a Good Egg

A washed or rinsed egg will keep for about a month in the fridge (or other cool place if you're off the grid). But freshly laid eggs have a natural coating that keeps them fresh for significantly longer—up to four months. Some eggs may have droppings on them and need to be washed, but many won't, so don't just do it by rote.

Also, natural eggshells are much thicker than storebought ones. Commercial eggs are actually buffed to make them prettier, which also ends up weakening the shell. Your home-grown eggs will be much sturdier and healthier.

152 Feed Free-Range Chickens

It's easy enough to buy giant bags of chicken feed from the store, but if you want to save money, or if you find yourself in circumstances in which commercial feed isn't readily available, remember that chickens were able to feed themselves for millennia before humans stepped in and opened the chow line. Here's how you can keep your chickens well fed au naturel.

DRIED CORN If you grow a large-ear feed corn, you can let it dry on the stalks, then store the ears in bins and distribute the corn to the chickens all winter. Chickens with access to grit (sand and pebbles they need to grind food in their gizzards) will have no trouble with whole, dried corn kernels (they're too much for baby chicks to handle, however).

SEEDS Millet, sorghum, and sunflowers are easy to grow and provide seeds that are nutritious for chickens. Just toss them the whole seeds—they'll know what to do. In addition, there are grains that you don't need to harvest or process in order for your chickens to benefit from them. You can plant alfalfa, clover, annual rye, cowpeas, and/or buckwheat, let them mature, and then allow your chickens to wander the garden, eating the

seeds straight from the source. Sprouting any seeds boosts their nutritional value, which is particalarly useful in winter when fresh foods are scarce.

GREENS Kale, turnips, and mustard greens are all great for chickens. Cut the greens and feed them to penned chickens, or let them graze at will. As they do, they'll also eat bugs and larvae that can devastate your garden (and, as ever, drop little fertilizer nuggets as they go).

FRUIT & VEGETABLES Most discarded fruits and vegetables (anything that's just a little too icky for your table, or that you grew too much of) can probably be safely added to a chicken's diet. In the winter, if you have stored up potatoes, beets, and winter squash, these are all great for your birds.

EGGS This sounds kind of gross, but it doesn't bother the chickens, and it shouldn't bother you. Never feed chickens raw eggs, as this may encourage them to cannibalize their own nests. However, if you have cracked, dirty, or excess eggs, just hard-boil them and then crumble them (shells and all) into the birds' feed to amp up their protein.

153 Kill a Chicken Humanely

You may have heard, if only from Iggy Pop, that it's relatively simple for you to hypnotize a chicken. This is, in fact, true and makes the job of dispatching one much simpler. Here's how to do the job as painlessly as possible for everyone.

STEP 1 Pound two long nails into a stump, far enough apart to span the chicken's neck but close enough together to keep its head from slipping through.

STEP 2 Lay the chicken on the block with one wing under it, placing its neck between the nails. Apply just enough tension to the legs to stretch the neck and keep the bird in place.

STEP 3 Tap your finger just in front of the bird's beak, then about 4 inches (10 cm) away from it. Keep alternating taps like this until the hypnotized bird relaxes.

STEP 4 Using a hatchet, chop the chicken's head off.

STEP 5 Hold it up by its legs to let the blood drain. Another common cliché, "running around just like a chicken with its head cut off," will come to mind, as the bird will likely flap its wings and seem to struggle, even after decapitation.

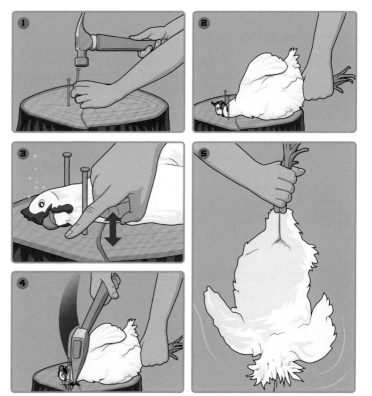

154 Prepare Your Chicken

When you go to behead your chicken, be sure you've got a pot of scalding water ready—it should be 140°–160°F (60°–70°C). Dip the decapitated bird into the hot water for 20–30 seconds. This should loosen the feathers to the point that you can easily remove them by hand with a firm wiping motion, rather than having to painstakingly pluck them. Chop off the chicken's feet, then cut around the cloaca (the bird's orifice), being careful not to cut into the intestines, as this will contaminate the

meat. Scoop the innards out with your hands and rinse the entire bird in cold water. If you can get all of this done in 20 minutes, you can then cook your bird before rigor mortis sets in. Otherwise, refrigerate the body for 24 hours before cooking.

155 Consider Other Fowl

Just because you're homesteading doesn't mean you shouldn't be able to eat well. In fact, some of the best meals you'll buy in that swanky restaurant are from some of the easiest and most productive types of livestock to raise. Just remember that unlike chickens, other birds will need to be trained not to fly away.

DUCKS Ducks bring some added benefits over chickens, such as laying larger eggs. Though they can thrive on the same feed as your chickens, they're much more efficient foragers, meaning less work for you—and they eat things that eat your garden, like snails and slugs. Ducks also don't scratch like chickens, making your garden safer.

GEESE Homesteaders with large grassy areas should think about geese as a meat option. They pick up a lot of their nutritional needs from grasses or windfalls, but they do need room to roam. An added benefit to geese is their ability to act as guards, sounding an alarm whenever something is amiss.

SQUAB A fancy word for pigeon, squab, once mated, will take care of their young quite ably and also produce eggs for up to five years. Squab aren't prone to some of the dangerous diseases associated with turkey, and they require very little space.

PHEASANTS If you want something a bit more exotic, there are several breeds of pheasant available. Many people consider them a hobby bird, with beautiful plumage and active personalities. They are a little higher maintenance, and you'll need to keep them apart from your chickens, but they're worth the effort.

TURKEYS A small flock of heritage turkeys can wow your friends. Though susceptible to infections in a flock, blackhead and coccidiosis can be treated if spotted early. Turkeys are excellent for pest control, and they provide a tasty meal. They're social, so you'll need a large space to keep them happy and healthy—but this bird is also well worth the effort.

156 Include Quail in Your Homestead

Keeping *Coturnix* quail will get you meat and eggs with minimal effort and little space—you only need 1 square foot (0.3 square m) for every bird. When housing your quail, you want to think vertically as well as horizontally. While you don't want to raise fliers (unless you're releasing them for hunting), you do want to have plenty of room at the top of their aviary. Use wire mesh to give air circulation and a solid roof to keep them out of the elements.

Quail droppings are high in ammonia, so you want to make sure you keep their enclosure clean at all times. A floor made of hardware cloth allows droppings to fall through to the ground (or other catchment system), while keeping the birds safe from predators like skunks, snakes, and foxes.

Quail eggs are small but delicious, and their delicate meat is also a favorite across the globe. The biggest reason to raise quail, however, is that they are quiet. Many cities have laws against chickens, but few have restrictions on smaller birds like quail.

When buying your quail, make sure you have two of the females for each male. They'll keep you happily supplied with a unique food source in even the the worst of times.

157 Avoid Salmonella

Salmonella is a rarely considered, but serious, risk for backyard breeders and homesteaders. Especially with chickens, but also with rabbits, droppings are everywhere, and working with the livestock (even indirectly) brings you into contact with potentially life-threatening illnesses. The solution is simple. If you own livestock of any sort, establish a cleaning routine with an antibacterial soap. Every time you go into the livestock area, even if you never touch the animals, wash your hands up to the elbows with hot water. Leave the soap in contact with the skin for at least 30 seconds before rinsing. And it's never a bad idea to wash twice.

158 Find the Right Feed

People homestead for different reasons, and being in control of their food supply is at the top of many lists. But choosing feeds for livestock can be tricky. Under ideal circumstances, processed foods provide balanced diets and ease of use, but a survival situation means many of these feeds may no longer be available. If non-GMO, organic ingredients matter to you, processed feeds may also give you pause.

The good news with small livestock like chickens and rabbits is that both are foragers, giving you ample opportunity to grow your own supplements or to let them range free.

PELLETS & CRUMBLES If you're going for cheap and easy methods of feeding your little farm, you'll want to rely on prefabricated pellets for rabbits and crumbles for chickens. While it's true that your forefathers fed their small livestock table scraps and leftovers, they also didn't have much choice. For rabbits, you can add in some easy supplements to provide dietary diversity. Just mix together 10 pounds (4.5 kg) of organic pellets, 4 pounds (1.8 kg) of calf manna (a dietary supplement of proteins and beneficial acids), 2 pounds (1 kg) of rolled oats, and a pound (0.5 kg) of black-oil sunflower seeds. For chickens, laying crumbles for hens will do the bulk of the work, but you can also feed them oyster shells, seaweeds, and greens.

SUPPLEMENTS If you have the space and availability, you can easily grow the plants your animals will love. Sunflowers are a great addition to your garden—and a good feed source—as are carrots and various green leafy vegetables like beets and kale. And when it comes time, don't compost allof your weeds—both chickens and rabbits love dandelions, clover, grass, and other yard clippings. You can extend the life of your fresh feed (and your pelleted feed for that matter) through the use of airtight, galvanized steel bins and cans. If you store everything in a cool, dry place, you can go a month or two without having to resupply.

Raise Rabbits

When it comes to providing a lot of meat for the table, don't think big. A single female rabbit (called a doe) can produce more than 300 pounds (135 kg) of meat a year in a very small space. Because rabbits for meat are cage-raised, they're the cleanest livestock choice. A 5-pound (2.3-kg) rabbit yields roughly 3.5 pounds (1.5 kg) of all-white meat when dressed. When choosing a breed of rabbit, consider these three primary meat breeds.

NEW ZEALAND WHITES This heavy breed can stand cold temperatures but, like most rabbits, will suffer in extreme heat. They have one of the best meat-to-bone ratios of any breed, and they reach processing age in 8–10 weeks. Additionally, it's the most common breed, so finding yourself some foundation stock should be simple regardless of location.

New Zealand White

CALIFORNIANS Similar in size to the NZ Whites, Californians are distinguished by their black ears and noses. They still grow out at about the same rate: 8–10 weeks. But some breeders think they are less robust than the Whites.

FLORIDA WHITES This smaller breed has the great advantage of needing less space on the far end of the growing cycle, but they still grow to fryer size at 8–10 weeks of age, and they're comparable in size at that age to their larger cousins.

160 Breed Rabbits the Right Way

Rabbits breed like—well, there's a reason for the expression. With a little oversight, you can feed a family of four indefinitely on a small stock. Just follow these simple rules for establishing and maintaining an efficient, safe rabbitry.

RULE 1 Begin with good breeding stock. Pay for pedigreed bucks and does from reputable breeders. The "meat pen," a buck and two does, is popular.

RULE 2 You can breed sire to daughter, dam to son, and grandparents to grandchildren, but not siblings.

RULE 3 Keep one rabbit in each cage. Does can be territorial, and bucks will fight. When breeding, always bring the doe to the buck's cage.

RULE 4 Keep a calendar. After breeding, expect your doe to kindle her litter 28 days later. Typically, a doe kindles eight kits per litter.

RULE 5 Keep records via hutch cards. This card should list sire, dam, date conceived, date born, etc.

RULE 6 You should process your rabbits when they are approximately 8 weeks old.

RULE 7 Wean kits at 4–5 weeks of age. You can rebreed your does before the litter is weaned, meaning a doe can have five or six litters every year. Most keepers time breeding to allow a doe a week or so of rest between weaning and kindling.

161 Build a Rabbit Hutch

Rabbits are low-maintenance livestock. Clean water and food are first and foremost concerns, followed by a hutch to protect the rabbits from the elements and predators. There are plenty of hutches available for purchase, but it's easy enough to build your own.

YOU'LL NEED

☐ **4 8-foot (2.4-m) 4x4 posts**

☐ **6 8-foot (2.4-m) 2x4s**

☐ **8 2x4 joist hangers**

☐ **4x8-foot (1.2x2.4 m) sheet of ½-inch (1.3 cm) plywood**

☐ **4 heavy-duty eye hooks per cage**

large-breed rabbit is 30x30x18 inches [80x80x50 cm]). The cages can then be hung freely from the top of the structure for both easy access and safety.

If your hutch is free-standing and exposed to the elements, you'll need to consider weather protection. A canvas tarp will serve, and it can be easily rolled up when the weather is nice. Additionally, you can hang a piece of corrugated metal underneath your hutch to catch any droppings.

STEP 1 Use 4x4 posts to anchor the corners. Space posts 8 feet (2.4 m) apart in length, 3 feet (1 m) apart in width. For stability and leveling, use a post-hole digger to sink the corners 10–12 inches (25–30 cm) into the ground. Fill the holes with concrete for extra support.

STEP 2 Use simple joist hangers to anchor 2x4 supports at the tops of the 4x4s. Additional joists can be hung between the 2x4s for added stability and more anchor points for the cages. (You also can use a simple 2x4 construction along the bottom of the hutch to add stability and to create a waste catchment box.)

STEP 3 Anchor the sheet of plywood atop the 4x4s for your roof. To help waterproof the hutch, you can finish the top with tar paper and asphalt shingles. Otherwise, use a sealant to extend the life of your roof.

STEP 4 Anchor your eye hooks from the bottoms of the 2x4 joists at the corners of your cages (a cage for a

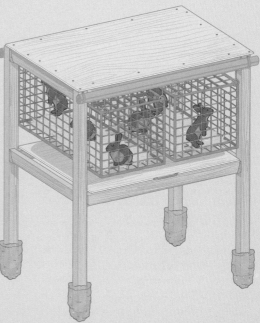

162 Raise a Cavy

If even rabbits are too space-intensive, another option is the cavy, also known as the guinea pig. These can be kept indoors, are easy to care for, and yield a small amount of meat that's considered a delicacy in some parts of the world. Unlike rabbits, cavy sows have a 16-day heat cycle, which means you have to

pay a bit closer attention for successful breeding. It's also fine to leave a mating pair alone until the sow is pregnant. The cavy will have from one to nine young which reach processing age at 8–10 weeks. They're small, but can still provide a vital amount of protein for your family.

163 Kill Small Animals Humanely

The hardest part of raising livestock for food is the humane slaughter and processing of the animal. Even the most hardened homesteader will develop some sort of bond with his hand-raised animals. A faster process means more humane results for the critter, and it's less unpleasant for you. Decide ahead of time which method works for you, and perfect it. You want to be as fast and as fluid as possible when the time comes.

The captive-bolt gun is a great tool for processing animals such as cavy or rabbits. This is a miniature version of what commercial slaughterhouses use for large animals like cattle or pigs. The bolt is placed on the middle of the head, just in front of the ears. A triggering mechanism releases a tensioned bolt, which impacts with enough force to kill the animal instantly. These devices don't come cheap, though.

Cervical dislocation is a preferred technique for most breeders. The old-school method involves using a broomstick to pin the head of the rabbit against the ground while pulling the hind legs upward until the skull is dislocated. Today, you can buy various types of commercially produced wringers, or you can make your own from welded metal or cut from wood. All you need is a deep-cut "V." Slide the head into that groove until it is immobilized and won't come out, then pull the hind legs to dislocate the skull from the spine. The animal dies instantly and without any suffering. The drawback here is potential bruising of the meat around the neck and shoulders.

One other option is to use a gun. You might hear people extol the virtues of a .22, but the cost of ammunition and the noise from the report make this method less than desirable. For killing small livestock, a break-action air rifle is more than sufficient. You'll want one that shoots above 900 fps for a killing shot, and use hunting pellets for your ammunition.

164 Build a Barrel Abattoir

For most homesteaders, space is at a premium. Instead of having to devote a whole structure or outbuilding to processing livestock, consider just constructing a small, portable station for your work. A 55-gallon (210-l) barrel can easily be repurposed for this design.

STEP 1 Use a jigsaw or handsaw to cut the barrel in half from the top down. Leave the bottom 12 inches (30 cm) of the barrel intact. You can either place a tub in the bottom to catch blood and entrails, or else you can simply line the bottom with a plastic garbage bag.

STEP 2 Build a simple 2x4 frame on the outside of the altered barrel. Place the flat side of the vertical 2x4s against the vertical sides of the barrel, and attach them with bolts and wing nuts.

STEP 3 Attach a 2x4 crossbeam to the 2x4 legs and the barrel top. Another 2x4 length is fastened as a face plate at the top of the frame.

STEP 4 Affix the wringer and hangers to the crossbeam. Your barrel is now ready for processing (see item 165).

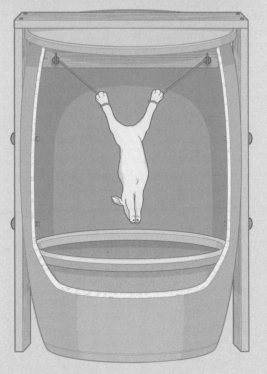

165 Dress a Rabbit

You can dress out a rabbit in under 10 minutes. With a typical litter of eight, a little more than an hour's worth of work will put protein on your table for a week or more. Compared to the skill and time required to butcher larger animals, this is yet another way to increase the return on your investment.

STEP 1 Hang the carcass by its hind legs. You can use either pegs, sticks, or strings inserted between the rear leg bone and the Achilles tendon.

STEP 2 Cut off the head and allow the carcass to bleed out (about 5 minutes). Use high-quality, very sharp garden shears to sever the front legs at the joint.

STEP 3 Cut the fur around the joint of each rear leg, and pull the skin as far down the leg as possible. Then, make a connecting cut from leg to leg, being careful not to nick the anus.

STEP 4 Make an incision around the anus and tail, then pull the skin completely down and off the carcass. If you're tanning the pelt (see item 291), slit the skin lengthwise along the belly. You can tan immediately, or roll it, fur side out, and freeze for handling later.

STEP 5 Make an incision in the muscle wall of the groin to begin gutting the carcass, being careful to keep all innards intact. This should be a careful slice.

STEP 6 Insert two fingers into the incision in a V to help pull the meat away from the guts. Cut the muscle wall carefully—don't damage the bladder or intestines, as that will taint the meat. Once your cut reaches the ribs, stick the blade in deeper and shear down through the ribs. All of the innards should be easy to pull free.

STEP 7 Pull the gallbladder off the liver (it looks like a pea), and set the giblets aside to add to the processed meat. Don't allow the liver, kidneys, or heart to fall into the waste bucket, as these giblets are edible.

STEP 8 Cut off the rear legs at the joint. Rinse off the carcass, then chill it in clean salted water or cook it immediately. You can keep the meat refrigerated up to 48 hours, or bag it for freezing. A vacuum sealer will also help keep the meat fresher longer.

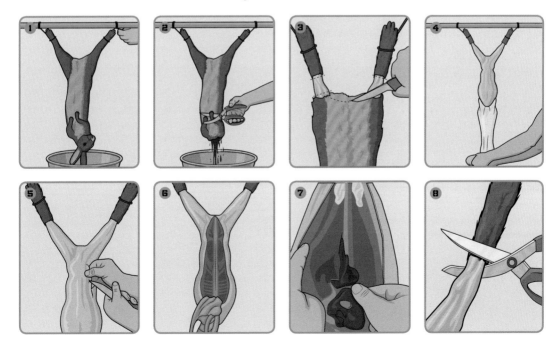

166 Create a Conflict-Free Homestead

The biggest challenge to raising livestock is figuring out what you're able to raise. After that, it's a matter of adequately housing your livestock. A good layout can make all the difference between creating a productive home ranch and losing your investment.

RULE 1 The more livestock you have, the greater interest predators take in their activity. When deciding how to house your livestock, consider how to protect them from predators. Chickens need a safe place to roost, but they also need protection from hawks and owls from above. You may need to clear branches or trees that overlook the chicken run.

RULE 2 Figure out which animals get along and which will fight. Pigs eat just about anything, including baby birds and rabbit kits. Ducks and chickens get along well, but chickens are aggressive toward small birds. Goats love to test fences, and they climb on everything—and can destroy even the sturdiest of structures.

RULE 3 Be creative with how you separate livestock. It's easy to cordon off each area with a fence and call it a day. But it's ugly and wastes space. Since most of your animals will want shade, grow squash vines at the base of the fencing. With a bit of encouragement to grow upwards (as though on a trellis), the squash will grow up and over the enclosures, providing vegetables that

remain out of reach of your animals and large leaves for their shade.

RULE 4 Consider how plants can have multiple uses. Those same squash blossoms shading your rabbits also provide a kind of perimeter defense against would-be predators. Raccoons love chickens and rabbits, but they hate squash plants with prickly edges.

RULE 5 Plant honeysuckle, jasmine, or other fragrant climbing plant vines where you want shade; these can help to eliminate any potential odor problems caused by large flocks of chickens or cages of rabbits.

167 Don't Forget the Poop

The greatest benefit to raising small livestock, apart from providing you with food, is providing you with an ample supply of fertilizer. Don't ever let the poop go to waste. Make sure when you're building your enclosure to include a catcher for the droppings.

CHICKEN MANURE One of the best fertilizers, chicken manure is so concentrated it will burn the roots of your plants if you incorporate it directly. You have two choices: composting or resting. If you choose to compost, include the straw or bedding until it has broken down completely. A tumbler or barrel-style composter will break everything down within 60–90 days. Keep it moist and hot, and it

should break down to a sweet-smelling black fertilizer at that time. If you aren't in a hurry, you can add the manure as a layer to your compost heap or else line it directly into your garden in the fall and give it the winter to fully decompose.

RABBIT DROPPINGS These are worth their weight in gold. Unlike chicken manure, rabbit droppings are "cold," meaning you can put them directly into the garden. If you want to increase the nitrogen levels in your compost, there's no rule against adding rabbit droppings to it. Otherwise, you can mix them directly into the soil around existing plants, or supplement the soil prior to planting.

168 Make Goat's-Milk Cheese

Raising goats can be challenging and costly. Most people interested in goats, though, are more interested in the milk than the potential for meat. Rather than raising a herd yourself, locate a source for goat milk. Under normal (pre-disaster) circumstances, you can find goat milk in most dairy markets. Better yet, make friends with a goat owner so you can get milk straight from the source. Here's an easy recipe for making cheese, one of the best uses for goat milk. Unlike other recipes that require a cheese base and special cultures, this approach will work anytime, as long as you have milk.

STEP 1 Heat a medium saucepan with goat's milk to 180°F (82°C). It should only take about 15 minutes.

STEP 2 Remove from heat and stir in ¼ cup (60 ml) freshly squeezed lemon juice. Let sit until it begins to curdle (about 20 seconds). The curds won't be overly large.

STEP 3 Line a colander with several sheets of cheesecloth. Don't scrimp on the cloth, otherwise you'll lose the curds. Place the colander in a large bowl. Ladle the milk into the cheesecloth.

STEP 4 Tie the four corners of the cheesecloth around a wooden spoon, and set it over a very deep bowl.

STEP 5 Let it drain for 1 to 1½ hours until what remains in the cheesecloth is a smooth, ricotta-like mixture.

STEP 6 Transfer this mixture into a fresh bowl and add coarse salt, a grated clove of garlic, and herbs of your choosing.

This cheese is best eaten immediately, because the herbs and curds can deteriorate. If stored in an airtight container, however, you can keep it a few days in the refrigerator.

169 Avoid Cattle. No Bull!

When it comes to raising meat for the table, some people make the mistake of thinking big. But raising a cow (or two) requires a lot of work and space. The upsides will include several hundred pounds of processed meat (depending on breed and age), a variety of uses for both meat and hide, and a dairy source. Cattle need very little in the way of shelter (a shed for the winter and a chute to help handle them)—but there are plenty of drawbacks.

SPACE You'll need an average of 2 acres (0.8 hectares) to raise a single cow to processing age.

TIME A cow won't be ready to process for 12–18 months.

FEEDING You'll need to provide your cattle both roughage and concentrates. Roughage includes grazable pastures, grasses, and hays. Concentrates include supplemental feeds like grains, brans, and meals. This can be costly.

BREEDING It's much more challenging to handle cattle breeding on a small homestead, as you'll need to safely house a bull. In most circumstances, ranchers turn to artificial insemination to breed their herds.

RISKS If a chicken is lost to a predator or disease, a well-managed flock can take the hit. Replacing a rabbit would take a few weeks, tops. But losing a cow means losing an enormous investment, not to mention the time and effort to replace that loss.

170 Make a Canning Kit

You really don't need much equipment for canning. All you really need are jars, a large pot, and a way to get your jars out of the boiling water. Start by buying a few items at a time until you have everything assembled.

CANNING JARS, METAL RINGS, & NEW LIDS These are essential supplies for canning. Make sure you use canning-jar lids, as the undercoating is designed to resist the corrosion from the high-acid foods inside. Always use new lids when you're canning, as the rubber seal is what allows the jar to stick to the rim, and you want to make sure your undercoating is strong.

DEEP POT Remember those old-school enamelware pots—those blue or black ones with the white dots? That's the kind you're after. You can find them in most hardware stores or kitchen outlets. Make sure the pot also comes with a canning rack that fits inside the base of the pot and holds the jars in place. If you don't want

to go with enamelware (or you're not canning very much), you can also use a 9-quart (8.5-l) stock pot.

8-QUART (7.5-L) PRESERVING PAN This will take care of most of your cooking. You want a wide pan so that jams and preserves can boil off liquids in a hurry.

WOODEN SPOON This is an essential item for every kitchen, whether you're canning or not. When canning preserves, you'll use the handle to remove air bubbles inside the jar.

MISCELLANEOUS OPTIONS Some optional elements that will make your canning easier include a scale for precise measuring of ingredients, a measuring cup or ladle, a large funnel to help fill your jars easily, a jar lifter (you can DIY one with rubber bands around metal tongs, but you'll be happier with a specifically designed tool), and a candy thermometer.

171 Can in a Water Bath

You should be canning by season to have year-round access to the fruits (and vegetables) of your labor. Water-bath canning is far and away the most common form of home-preserving food stores. Fortunately, it's also easy as pie.

STEP 1 Fill your canning pot with water and turn the burner on high. The water will reach a boil in about a half hour.

STEP 2 While your water is heating, thoroughly wash your canning jars, rings, and lids, even if they're new. Put them in the canning pot and let them heat up along with the water. If a recipe calls for sterilizing a jar (just make this part a habit in any case), be sure the jar, lids, and rings are submerged in a rolling boil for a full 10 minutes.

STEP 3 Use your jar-lifter to remove the lids and rings from the boiling water, and set them aside in a heatproof bowl. Leave the jars in the boiling water until ready to fill.

STEP 4 Make the preserve or pickle as called for in the recipe. You'll actually be performing this step during the time the water is boiling and your jars are sterilizing.

STEP 5 Fill your jars. Use a ladle or measuring cup to pour the contents slowly into your funnel. Make sure to pour the contents as close to the bottom of the funnel as possible to limit air bubbles. To fill, pull a jar out with your lifter, empty the boiling water back into the pot, then immediately fill with preserves.

STEP 6 After eliminating large air bubbles with your wooden spoon handle, put the jar lids and rings on, and tighten them down (but not too tightly). Wipe the edges clean.

STEP 7 Put your jars into the hot water bath, then turn the heat up and put the lid back on. Leave things boiling for the amount of time indicated in the recipe.

STEP 8 Remove the jars and set them aside to cool. You'll need to leave them alone for 12 hours, undisturbed, so have a space set up out of the way for them to cool.

STEP 9 Check that all your jars have a good seal. Push down on the lid. If it doesn't move, you have a good seal. If it "pops" up and down easily, put it in the refrigerator and eat it immediately.

172

Learn to Pressure-Can

If you want to can unpickled vegetables, soup stocks, meats, or beans, you must use a pressure canner. Of all the rules of canning, this one is nonnegotiable.

STEP 1 Make sure the jar rack is in the bottom of the pressure canner, then fill the canner with water to the manufacturer's specifications. If an amount isn't specified, start with 3 inches (8 cm) of water. If the pressure canner will be working more than 40 minutes, you'll want to add even more.

STEP 2 If hot-packing the jars, go ahead and turn the heat on under the pressure canner. If cold-packing jars, don't turn the heat on yet. You can crack the jars when you place them in the water.

STEP 3 Fill your clean jars no fuller than $^{1}/_{2}$ inch (1.3 cm) from the top, then affix the lid and ring.

STEP 4 Close and seal the lid of the pressure canner, making sure to leave the petcock open in order to vent steam. When steam begins escaping vigorously, allow it to exhaust for 10 minutes.

STEP 5 Put the weighted gauge on top of the lid or close the petcock. Follow instructions for timing once the pressure canner has reached the appropriate amount of pressure (typically 10 pounds, or 4.5 kg). If the pressure drops, turn the heat up.

STEP 6 After the prescribed duration, turn off the heat and allow to cool 5 minutes. When the pressure gauge reads zero, remove the weighted gauge or open the petcock slowly. If it hisses, the canner is still under pressure and needs to cool another 5 minutes.

STEP 7 Open the lid of the canner slowly from the side away from your face. Use your jar lifter to remove the jars, then set aside to cool for 12 hours. Check for a proper seal at that time.

173 Get a Lift

If you don't have a jar lifter, you can use aluminum foil to fashion one—they're essential for placing and removing jars or pans in your pressure cooker. Get a piece of aluminum foil that will fit all the way around the bottom of the jar, plus an additional 8 inches (20 cm). It should be long enough to loop underneath and give you handles on each side. Fold the foil lengthwise until it is about 3 inches (8 cm) wide, then grab the sides and lower the filled jar or pan into the pressure cooker. Gently fold down the handles during cooking, and use the same handles to effortlessly lift out the hot jar.

174 Yes You Can . . . Meat

If canning vegetables makes you nervous, packing jars full of meat probably terrifies you. The reality, though, is that canning is an excellent way for you to preserve beef, chicken, pork, and fish. You don't have to be a rancher for preserving meat to be in your best interest. If you're confident in your canning abilities, your options for ensuring you have enough protein in an emergency situation increase exponentially.

STEP 1 You must use a pressure canner. Under no circumstances should you use a water-bath canning method. Set up your equipment and counter space as previously described (see item 172).

STEP 2 Trim the fat from your cuts. Fat takes up valuable canning space, and it also has a tendency to coat the lid of the jar, preventing a good seal.

STEP 3 Cut the meat into cubes or strips. You'll be able to more economically pack your jars this way,

rather than trying to stuff an entire steak into them.

STEP 4 Loosely pack the meat into the jars, then fill with water, brine, or stock. Stop filling about 1 inch (2.5 cm) from the top. A good guide is no higher than the lowest thread of the jar's mouth.

STEP 5 Follow instructions for pressure canning. When you store the canned meat, make sure it is out of sunlight and in a cool, dry place.

175 Plant a Canning Garden

When it comes to canning, two things can intimidate newcomers: the canning process and growing the stuff to can. The trick is getting your garden to grow the way you want it to. If you've been planting and cultivating a garden for some time, you already know what grows well where you live. If you're just getting started, cut yourself some slack and follow these steps for long-term success. And remember, if you can eat it raw, you can easily pickle and preserve it.

START WITH TOMATOES These are the root of many sauces and meals, so try planting a whole row of them.

KNOW WHAT GROWS Expect it to take you an entire growing season to figure out what thrives in your soil. If a plant won't grow, no amount of loving it will fill your jars.

KNOW WHAT YOU LIKE There's nothing wrong with planting the old standbys. Tomatoes, beans, and squash will keep you happy, and they're usually easy to grow. But if you're testing the soil, you should buy anything

you find appealing, interesting, or even intimidating. You just might surprise yourself.

PLANT YOUR MENU If you love spaghetti, then break down all the ingredients from sauce to pasta. With fresh eggs, you can grow your dinner from scratch.

KEEP A JOURNAL Track the things you eat, and try to plan ahead for the things you love in the quantities you want. If those spicy canned green beans are a family favorite, plant enough for a jar per week—or more.

GROW MORE The basic rules for a canning garden are no different than for your vegetable garden. But instead of worrying about overproduction or food going to waste, you anticipate the surplus and can it when it's ready.

176 Follow These Golden Rules for Pickling Produce

Our ancestors had preserving (and life without modern refrigeration) perfected. We've unfortunately forgotten many of their lessons. However, there are plenty of resources available to us in the pursuit of rediscovering some of those lost secrets. Almanacs and farm guides often provide tips for pickling, including recipes for specific types of produce.

PICK IT FRESH Always can fresh produce. The fruits and vegetables from the market may look great, but they're usually coated with wax, which will spoil your efforts.

KEEP IT CRISPY Cut off the blossom end of cucumbers and squashes, as they can contain an enzyme that will turn a crisp pickle to mush in the jar. For crisper pickles, spread your cucumbers out on a baking sheet and cover with canning salt. Let them sit overnight, which draws a lot of moisture out of the vegetables, then rinse and dry them before canning.

GET ACID RIGHT Control both acidity and food appearance with with the right vinegar. White vinegar at 5 percent acidity is the best bet.

MIND YOUR SALT Never use iodized salt in your pickling. It clouds your brine and can adversely affect the consistency and color of your pickles. Canning or pickling salt is easy enough to find.

WAIT TO EAT After pickling foods, wait at least three weeks before eating to allow the flavors to mix and mellow.

177 Jam or Jelly Your Favorite Fruits

There's little difference between making pickles and making jams or jellies. The technical process remains the same, with the obvious variation in the use of sugars. When canning your favorite fruits, use white granulated sugar, as it is the least likely to alter the fruit's natural flavors. If you're truly curious about the differences between jams and preserves, it's really all about the fruit. Jams use smaller bits of a fruit, whereas preserves have larger chunks or whole pieces. Jellies use a gelatin base to congeal the fruit.

PICK THE RIGHT FRUIT When you're preparing your produce, make sure it's at room temperature to help more quickly and efficiently dissolve sugars. Also be sure the fruits are free of bruises or blemishes. Avoid soaking berries prior to canning to keep them from turning soft. Simply wash and dry them.

DON'T SKIMP ON SUGAR The sugar in your canning acts as a preservative against harmful microorganisms. If a sugar-free or lower-sugar product is what you're after, find a recipe to account for that at the outset.

GIVE THEM A BATH Water-bath canning is fine for jams and jellies. You can also freeze uncooked products in canning jars or airtight plastic containers. Freezer-stored preserves should be good for a year, and, if refrigerated, will last a month or more. If making preserves from frozen stock, simply defrost thoroughly before following your normal canning procedure.

178 Dry Out Your Fruits

Fruits and vegetables are essential to a healthy diet, but dried fruit has a lot of sugar. Don't let that deter you; instead of avoiding dried fruit due to high sugar content, moderate your intake by eating it mixed with nuts for a trail mix, or with healthier, low-sugar foods like yogurt. Also, remember that in a survival situation, calories are your friends.

Once you've selected your fresh fruit, thoroughly wash it and make sure it's free of marks and blemishes. (If you are not sure what fruits are best to use for dehydrating, just take a trip to your local market and see what's common.) Then pit and slice the fruit accordingly. If you're drying larger berries, make sure to cut them in half.

With your fruit prepared, it's time to pretreat it. Most store-bought dried goods use sulfur to maintain color throughout the dehydrating process. You can skip the sulfur by creating a bath of ascorbic acid. You want 2 tablespoons (30 g) ascorbic acid for every quart or liter of water. And if you don't have ascorbic acid on hand, crush Vitamin C tabs (you'll want 5 g).

If you live in a very hot environment, use the sun. Line a cookie sheet with cheesecloth, then lay out the fruit and let dry in the sun. Bring it in overnight to keep it from forming dew.

If you want to use your oven, keep it at its lowest setting, making sure internal temperatures don't rise above 145°F (63°C). Keep the oven door slightly ajar to allow any steam or moisture to escape. Drying times vary by fruit, so monitor closely. Successfully dried fruit should be leathery and not brittle to the touch.

179 Drop Some Acid

When it comes to canning, acid is your friend. Forget reflux. You're out to prevent botulism, which is a very serious and sometimes deadly illness in the best of times. If you're in a survival situation, you have to be able to trust your food. The most common cause of cases of botulism in canning is eating improperly canned low-acid foods such as plain, unpickled vegetables. Botulism is a threat because of its origin: the *Clostridium botulinum* spores themselves, which produce neurotoxins. Boiling water will kill the bacteria itself, but it won't harm the spores. What's more, the spores are activated in oxygen-free environments—like the inside of a canning jar. Even if you've boiled, processed, and sealed those yummy green beans inside your jar, you can still be ingesting active botulism spores when you eat them.

Fortunately, the spores can't tolerate acid, so pay close attention to the pH level. For foods to be safely canned in the water-bath method, you need to achieve a pH level lower than 4.6. If you're following a recipe that calls for a specific type of vinegar, make sure that you follow the recipe—to the letter—and use the exact acidity percentage specified. In the event you are canning low-acid foods that have not been pickled, including meats, you have no choice but to use a pressure canner, which processes jars at temperatures much higher than boiling water (temps high enough not only to kill the bacteria but also to kill the spores) and removes the air from inside the cans.

Survivalist Rick "Hue" Hueston is an explorer and naturalist of a different breed. He is a former military man exploring our natural world with predator vision and intuition—and he has the wild-food foraging skills to show for it.

180 Survive the End Times with Hue

My friends have voted me most likely to survive the apocalypse without having to eat one of the neighbors, since I can easily turn backyard foraged plants into a gourmet meal.

My name is Hue, and I have been a lifelong wild-food and primitive skills enthusiast with a passion for teaching foraging skills—particularly how to turn wild edible plants into a gourmet meal. I began exploring wild foods at an early age when the promise of excitement and adventure drew me to the wild places in the Northeast without a lunch sack, leaving me extremely hungry. Since then, I have spent many years becoming a seasoned forager, with extensive wild-food experience in a variety of North America's temperate, boreal, mountain, grassland, and desert eco-regions and biomes. Twenty years in the military also gave me ample opportunity to experience wild food in differing environments. It's available everywhere, and if I can learn, so can you.

When creating your own foraged meals, remember the rule of 2T: Wild food needs to be Tantalizing on the plate and Tempting to the taste buds. That's how to create an authentic meal rather than the more common hand-to-mouth survival food. Learn your area, brew up some recipes, and experiment!

You can follow my foraging and epicurean explorations at Primitive Café on Facebook.

181 Forage Hue's Top 10 Wild Foods

These tasty wild foods can be found in the city and the country. Get yourself an identification guide and sample some on your next outing.

1 GARLIC MUSTARD (*Alliaria petiolata*) A widely distributed invasive that is the most nutritious wild green available.

2 DANDELION (*Taraxacum officinale*) This healthy bitter herb is packed with vitamins, minerals, and antioxidants.

3 WILD GARLIC (*Allium* various species) Flavor is paramount in wild food meals—here is where you find it.

4 CHICORY (*Cichorium intybus*) Bitter herb similar in usage to dandelion.

5 LAMB'S-QUARTERS (*Chenopodium album*) Best spinach substitute available throughout its growing season.

6 EVENING PRIMROSE (*Oenothera biennis*) A versatile wild food with spicy hot roots, young leaves and flowers for salads, and abundant seeds.

7 WILD CARROT (*Daucus carota*) Provides a flavor additive and some starchy calories.

8 BURDOCK (*Arctium* various species) Provides starchy calories from root and stalk.

9 CATTAIL (*Typha latifolia*) If you can find it pollution-free in the urban environment, the roots can be cooked up like vegetables, as well as the green heads and shoots in spring.

10 ACORN (*Quercus* various species) Calories are king and acorns pack a punch. Easy to gather in quantity, they do require processing in water to remove tannic acid before consumption.

182 Cook Hue's Squirrel Stew

Critters are the essential foundation of a perfect wild meal, especially the easy-to-find urban tree rat—or, more appropriately, "chicken of the tree." Squirrel is an overlooked sustainable wild meat: Gamey in a good way but sweet, it's like a cross between lamb and duck with a slight nuttiness. Nutritionally, squirrel meat is 21.4 percent protein and 3.2 percent fat, and each average-size squirrel is about 800 calories a pop. Here's my recipe for Squirrel Stew with Wild Garlic Dumplings.

STEP 1 Break down the squirrel: Skin it, remove the insides, and cut off feet and head. Clean the meat inside and out, and soak 5–8 hours in lightly salted water.

STEP 2 Cover with water and boil the soaked squirrel for about 10 minutes, then discard the water. Boil again in fresh water with a little salt for about 2 more hours. Let cool, saving the broth.

STEP 3 Bone the squirrel, and cut the meat into bite-size pieces.

STEP 4 Add the following to the broth: a handful of wild greens like new-growth dandelion or chicory; wild garlic bulbs, onion, or ramps; wild carrot roots (first year's growth) and wild carrot greens; wild roots like evening primrose or burdock; and bay leaves (optional).

STEP 5 Return the meat to the broth and cook until vegetables are almost done. Season with salt and pepper to taste.

STEP 6 Prepare the dumplings: Mix together 1 cup (140 g) all-purpose flour, 1 cup (100 g) acorn flour, $1/2$ teaspoon (3 g) salt, 4 teaspoons (23 g) baking powder, and chopped sautéed wild garlic bulbs. Gradually add $3/4$ cup (177 ml) milk until doughy. Roll dough out to $1/2$-inch (1-cm) thickness and cut into small squares. Place on top of stew in pot, cover tightly, and cook an additional 15 minutes. Serve and enjoy!

183 Make a Cardboard Box Smoker

When it comes to smokers, you can spend a lot of money buying one in a store. Restaurants will spend thousands on elaborate smokers. But you can make a backyard smoker out of just about any box, including cardboard.

First, you need a box no more than 4 feet (1.2 m) tall and 2 feet (0.6 m) wide. Cut a door in the bottom of one side to remove and reload wood chips during cooking.

Next, insert two parallel dowel rods through the box at 12 and 36 inches (30 and 90 cm). You'll place your racks (one pan to catch drippings and a wire rack to hold food) on top of the dowels.

Insert your heat source and wood chips into the bottom door. You can use a hot plate and wood chips in a cast-iron skillet, or similar arrangement.

Set a similarly-sized box over the top once you have your fish or meat safely on the rack and your smoke source going. Then monitor the temperature as closely as possible. A probe thermometer inserted at food level works well.

Change your wood chips as needed, and follow the recipe for internal meat temperature and smoke time. It should go without saying that monitoring a smoke source inside a cardboard box is essential.

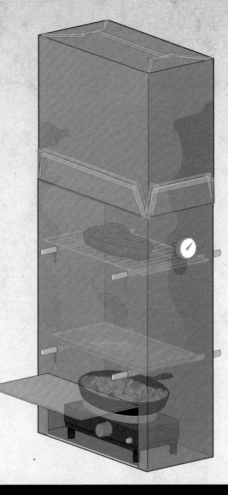

184 Smoke Out Your Vegetarians

In times of crisis, most people will eat whatever is handy. But there's always the chance a vegetarian in the bunker will turn up their nose at all the smoky meat products you're bestowing on the community. Now, these folks can get their protein from the buckets of rice and beans you have stored up, but, if you want to toss them a bone (or, rather, something boneless), you can actually make smoked tofu using a variation of the method above.

To smoke tofu, rub a block of it with a dry spice rub, and let it sit for a few hours to drain and dry.

Smoke on an oiled grill for about 20 minutes, then flip carefully with a spatula and cook, another 20 minutes, until the exterior is brown and slightly tacky. What's that? Cooking tofu in a smoker is always tacky? Hey, no argument here. But hopefully the vegans will think it's delicious and you'll be lauded for your generous, people-pleasing efforts. Now, pass the brisket.

185 Get Fishy

If you're fortunate enough to live near fishable waters, then you have the opportunity to smoke fish. A lot of people are afraid of handling fish for fear of spoilage, but it's a lot easier than you think—and makes for a flavorful and long-lasting protein source.

STEP 1 Create a basic brine consisting of 4 cups (1 l) water, 1/4 cup (59 g) each salt and brown sugar, 1/2 cup (118 g) chopped onion, 1/2 cup (118 g) fennel, a couple bay leaves, a crushed clove or two of garlic, and some celery. Mix together in a sealable glass container and add your cuts of fish, then refrigerate overnight. At this stage, you're dehydrating the fish to prep it for smoking while also pickling it. The longer you leave it in the brine, the saltier it will be. Don't leave it for more than a couple of days.

STEP 2 Add a varnish-like seal, called a pellicle, by allowing the fish to air-dry a minimum of 2 hours in a cool (lower than 65°F, or 18°C), well-ventilated area. You can even use a small fan set on low. Most smokers forget this step, which is unfortunate. The sticky film gives the smoke something to adhere to, making a more flavorful and longer-lasting product.

STEP 3 Use a box smoker to cure your fillets. How long this process takes depends on the thickness of the cuts, but figure a minimum of 2 hours for thin fillets. Aim for an internal temperature of 140°F (60°C). The type of wood you use to smoke the fish is entirely up to you, but most fruit or nut woods are popular. Once you're finished smoking the fish, it will be good for 7–10 days in the fridge, or up to six months in the freezer.

186 Make Jerky

Before refrigeration and canning, humans figured out how to dry meats as jerky. Most of us only know about beef jerky, but any lean meat can and should be used. Turkey, for instance, is naturally lean and mildly flavored, making it perfect for seasoned jerky. Nearly any hunted game and fish can be turned into jerky following a few easy steps.

STEP 1 Select a lean cut of meat. The less fat, the better, so go for a lean sirloin or similar cut.

STEP 2 Remove all visible fat (fat makes the jerky spoil faster), then cut the meat into thin strips no thicker than 1/2 inch (13 mm). If you're buying meat from a market, ask the butcher to cut the strips for you. Otherwise, freeze the meat for 5 minutes to make it easier to cut on your own.

STEP 3 Marinate the strips of meat with olive oil and sea salt or a recipe of your choice, then let them refrigerate overnight.

STEP 4 Rub dry spices over the marinated cuts before baking. Don't be afraid to experiment, and don't shy away from salt—it will aid in the drying process.

STEP 5 If you're lucky, you have a dehydrator for this step. But if you don't, your oven will suffice: Preheat it to 165°F (74°C). Remember the goal is to dry, not cook. Set the strips atop a wire rack in the oven, and catch any drippings. Then bake 1–3 hours, or until the jerky is dry to the touch.

STEP 6 You should eat your jerky within two weeks of making it. Store it in an airtight container (a vacuum sealer is ideal) and refrigerate until ready to eat.

187 Brew Your Own Alcohol

Home brewing is much easier than you think, and once you stock up on the right yeast, the rest of the supplies are probably close at hand. The resulting brew could be worth a lot in tough times—homespun alcohol can disinfect, anesthetize, and lubricate bartering deals, to name just a few of its many uses.

To put it briefly, you're going to add yeast to a sugar-water solution, which is kept at room temperature. The yeast is going to eat the sugar, producing carbon dioxide and alcohol. This is the process of fermentation, which will last about a month. During this time, a special cap will let the CO_2 bubble out but keep oxygen from entering the brewing jug. Sounds simple, right? It is.

COLLECT YOUR SUPPLIES You'll need a 1-gallon (4-l) glass jug, yeast, a sugar source (honey, malt, table sugar, molasses), clean water, and a wine lock cap for the jug. One other item of note is a sanitizer; a quick fix is cheap vodka. The wine lock is the only part that may need to be improvised (if you don't pick one up when you buy your yeast). It can be a vinyl hose that fits into or over the mouth of the jug. Another popular option is a balloon that has been pierced by a needle. When the balloon fills with CO_2, the needle hole opens and relieves the pressure like a valve.

BE SWEET If you intend to brew beer that tastes like beer, you'll need malt. This can be found in a can with hops already added or as a powdered extract. For old-school brewing, you could sprout some grains like wheat or barley, then toast and grind them. Simmer the ground grain in water for an hour, and filter out the malt-rich

water, which then boils with the hops for another hour. If you're making wine, you can use a mix of fruit and table sugar. For mead, all you need is honey and water (plus wine yeast). Almost any sugar will ferment.

GET CARBONATED To make your beer bubble or your Champagne fizz, you will need to carbonate it after fermentation. This can be done by adding more sugar to the brew and sealing it in a pressure-safe vessel. The dormant yeast will wake up to produce a little more CO_2, carbonating the beverage. Add an ounce of table sugar or corn sugar to each gallon of brew, and seal it in bottles. Clean soda bottles and self-capping ones will work fine. Let it sit for one week, then chill and enjoy.

188 Brew Mead

YOU'LL NEED
☐ 2.5 pounds (1 kg) honey
☐ 1 gallon (4 l) water
☐ 1 package Champagne yeast

In a large stainless-steel or enamel pot, bring the honey and water to a boil. Boil for 10 minutes, skimming off any foam that forms on top (you can eat this; it's tasty). Cool the liquid to room temperature, then add the Champagne yeast. Use a sanitized funnel to pour the brew into a sanitized glass or food-grade plastic fermentation vessel, and attach the wine lock. Let it ferment for six weeks (honey is slow).

After it has fermented and cleared, drain the mead into a sanitized jug and cork or cap it securely. Age for a few months in a cool, dark place, then enjoy the king's nectar.

189 Craft an Amber American Ale

YOU'LL NEED

- ☐ 1 pound (450 g) dried amber malt extract
- ☐ ¼ ounce (7 g) Cascade hops
- ☐ 1 package ale yeast
- ☐ 1 ounce (28 g) sugar to carbonate the ale, and bottles to handle the pressure of carbonation

STEP 1 In a big stainless-steel or enamel pot, boil 1 gallon (4 l) of water with the malt extract and the Cascade hops for 60 minutes. (Watch that it doesn't boil over!)

STEP 2 Cool and strain the brew into a clean jug. Let it cool to room temperature, as it needs to be below 80°F (27°C) before adding the yeast.

STEP 3 Add the dried yeast to the brew and shake it up. Use ale yeast to brew at room temperature. Lager yeast will require holding the temp at 50°–55°F (10°–13°C) for an extended two-month fermentation.

STEP 4 Add the sanitized fermentation lock to the vessel. Watch carefully for a few days. If bubbling (fermentation) doesn't occur in 12 to 24 hours, your yeast

was dead, or the too-hot heat killed it. Add more yeast to save the batch.

STEP 5 Set the jug in a sink for a few days, as the malt and hops combo will foam over. After a week, clean the airlock and replace it. Three weeks later, the sediment should be thick at the bottom, the bubbling should have stopped, and the ale should be clearing.

STEP 6 Carefully pour the flat beer into a clean container, leaving the sediment in the jug. Add 1 ounce of sugar per gallon of beer and mix. Funnel into sanitized bottles and cap them. You'll need about 10 bottles (12-ounce size) and caps for 1 gallon of ale. Keep the beer at room temperature for one week to carbonate, then chill for one more week and enjoy.

190 Make Blackberry Wine

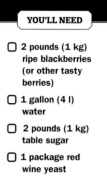

YOU'LL NEED

- ☐ 2 pounds (1 kg) ripe blackberries (or other tasty berries)
- ☐ 1 gallon (4 l) water
- ☐ 2 pounds (1 kg) table sugar
- ☐ 1 package red wine yeast

In a several-gallon stainless-steel or enamel pot, bring the berries, sugar, and water to a boil. Continue the boil for 15 minutes, mashing the berries with a spoon as you go. Cool the liquid to room temperature, pour through a sanitized strainer, and add the red wine yeast. Use a sanitized funnel to help pour the brew into a sanitized glass or food-grade plastic fermentation vessel and attach the wine lock. Let it ferment 4–5 weeks, or until it stops bubbling. After it has fermented and cleared, drain the wine into a sanitized bottle or jug, and cork or cap it securely. Age for a few months in a cool, dark place, and enjoy your sweet berry wine.

191 Tie 7 Helpful Knots

So you've mastered the basic knots, or you grew up on a hauler and can't remember a time you didn't know them. Time to focus on a few more sophisticated knots so you'll be armed with the know-how for any job that might come up.

Whether you're joining two materials that don't want to be joined or adding a new segment to an existing line, these seven knots will serve you well. See items 65 and 315 for more knots that can help you survive a wide range of situations.

SHEET BEND

This one is a little weird, but nothing works better for tying different types of material together and joining different thicknesses. This knot even joins together lines or materials that normally couldn't be joined together.

HOW TO TIE Start by bending the thicker or more slippery rope into a J shape (like a fish hook). You then pass the other rope through the fish hook from behind, wrap around the entire fish hook once, and then tuck the smaller line under itself.

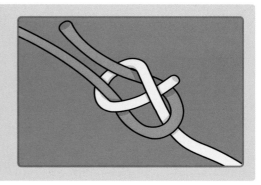

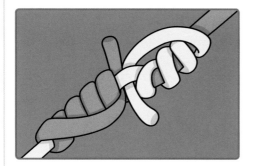

BLOOD KNOT

This little gem of a knot is used on fishing line to secure two lines together. It can mend a broken line or attach leaders and tippets.

HOW TO TIE Overlap the two lines and wrap one free end around the other line five or six times. Pass the free end between the two lines. Wrap the other line the same number of times, and tuck the free end between the two lines in the opposite direction of the other free end. If using fishing line, add saliva to reduce friction damage.

TAUT LINE HITCH

This hitch takes the place of a slide to tighten or loosen a loop in a line (like a tent guyline). This knot grips well as long as there's tension on the taut side of the loop.

HOW TO TIE Create a loop by wrapping around something like a tent stake. With the free end of the rope, wrap toward the stake twice. Then wrap the free end over everything, toward you one time around the rope, and cinch these wraps tight. Pull on the standing line and the hitch should grip the loaded line.

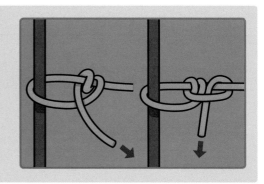

MAN HARNESS

This crafty knot puts a loop in a line when neither end of the line is free. This one is great in a wide range of possible situations.

HOW TO TIE Once you have a little slack, make a loop so that part of the line runs through the middle of the loop. Grab the side of the loop and pull it through the gap between the line in the middle and the other side of the loop. Pull the new loop tight, then pull the line to cinch. This one can slip without constant tension on the loop.

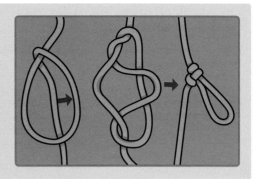

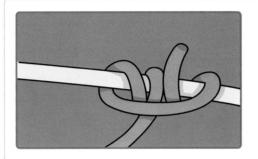

ROLLING HITCH

This hitch uses the basic knot behind a taut-line hitch to add a leg to any existing line. This was often used historically to hook more dogs to a dogsled main line.

HOW TO TIE Wrap the free end of one rope around the main rope to create a half hitch. Make a second half hitch and then wrap over the entire knot—finishing it off with a final half hitch to the other side from your starting place.

CARRICK BEND

This alternate to a square knot joins two ropes together securely and is easier to untie.

HOW TO TIE Form a loop with the free end of one rope. Pass the other rope's end under the first loop, then over, then under, as seen in the picture. Thread the free end across the loop passing under itself, and pull the ends.

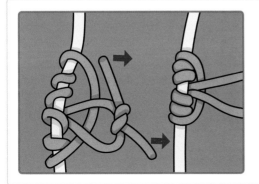

PRUSIK KNOT

This knot creates a loop that can be used as an ascender or descender. This slide-and-grip knot can be handy for adding a loop to a rope when neither end is free.

HOW TO TIE Take a short rope and a separate long rope. Tie a loop in the short rope with a solid knot. Wrap the loop around the long rope three times, so each wrap lies flat against the long rope. Pass the loop of short rope under itself and tighten. If there's weight on the loop, the prusik will grip the long rope. Slide up or down by taking the weight off the loop and pushing the wraps.

192 Improvise a Solar Lightbulb

If you have a garage, shelter, shed, or outbuilding that could use some light and you don't have a way to provide electricity, you can channel the sun instead. This idea was originally pioneered in shanty towns that lacked utilities, but it can be put to use anywhere sunny.

YOU'LL NEED

- ☐ Roofing material to match your structure (aluminum siding, plastic panel, etc.)
- ☐ 2-liter plastic water or soda bottle
- ☐ 1 tablespoon (15 ml) bleach
- ☐ Heavy-duty weatherproof caulking or sealant

STEP 1 Cut a 1-foot (0.3-m) square of your roofing material, then measure and cut a hole in its center to match the widest part of your plastic bottle. You can also cut a slightly smaller hole, then trim its edges to fold down into little flaps to help support the weight of the bottle.

STEP 2 Fill your bottle near to the brim with water, and add bleach. Close its cap and cover its edges with sealant.

STEP 3 Slide the bottle through the hole in the roofing material, about halfway, with its top facing up. Add more sealant around both sides of the panel and allow it to dry to anchor the bottle in place.

STEP 4 Find a place on the roof of your structure where the light will be cast most widely inside. Mark and cut a hole large enough for the bottle's widest point.

STEP 5 Apply more sealant around the hole, and slide the bottle through, pressing the panel firmly into place to seal thoroughly. Add more sealant to weatherproof. You now have the equivalent of a 60-watt lightbulb.

193 Make Your Own Fuel

Whether serving as a small light source or powering an improvised camping stove, those cans of Sterno are a great resource. With a few household ingredients, you can make your own by creating a substance that binds with alcohol to make a gel.

YOU'LL NEED

- ☐ Antacid tablets with a minimum of 1,000 mg calcium carbonate each
- ☐ White vinegar
- ☐ Alcohol of at least 95% (either ethanol or grain alcohol, or isopropyl rubbing alcohol)

STEP 1 Crush your antacid tablets into fine powder. (You can substitute crushed eggshells, powdered gardener's lime, or calcium supplements.)

STEP 2 Add vinegar to the powder, about 2 teaspoons (10 ml) per tablet, and stir the mixture together until the powder dissolves and the fizzing stops. Allow it to dry overnight and thicken into a slurry; its volume will shrink by half.

STEP 3 Measure out an amount of alcohol about twice the volume of the slurry, and stir in slowly and thoroughly, a bit at a time. The mixture will thicken into a jelly.

STEP 4 Collect into a container and seal it airtight to avoid any alcohol evaporation. When needed, you can open the container and light the material (after placing into a fireproof vessel, if needed).

194 Assemble an Oil Lamp

Need a light? You don't necessarily have to fill up a lantern with gas, petroleum, or paraffin oil; you don't even need a specially built lantern. People have been lighting their way with lamps for millennia, fueled by oils from plants (most notably, olive oil). All you need is a sturdy container, a fuel source, and a wick to draw it up.

STEP 1 Get a jar or bottle to hold your fuel. (You can even use the container that holds your olive oil.) Puncture a hole through the lid to hold your wick, and make one more hole to avoid a vacuum effect when the wick burns later.

STEP 2 Acquire a wick (you can find various sizes in craft stores), or make your own from an absorbent cotton or linen cord. You can also cut a long, thin strip from an article of clothing.

STEP 3 Soak the wick in a mixture of 1 tablespoon (15 g) salt per 8 ounces (230 ml) water, which will help keep the wick from charring. Gently wring out the wick and dry overnight.

STEP 4 Fill your container with whatever oil you're using as fuel. You can use olive oil, paraffin lamp oil, vegetable oil, or even used cooking oil. Pure olive oil or paraffin burns the most cleanly, with the least smoke, while other vegetable oil types will smoke more. Dip the wick into the oil to soak it, and then feed it through the opening on the lid. Screw the lid on firmly.

STEP 5 Pull up between ¼ inch (6 mm) and ½ inch (12 mm) of wick and light it. As the oil burns, more should be drawn up through the wick, assisted by air flow through the second hole, and continue feeding the lamp.

vent hole

195 Make Candles

An ideal emergency light source, candles can be stored for years at a time, and aside from whatever part is melted while lit, their fuel cannot be spilled. There are plenty of substances that can be used for the body of the candle: the remnants of other candles, beeswax, paraffin, or tallow (a solid, whitish animal fat). You can even use lard like the kind found in bacon or cooking grease, although it is softer and will need to stay in a container. To make candles, all you really need is the wax, a heat source, a container, and a wick. There are two main methods to making candles:

DIPPING This method starts with a long wick dipped into a container of hot, liquid wax (either in a special heater or a double boiler—such as a pot full of wax in a larger pot filled with hot water). Layers of wax are built up around the wick with each successive dipping, creating a broader, heavier candle as you go.

MOLDING A container is used to hold this sort of candle—a jar, can, or similar container (sometimes disposable, like votive candles in small aluminum cups)—or a mold that can be reused or discarded (such as a paper cup). You can tie the end of the wick around a stick and let it hang down into the mold while it is filled with wax, or drill a hole into the wax after pouring, and thread the wick into it.

196 Build a Bicycle-Powered Generator

When the lights go out and your appliances stop working, you can of course resort to a gas-powered generator. But if you're short on fuel, or don't have solar power as a fallback, you can gather a few spare parts and create a power supply fueled by your muscles instead.

drive belt

12-volt motor

197 Power Up

At a steady pace, your average bicyclist could pedal out between 120 and 300 watts of power in a 20-minute session on this generator. Your typical 12-volt car battery holds up to 500 watts, so you could fully charge it (and get some serious cardio, too) with a little time on the bike.

Most small household appliances don't draw a lot of power. Your laptop runs on 50 watts, so 20 minutes of cycling will run it for almost an hour. Lightbulbs start at 25 watts, but LEDs and fluorescents have a base of 5 watts—and give 2½ hours of light! Your morning coffeemaker needs about 130 watts to brew you a full pot in 10 minutes. Consider the wide range of your power needs, and make sure your battery can handle several recharges.

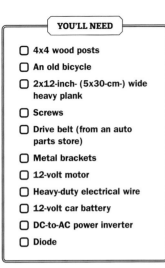
STEP 1 Measure and cut two 4x4 posts of equal length, tall enough to keep the back wheel of your bicycle at least a couple of inches off the ground when its axle is rested on top of the posts. Cut grooves into the posts for the axles to rest on.

STEP 2 Fasten the posts onto the plank with screws through their undersides, leaving enough space between them to accommodate the bike's frame.

STEP 3 Remove the bicycle's back tire, and replace it with the drive belt. Set the bike's rear axle on top of the posts and secure in place with metal brackets.

STEP 4 Attach the 12-volt motor to the plank (add brackets if the motor has none), in line with the bicycle's rear wheel, and wrap the drive belt around the motor's axle. Make sure the drive belt has no slack.

STEP 5 Attach electrical wire between the negative terminal of the motor and the 12-volt battery, then connect the battery to the inverter's negative terminal.

STEP 6 Run wire from the motor's positive terminal to the anode end of the diode. Connect another length of wire from the diode's cathode end to the battery's positive terminal, and wire the battery to the inverter's positive terminal.

STEP 7 Plug in your appliance to the inverter, climb on your bike, and pedal away.

198

Brew Coffee Without Power

Even if you're short on electricity, you still need to get up and at 'em in the morning. But how, without your favorite electric grinder and espresso machine? Here are a few ways to get your morning Joe.

COWBOY Rough-grind your coffee beans with a hand grinder or mortar and pestle, then throw them into a pot of water. Heat to simmering, then let cool as the grounds settle before pouring off the coffee (optional: use a filter to remove loose grounds).

TURKISH To make Turkish coffee, also known as mud coffee, grind your beans into a fine powder, then add to water. Bring to a boil, then remove from the heat. A layer of foam covers the top of the coffee, and the fine grounds sink to the bottom.

FRENCH PRESS You can find French presses made of sturdy plastic instead of costly glass. Add grounds and boiled water, steep for a few minutes, then press the sieve down to filter.

VIETNAMESE Place grounds in a small single-serve metal filter, then pour hot water over them. The coffee seeps through the filter into a cup below.

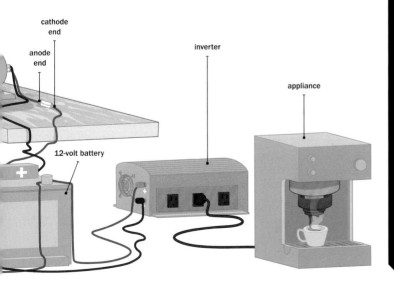

199 Make Power with Water

Since ancient times, people have harnessed the power of water to provide energy. Old-fashioned water wheels in rivers can produce low-speed, high-torque mechanical energy, sufficient to power a millstone to grind grain. But this barely scratches the surface of water's potential energy. Even a small amount of water flow over a short drop in height can create power, and an electrical generator can convert the turbine's spinning mechanical force into the infinitely versatile power of electricity. All you need are the right parts and the flowing water. As a bonus, the water goes right back to the waterway after your detour, making for minimal or no impact on the local ecology.

Homemade hydropower systems are not as out of reach as they may seem. While it's true that they can be fickle, tricky to build, and vulnerable to storms, you may be surprised by how accessible they are. Here are a few things to consider.

SCALE You're not trying to power a whole state, which means you don't need a reservoir. You can successfully make small-scale hydro systems without one. Though you require a good flow of water, small streams do provide enough force. The only time they're unreliable is during a drought or during dry summer months.

OUTPUT Micro hydro systems generally create less than 100 watts of energy, but a battery bank and the latest electronic control equipment will still power a modest house. Your homemade power will involve fewer surges than the main grid.

COST This is neither a cheap nor an effortless way to get power. That said, if you have a steady source of running water and sufficient engineerging (or old-fashioned tinkering) ability, you can create an energy source that can take you off the grid forever.

200 Build a Water Turbine

Like spraying a garden hose at a toy pinwheel, a focused jet of high-pressure water can cause a turbine to spin at an unbelievable speed. To do this right, you'll need plumbing, electrical, and engineering skills, or a whole lot of trial and error. Here's how you can do it yourself, with the right equipment and a hilly property that has a steady flow of water.

STEP 1 Assemble the materials. For a typical micro hydro setup, you'll need a pre-2000 car or truck alternator (these have a simpler construction), a turbine to attach to it (this could be made from a heat-reshaped plastic fan blade assembly), a housing for the turbine (like a plastic barrel), piping, valves, fasteners (like nuts, bolts, screws, etc.), electrical wiring, a shunt-load regulator to keep the batteries from overcharging, and a bank of 12-volt batteries—just as a minimum of supplies.

STEP 2 Build an intake structure to catch the water at a high point in the waterway. This structure should receive water for the system and screen out debris, sticks, frogs, and fish. It should be sturdy against flooding, easy to clean out, and freeze resistant.

STEP 3 Pipe out the steepest route through a pipeline (penstock) to the turbine site. The greater the drop in elevation, the better the turbine will function. Install a valve (any kind) in front of the turbine to control the water flow and the speed of the turbine.

STEP 4 Build and install the turbine and generator. Depending on the fall and flow of water, you'll have to select the best type of water turbine for your micro hydro installation. With elevation drops greater than 100 feet (30 m), a Pelton wheel provides a very high RPM turbine. For less steep installations, a propeller-type turbine will be the best choice. And for very flat, low-head installations, a propeller-type turbine in a pit will be your best option. A drop of less than 2 feet (0.6 m) may not be usable for hydroelectric.

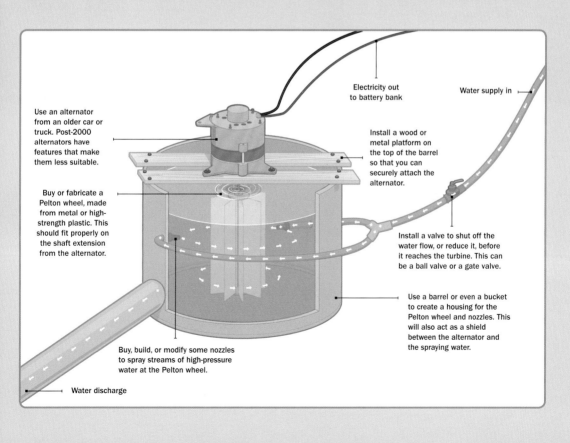

Use an alternator from an older car or truck. Post-2000 alternators have features that make them less suitable.

Buy or fabricate a Pelton wheel, made from metal or high-strength plastic. This should fit properly on the shaft extension from the alternator.

Buy, build, or modify some nozzles to spray streams of high-pressure water at the Pelton wheel.

Water discharge

Electricity out to battery bank

Water supply in

Install a wood or metal platform on the top of the barrel so that you can securely attach the alternator.

Install a valve to shut off the water flow, or reduce it, before it reaches the turbine. This can be a ball valve or a gate valve.

Use a barrel or even a bucket to create a housing for the Pelton wheel and nozzles. This will also act as a shield between the alternator and the spraying water.

201 Consider the Biodiesel Switch

Almost any diesel car can run on biodiesel without major modifications. Biodiesel is simple to use, biodegradable, nontoxic, and essentially free of sulfur and aromatics. Only diesel engines can run on biodiesel, so if you're not already behind the wheel of a diesel car, you may want to consider trading in. Other engines that run on #2 diesel can also be run on biodiesel, such as home furnaces, generators, and fishing boats.

202 Know Your Diesels

The term "biodiesel" is thrown around a lot these days and can mistakenly refer to more than one thing. If you're interested in running your engine on a different fuel type, get familiar with the options available to you.

PETROLEUM DIESEL (PETRODIESEL) This is the regular diesel you'll find at gas stations—the kind your engine was designed for. In addition to supply advantages, petrodiesel is also better suited for colder temperatures than its bio cousins.

BIODIESEL Biodiesel is made from vegetable oil rather than crude petroleum. It's a clean-burning alternative produced from renewable resources through a process in which the oil reacts chemically with alcohol. You can find petrodiesel and biodiesel mixtures more easily than you might think. The "B factor" is used to denote the percentage of biodiesel contained within a mix—biodiesel rated B5, B20, or B100 contains 5 percent, 20 percent, and 100 percent biodiesel, respectively. These percentages are worth noting because some newer diesel engines have problems running on pure biodiesel (B100) for extended periods of time.

STRAIGHT VEGETABLE OIL (SVO) If you've stepped foot in a kitchen, chances are you've encountered straight vegetable oil. It's commonly derived from soy, corn, palm, or other vegetable sources. Despite being the brass ring for biodiesel aficionados, the setbacks for this fuel source are numerous. For starters, it's extremely expensive, and because it hasn't been chemically treated it can turn into a gel at low temperatures. However, it can be done—see item 204.

203 Make the Conversion to Bio

No major conversion is needed if your car has a diesel engine. You will, however, need to replace the rubber fuel lines with metal ones, since biodiesel is known to wear rubber fuel lines down. However, your car may not agree. In some models, like light-duty diesel trucks, any form of biodiesel will dilute your motor oil. In others, your "check engine" light may turn on—so change your oil frequently. Visit your local biodiesel retailer to get the scoop on particulars relating to your vehicle.

204 Get Running on French-Fry Oil

If you're planning to go all in with SVO, know that vegetable oil is very different from biodiesel, and an expensive conversion kit is mandatory for SVO-only operation. SVO cannot meet biodiesel fuel specifications, it is not registered with the EPA, and it is not a legal motor fuel anywhere in the country. That said, it's still possible.

FIND A SOURCE You can use waste vegetable oil (as in, the stuff the French fries were in). It may not be clean or pretty, but it's cheap, and you get points for recycling. Unsurprisingly, the best starting point for large amounts of vegetable oil is restaurants. Local fast food joints should have vats of the used stuff sitting out back. Talk to the manager and get a feel for how much SVO the business generates; then try to arrange a pickup schedule.

PROCURE A CONVERSION KIT Hit up online biodiesel communities before making a purchase, and shop around. This is not a small purchase, and prices can vary. There's likely a specific kit that works best with the make and model of your car, so firsthand accounts are priceless.

CHOOSE YOUR INSTALLATION You can hire an experienced mechanic or install the kit yourself. Many kits are user-friendly, but chances are you're voiding the vehicle's warranty, so it's good to have someone skilled in your corner in case something goes wrong. If you do go the DIY route, a good kit should have a two-tank system for separating the fuels; a pumping system for removing the SVO when the car is no longer in use; SVO-safe hoses, seals, and filters; and a heating system to keep the oil at the right temperature.

FILTER AND FILL The final hurdle is filtering your SVO. The simplest filtration method is to heat the oil in a metal bucket and then pour it through a series of cheap household filters (large coffee filters or mesh strainers). You want to remove any visible leftover food particles and debris before loading it into your system.

205 Turn the Right Oils into Fuel

A wide variety of oils (both vegetable and animal) can be turned into biodiesel. Olive oil, corn oil, lard, peanut oil, and even recycled oil from restaurants can be used—the list is quite extensive. For the easiest way to produce this high-energy fuel source at home, start with unused vegetable oil that is a liquid at room temperature.

206

Be Safe with Home Chemistry

The many remarkable processes involved in biodiesel production, as well as the dangerous materials, are not for amateurs. Always wear thick rubber gloves, safety glasses, and a dust mask when handling the lye, methanol (methyl alcohol), and the solution they make. All of these substances are very harmful if they touch your skin or eyes, or are inhaled or swallowed. Methanol is readily absorbed through the skin and quite toxic. Drinking just a few ounces would be fatal. Lye is extremely caustic, giving severe chemical burns to exposed skin (like that scene in *Fight Club*). Finally, methoxide (the substance produced from lye and methanol) is an extremely toxic nerve agent.

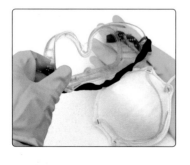

207 Get the Supplies

The materials for making 1 gallon (3.8 l) of biodiesel can be found by taking a trip to the grocery store and the hardware store. You'll need 1 gallon (3.8 l) of new vegetable oil (canola oil, corn oil, and soybean oil are the best). You'll also need $^{1}/_{2}$ ounce (14 g) of lye in the form of sodium hydroxide. Sodium hydroxide is used in certain drain cleaners—check the label to make sure it's in there, as some have other main ingredients. The final material is 27 ounces (800 ml) of methanol (methyl alcohol). This is commonly available as a fuel treatment. Make sure the label says methanol, as isopropyl alcohol won't work.

208 Learn the Process

Solid oils and used oils require some additional steps and extra equipment, so they are more challenging for the beginner. If clean, new liquid oil is used, your process can be very simple.

STEP 1 While wearing gloves and goggles, carefully pour the methanol and sodium hydroxide into a large glass jar. Stir the jar about 2 minutes, until the sodium hydroxide has completely dissolved. Do this outside, as the vapors are toxic, and use within an hour, as the solution has a short window of activity.

STEP 2 Warm your oil in a cooking pot on a stove or heater, until it is roughly 100°F (38°C). Then pour your vegetable oil into a bucket (or other plastic or glass container) with a tight-fitting lid. Add the methanol and lye mixture—very carefully—and seal.

STEP 3 Shake or roll the container gently 20–30 minutes, then allow it to sit for two days in a warm spot. During this time, the fluids will separate into two layers. The bottom layer will be glycerin, and the top layer will be your biodiesel. Carefully pour the biodiesel off into a fuel jug, leaving behind a tiny bit of biodiesel with the glycerin.

STEP 4 Blend the biodiesel with regular diesel (up to 50/50) for use in newer, high-efficiency engines. During warm weather, you could also burn the biodiesel straight in older engines (those built before 2000, which have hardier systems than the newer, computer-controlled diesel engines).

209 Be Biodiesel Smart

There are right and wrong ways to use biodiesel—if you're cooking it, you shold know them all. First and foremost, use it soon. The quality can diminish after just 10 days, and the fuel may not be usable after a month or two. Remember to use it in warm weather, or blend it in cold. Pure biodiesel will thicken at 55°F (13°C), which could clog your fuel lines and kill your engine. When making biodiesel, work outdoors or in a well-ventilated space with breathing protection. Buying all new oil, plus the expense of the lye and methanol, will cause a gallon of your biodiesel to cost much more than a gallon of store-bought diesel. But once you get the hang of producing this fuel, you can add the extra steps to process free waste cooking oil, dropping your fuel costs to pennies per gallon. Last, if you try used oil, filter it thoroughly to remove as many food particles as possible. Also heat it to 200°F (93°C) for 10 minutes to drive off water that was introduced in the oil's use. And get the supplies to titrate so you can determine the pH of the oil (used oil is often more acidic than new oil).

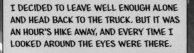
I DECIDED TO LEAVE WELL ENOUGH ALONE AND HEAD BACK TO THE TRUCK. BUT IT WAS AN HOUR'S HIKE AWAY, AND EVERY TIME I LOOKED AROUND THE EYES WERE THERE.

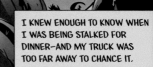

I KNEW ENOUGH TO KNOW WHEN I WAS BEING STALKED FOR DINNER—AND MY TRUCK WAS TOO FAR AWAY TO CHANCE IT.

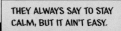

THEY ALWAYS SAY TO STAY CALM, BUT IT AIN'T EASY.

SO I STOOD MY GROUND, RAISED MY ARMS, AND GAVE HER A GOOD FIRM SHOUT OR TWO. I CLAPPED LOUDLY AND TRIED TO LOOK IMPOSING.

I PREPARED TO HIT HER WITH EVERYTHING I HAD—AND JUST LIKE THAT, SHE TURNED AND STALKED OFF.

I MADE IT BACK TO MY TRUCK AND FLOORED IT, JUST IN CASE SHE WAS LOOKING FOR DESSERT.

211 Avoid Conflict

If you're learning how to fight from a book, you're probably in trouble, but it's a start. The best defense is distance, so learn to spot potential trouble before you need to fight your way out of it. Honing your situational awareness is crucial, especially when emergency services and police presence might be limited or unavailable.

- Vary your patterns and routines to make yourself or your property a less likely target.
- Always walk with your head up, and be aware of anything and everything going on around you.
- Keep your keys handy and always ready, so that you can open a car or building door quickly—or use them as an improvised weapon if needed.
- Wear shoes that allow you to run in the event of an attack.
- Wear clothes that are loose enough to wriggle out of if someone grabs you.
- Never be empty-handed. Carry a rolled magazine with you. It makes a handy club and also can protect you from a knife.

It's no fun going through life with paranoid tendencies, but a little bit of awareness, even in familiar surroundings, can make a big difference. Stay alert to avoid becoming a target.

212 Throw a Power Punch

If you have to punch someone, know what you're doing. The difference between a power punch and a weak swat can mean ending a fight quickly or getting beaten up. If you want to pack a wallop, follow these steps.

STEP 1 Choose a target (see below). You can hit any part of the body, but you won't always have time to select the ideal spot. The good news is that the face comes prepackaged with a perfectly centered target: the nose. A well-landed blow will make his eyes water and ring his bell.

STEP 2 Remember your feet; throwing a punch depends on a solid stance. If you're right-handed, stand with your feet shoulder width apart, your left foot forward and your body turned at an angle to the attacker. For lefties, reverse it. Your back leg should support your weight.

STEP 3 Put your weight behind the punch rather than just using your arm strength. Push off from your back foot, and as your arm uncoils, swivel your torso to drive your arm. As your punch extends, shift your weight forward to your front foot, which should come naturally.

213 Hit the Spot

Where to aim those punches? Target the most fragile areas of your attacker's body with a fist or elbow strike, and you might stun him long enough to get away. Here are some sweet spots:

- Temple
- Below ear
- Side of neck
- Base of throat
- Solar plexus
- Armpit
- Lower abs
- Groin

214 Block and Counter

The easiest way to defend yourself from a flying fist is to avoid standing still in front of it. If you do have to fight, here are some tips to prepare you.

Stay steady and light on your feet. Most fistfights aren't boxing matches; they're wild frenzies. But if someone wants to stand in front of you and duke it out, it's important to move quickly in and out of range, as well as to step side to side to minimize damage.

Remember to "peek-a-boo" your defenses: Hold your fists close together in front of your face. This defense is almost universal in boxing, and it keeps vulnerable areas covered by less-vulnerable ones. It's also easier to throw quick punches from this position.

Watch your opponent's shoulders to see what kind of punch is being thrown. Little movement means it's coming straight at you. Larger, circular motions mean a looping punch. A cocked arm usually means an uppercut. For jabs and uppercuts, lean back to maximize the distance between your head (the target) and your opponent's fists. For looping haymakers, sidestep in the direction of the punch. You may still get tagged, but your movement will lessen the impact.

215 Choose the Right Knife

Who doesn't want to be the guy with the biggest knife—one so intimidating it makes everyone else flee in terror? But choosing the right knife for self-defense can be tricky. If you're dead set on a blade, consider these two criteria.

HANDLE As important as the blade is where you hold onto it. Choose a handle a little longer than your grip so you can strike with the handle as well as the blade. Go for a handle with a pommel (a knob on the hilt) for this purpose. Make sure the grip doesn't get slippery when it gets wet. You'll also have a firmer grip with an oval handle rather than a round one. Look for a hilt guard to help protect your hand from your opponent's blade.

BLADE Look for a double-edged blade to give you greater versatility and a longer edge. Be sure the point doesn't taper too sharply, so that the tip doesn't break if you strike something hard. And consider the finish—if concealment is a concern, then go with something matte, but a bright, polished blade is more intimidating. Keep in mind that fixed blades beat folding blades for strength and speed.

216 Stand and Deliver

The biggest, baddest knife won't help you at all if you don't know how to wield it. That knowledge starts with a solid base, or fighting stance. The key to this is to maintain your balance. Keep your feet shoulder width apart, weight evenly distributed between the legs, and knees slightly bent. Try to turn your body sideways to your opponent, which makes you a smaller target.

Too many people focus too intently on the knife hand. The real game-changer comes from your free hand. In an extreme survival situation, you may need to think of this hand as expendable; keep it close to your torso as a shield for vital organs. You can also use it as a distraction, throwing things at your opponent or grabbing his blade. This hand also will help you keep your balance if you're moving over unstable terrain. Don't forget, there's no such thing as a clean technique here. Cut and cut often. And if you see an opportunity to land a punch with your free hand, make it count.

217 Get a Grip

You have four choices when it comes to gripping your knife for combat, but only one of them is really ideal. If you're caught unawares or fighting a novice, it can be useful to understand the reasons that some grips are not so great—especially since you may have seen (or used) them in the past, or might be up against someone who "learned" to fight from the movies. See the chart below to learn the right way to hold onto your blade, how to make the wrong ways work for you if you must, and how to use your opponent's grip against him.

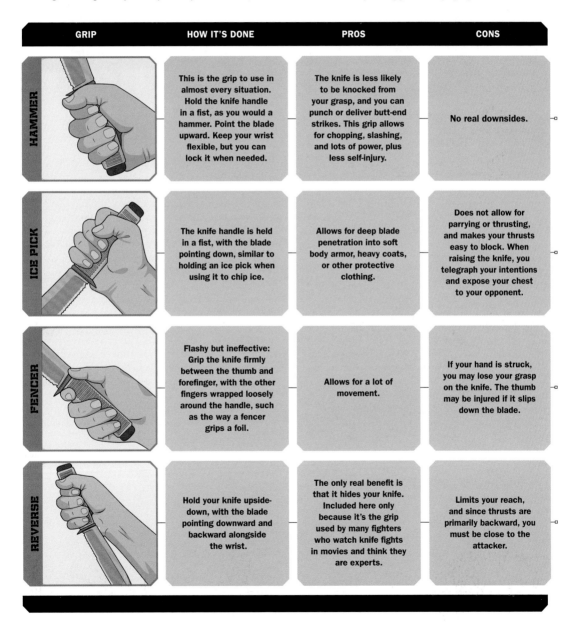

GRIP	HOW IT'S DONE	PROS	CONS
HAMMER	This is the grip to use in almost every situation. Hold the knife handle in a fist, as you would a hammer. Point the blade upward. Keep your wrist flexible, but you can lock it when needed.	The knife is less likely to be knocked from your grasp, and you can punch or deliver butt-end strikes. This grip allows for chopping, slashing, and lots of power, plus less self-injury.	No real downsides.
ICE PICK	The knife handle is held in a fist, with the blade pointing down, similar to holding an ice pick when using it to chip ice.	Allows for deep blade penetration into soft body armor, heavy coats, or other protective clothing.	Does not allow for parrying or thrusting, and makes your thrusts easy to block. When raising the knife, you telegraph your intentions and expose your chest to your opponent.
FENCER	Flashy but ineffective: Grip the knife firmly between the thumb and forefinger, with the other fingers wrapped loosely around the handle, such as the way a fencer grips a foil.	Allows for a lot of movement.	If your hand is struck, you may lose your grasp on the knife. The thumb may be injured if it slips down the blade.
REVERSE	Hold your knife upside-down, with the blade pointing downward and backward alongside the wrist.	The only real benefit is that it hides your knife. Included here only because it's the grip used by many fighters who watch knife fights in movies and think they are experts.	Limits your reach, and since thrusts are primarily backward, you must be close to the attacker.

218 Throw a Knife

Often relegated to the balloon-popping world of a sideshow act or a pivotal scene in an action flick, knife throwing does have a legitimate place in your real-world self-defense skills. And while you don't usually want to throw away your weapon, there are times when you might need to fight at a distance or skewer a small game animal, both of which can be accomplished with the art of knife throwing.

UNDERHANDED OR OVERHANDED Only experience will tell you whether you are naturally better at underhanded or overhanded knife throwing. Both can work, and both should be practiced, but it makes sense to know where your strengths lie. Select a well-balanced knife or, better yet, a set of throwing knives. Spend a few hours practicing to develop your aiming and throwing skills, and then keep going until you become proficient. Every knife throws differently, and range has a great bearing on your throwing as well. Close range may only require a light flick of the knife, while longer range will be more like a baseball throw.

OVERHANDED TECHNIQUE Grip a normal knife by the blade, with the knife's spine (the square edge) against your hand. Hold the knife up, with the knife handle up by your ear. Take aim at your target, and bring your arm down as if you were swinging a hammer to drive a nail. The timing of the knife release is critical, and after a few minutes, you'll start to get the hang of it. Pay close attention to the distance from your target, and get a feel for throwing at different distances. If you are using a throwing knife, you will want to learn to throw by both the handle and the blade.

UNDERHANDED TECHNIQUE This can allow you to attempt something of a surprise attack, as the knife is often hard to spot when held in this low position. Grip the blade similarly to the overhanded technique, this time holding the knife down by your knee, with the handle pointed toward the ground. Move your arm quickly upward, and release just before your arm lines up with the target.

Overhanded

Underhanded

219 Sharpen Your Blade

Putting a keen edge on your knife is almost as important as carrying the knife in the first place. A dull knife won't cut very much and is more likely to cause injury to its owner. Good equipment is an important part of the task, but with the right technique you can literally sharpen a knife on a rock.

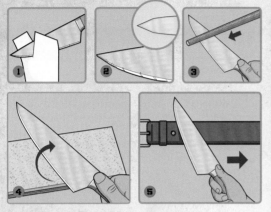

STEP 1 Survey the damage to see just how dull your knife really is. Look for nicks in the edge, and try cutting a piece of paper to test the edge. Deep nicks and no paper cutting mean you're going to have a lot of sharpening ahead of you.

STEP 2 Determine the edge angle of your knife. Depending on the make and model, the actual edge may have a different angle than the sides of the knife blade.

STEP 3 File away any nicks with a bastard file or a coarse sharpening stone, while maintaining the proper edge angle (most knives have a bevel angle of roughly 20 to 23 degrees). If there are no nicks, go down each side of the edge twice with a coarse stone.

STEP 4 Sharpen with a medium grit sharpening stone, twice on each side, and finish by doing the same with a fine stone. Grind the edge using little circles and count as you go, making the same number of strokes on each side of the blade.

STEP 5 Finally, to remove burrs and polish the edge, strop the blade against a leather belt or a smooth log. Draw the spine of the knife forward, dragging the sharp edge against the stropping surface. Strop each side several times, then test for sharpness.

220 Don't Get in a Knife Fight

Many people carry a knife thinking it ups their chances for survival in, well, a knife fight. But movies about gangs aside, chances are slim that you'll be cornered in an alley by a handful of knife-wielding thugs looking for a rumble. Knife cultures are rare, and if you do find yourself in a knife fight, you'll probably only realize it after you've been stabbed.

In most cases, you won't have time to draw your knife. Someone armed with a knife is unlikely to give you time to level the playing field, so go with a sheath knife if you must carry one. You'll eliminate the steps of unfolding or extracting the blade. While you're at it, spend time practicing your quick draw.

Don't think of it as a "fight" at all. When was the last time you saw a news story about two hombres going at it with blades? Fights escalate. You don't want to be the guy expecting a knife fight against a guy with a club or a gun. If a knife is your best option, you'd better know it fast and act before your adversary has a chance to reveal his weapon of choice.

Last, there's always a better option than going with a knife for self-defense. Your opponent will attack unpredictably. Even if you "win," you'll more than likely emerge with some bad injuries yourself. Depending on the context, these wounds could spell the end of your survival efforts. Most knife-fighting techniques evolved from martial arts. Unless you're equally proficient in that art, your best defense is running away as fast as you can.

Make a PVC Bow

Whether you need to hunt for food or fend off post-apocalyptic barbarian hordes, a bow is a good, versatile weapon and tool. Building a simple wooden longbow takes a fair amount of know-how, but with these directions and a length of PVC pipe, you can improvise a bow with a draw of up to 60 pounds (27 kg).

YOU'LL NEED

- ☐ ³/₄-inch- (2-cm-) wide, 5-foot- (1.5-m-) long PVC pipe (schedule 40 white pipe is stiffer but prone to cracking from UV exposure or cold; schedule 80 gray pipe is softer but may weaken over time if the bow stays strung constantly)
- ☐ Two 5-foot (1.5-m) lengths of ¹/₄-inch (0.6-cm) fiberglass rod (from farm/garden/hardware supply stores)
- ☐ ⁵/₈-inch (1.6-cm) rubber heater hose (from auto parts store)
- ☐ Athletic tape
- ☐ 56-inch (1.4-m) bow string (from sporting goods stores; you can improvise one from high tensile cord, but better to buy one)
- ☐ Self-adhering medical wrap

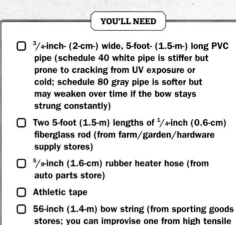

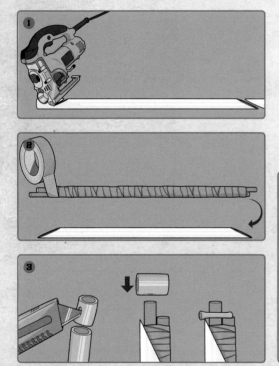

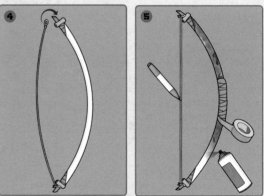

STEP 1 Cut the ends of the PVC pipe at about a 30-degree angle (tilting toward each other) and sand smooth.

STEP 2 Mark the two fiberglass rods at about 1¹/₈ inch (3 cm), and tape them together with athletic tape, leaving just the measured length of each rod sticking out of the tape. Feed the rods into the PVC pipe; the marked length should be showing at each end.

STEP 3 Cut two 1-inch (2.5-cm) pieces from the ⁵/₈-inch (1.5-cm) heater hose, and punch a hole through both sides midway. Put a hose piece on each end of the fiberglass rods to act as a protector for your bow string.

STEP 4 String your bow by hooking one end of your bow string over the fiberglass rod sticking out of one end of the pipe, bending the bow slowly, and slipping the other end of the bow string onto the other fiberglass rod tip. Be sure the rubber heater hose protects the string from fraying against the pipe.

STEP 5 Mark the center of the bow and wrap the handle in self-adhering medical wrap to improve your grip. Mark the middle of the string to locate where the arrow will be nocked. Cover the bow in tape or paint to protect from wear.

222 Fletch Your Own Arrows

Now that you have a bow, you still need ammunition, and that means making your own arrows. You'll need strong wooden shafts to safely accommodate the bow's draw, but with a little work and the right supplies, you'll be on your way to being an urban ranger.

YOU'LL NEED

- ☐ Duct tape and electrical tape
- ☐ ³/₈-inch (1-cm) hardwood dowels (e.g. birch, cedar, poplar, or ramon), about 29 inches (74 cm) in length (make sure the grain of the dowel goes its full length with no knots to avoid breakage)
- ☐ ¹/₁₆-inch (1.6-mm) sheet metal (aluminum or steel)
- ☐ Epoxy and varnish or beeswax

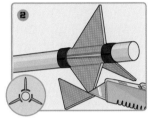

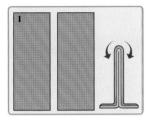

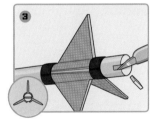

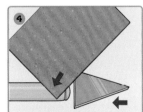

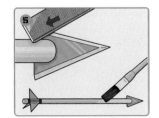

STEP 1 Cut three pieces of duct tape about 1¹/₂ inches (4 cm) wide by 4 inches (10 cm) long. Fold each piece in half, leaving a total of about ¹/₂ inch (1.3 cm) wide open at the bottom or ¹/₄ inch (0.6 cm) from each side.

STEP 2 Attach tape to dowel with these flaps, about 1¹/₂ inches (4 cm) behind the end of the dowel, evenly spaced around the shaft. Trim the pieces of tape into triangles or shield shapes to make fletchings. Wrap a bit of the fletching ends in electrical tape so they bend against the shaft, to stabilize.

STEP 3 Cut a ¹/₄-inch- (0.6-cm-) deep notch on the back of the wooden dowel (about half that wide at the most) to make a nock for your arrow, with one fletching perpendicular to it. Sand the wood.

STEP 4 Cut arrowheads from sheet metal in about a 1-inch- (2.5-cm-) wide by 2-inch- (5-cm-) long triangle. Cut a notch into the front of the arrow shaft and sand smooth and round. Slide arrowhead into place and secure with epoxy.

STEP 5 Sharpen arrowhead edges and coat wood in varnish or beeswax.

223

Shoot Your Bow Properly

Whatever bow you're using, you should definitely learn to shoot your arrows correctly. Here are the basic steps.

STEP 1 Stand with your body perpendicular to the target, turning your chin over your shoulder toward it.

STEP 2 Nock your arrow with one fletching facing outward from the bow, holding one finger above and two (or three) below it.

STEP 3 Draw the string, holding it at the first knuckle of your fingers. Keep your elbow up as you pull the string to the corner of your mouth, and hold your bow arm out stiff, but don't squeeze the bow.

STEP 4 Aim down the length of the shaft and set its point on your target.

STEP 5 Loose the arrow by relaxing your fingers and letting the string slip free. Hold still until the arrow hits its mark.

If you need to readjust, stop and start over. You can protect your fingers and forearms with gloves or guards. Keep practicing and you'll consistently hit your target.

Don't Get Caught Without:
DUCT TAPE

If there ever was a miracle product, it's duct tape. In existence for more than 70 years, this staple product of fix-it-yourselfers has been used by everyone and for everything. Here are some of the things duct tape can do in a pinch.

❶ REPAIR CRACKS

Repairing a cracked water bottle or a pierced hydration bladder? A strip of DT is the next best thing for an ailing water vessel. Just dry the surface before you try to tape your patch in place, as most forms of duct tape won't stick to moisture.

❷ MAKE CORDAGE

Twist one or several lengths of duct tape into a cord or rope.

❸ CRAFT A SPEAR

Cut a branch about 3 to 6 feet (1 to 2 m) long, and tape your knife to it firmly. Presto! You have a spear for hunting, fishing, or defense.

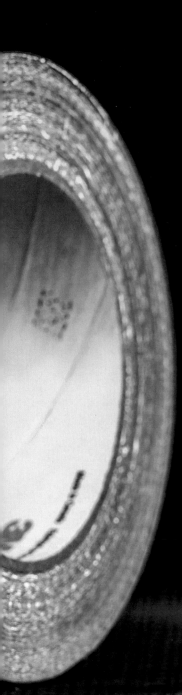

CUFF 'EM

If someone is acting up during a survival emergency, you can duct tape his hands together around a tree to prevent him from becoming a danger to himself or others.

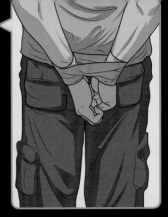

⑤ CATCH INSECTS

Who needs flypaper when you have duct tape? Tear off a few strips and hang them around your bed and eating area to catch those annoying bugs.

⑥ REINFORCE KNOTS

If you're worried about your knots slipping, wrapping them in duct tape will help keep them fast. You'll need to cut the tape away with a knife or scissors to untie the knot.

⑦ INSULATE CLOTHING

Layer the inside of your shoes and clothing to keep water out and seal body heat in.

⑧ AFFIX BANDAGES

Place a sterile dressing over your wound, and strap it in place with DT. Hopefully you're not too hairy where you got injured.

⑨ MAKE A HAT

If you're in danger of getting sunstroke and all you have is duct tape, you can fashion a makeshift hat to reflect away the sun's rays. So much more stylish than tinfoil.

⑩ CRAFT A SLING

Fold a length of DT down the middle, so that it is half the original width and no longer exposing a sticky side. Use the strap to make a sling for a busted arm.

225

Learn Safe Gun Handling

It's not hard to find examples of people misusing firearms. Regardless of the circumstances, and especially in survival situations when an injury could spell disaster, knowing basic rules of gun safety is a must. Here are nine rules for gun safety that you should absolutely know.

SAFETY RULES

- Keep the muzzle pointed in a safe direction.
- Unload any firearm when not actually in use.
- Treat every gun as though it were loaded.
- Be sure of your target and what's beyond it.
- Use correct ammunition.
- Always wear eye and ear protection when shooting.
- Be sure the barrel is clear of obstructions before shooting.
- Don't alter or modify your gun, and have guns serviced regularly. In a long-term survival situation, find someone trained in gunsmithing rather than trying to do it yourself.
- Learn the mechanical and handling characteristics of the firearm you are using.

226 Stand and Shoot

When it comes to choosing a stance for shooting, you really only have two sound choices.

THE ISOSCELES
To take the isosceles stance, start by standing with your feet shoulder width apart, facing the target. Bend your knees slightly, and extend the handgun fully toward the target, keeping your arms straight and locked. With your shoulders squared, your arms will form a perfect isosceles triangle. The isosceles stance is usually the first two-handed stance taught in most firearms training classes. It provides a strong, simple stance that is easy to remember under stress.

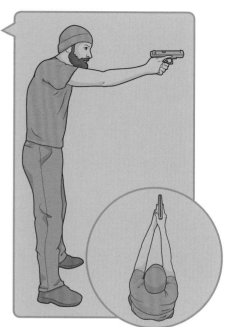

THE WEAVER
Stand with your feet shoulder width apart with your strong-side leg slightly back—this is called a boxer's stance. Next, angle your supporting arm's shoulder toward the target. Bend your knees while keeping your body weight slightly forward, and grasp the gun using opposite pressure with both hands. Keep both elbows bent with the support elbow pointing downward. This push-pull grip stance provides speed, stability, and accuracy.

227 Avoid Four Common Trigger Mistakes

If you're missing, chances are you're missing in the same spots. It's not enough to simply "aim lower." You want to hit where you're aiming. So aim for the center of the target each time, then pay attention to where your rounds are missing. If you're sighted in correctly, the issue lies in proper trigger control.

◄ **JERKING** If all your shots are missing low, you're jerking the trigger. Rather than squeezing the trigger with balanced pressure, you're likely jerking it with abrupt force, causing the barrel to dip as the round is fired.

► **PUSHING** If you have just the tip of your finger on the trigger, you may push the gun to the left (for a righty) when you apply pressure to the trigger. Center the pad of your finger on the trigger, and try a straighter squeeze.

◄ **HEELING** The opposite of jerking. If you're anticipating the pull, you may be overcompensating by pushing forward with the heel of your hand. This pressure causes the barrel of the gun to elevate.

► **SNATCHING** The opposite of pushing, you likely have too much of your index finger on the trigger. Snatching the trigger will cause the muzzle to drift toward your dominant side at at the point of fire.

228 Drill Home Accuracy

Shooting a handgun accurately takes a lot of practice. Yes, good-quality ammunition goes a long way toward marksmanship. But before you ever sight down a target, you can study some common mistakes and help diagnose problems as (or even before) they occur.

First, you need to understand sight alignment and picture. To align your handgun's sights properly, you must confirm that the top of the front sight is level with the notch in the rear sight. This ensures proper elevation, meaning that your aim is neither too high nor too low. Of course, you must also align the sights horizontally. A good way to practice without even using a gun is to have the shooter hold a pen and extend her arm out front. The shooter can pick a target in the distance and practice transferring her gaze from the tip of the pen to the target and back again. This focusing trains the shooter's eye to transition between the front sight and the target. Remember that when the shot breaks, the focus should be on the tip of the front sight or, in this case, the tip of the pen.

Second, learn trigger control. If you don't properly pull the trigger, the most well-sighted shot will be off target. In order to develop good trigger-pull mechanics, try balancing a penny on the end of the barrel. Now practice dry-firing the pistol until the penny remains balanced. If the penny keeps falling off, pay close attention to the direction it falls. This observation can tell you if you're pushing or jerking the trigger, and you can correct targeting issues before ever squeezing off a valuable round.

229 Build Your Own Blowgun

Cultures around the world have used blowguns as hunting tools for thousands of years, and there is no shortage of modern fans in the sport of blowgun target shooting. This particular plan doesn't include poison, but with these instructions, you can go after small game with your own homemade blowgun and darts.

YOU'LL NEED

- ☐ Schedule 40 ½-inch- (1-cm-) diameter PVC pipe or threaded PVC (optional)
- ☐ ½-inch (1-cm) female PVC pipe adapters (optional)
- ☐ 1 x ¾ inch (2.5 x 2 cm) PVC pipe adapter
- ☐ 1 x ½ inch (2.5 x 1 cm) PVC pipe bushing
- ☐ Superglue or PVC cement
- ☐ Wooden or metal skewers
- ☐ Thin twine, thread, or string
- ☐ Cotton balls

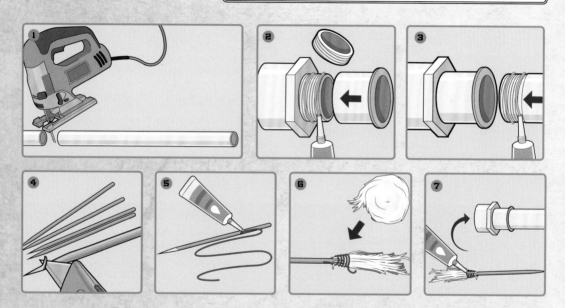

STEP 1 Measure a length of PVC pipe to make the body of your blowgun—generally about 3–6 feet (1–2 m). You can also make a "takedown" version by assembling multiple lengths of threaded PVC pipe and female adapters. Cut the ends of your pipe (including removing any threading if necessary) and sand smooth.

STEP 2 Create a mouthpiece by cutting down the threads on the ¾-inch adapter, leaving about ¼ to ½ inch (0.6 to 1.2 cm). Screw the adapter into the ½-inch (1.2-cm) bushing, securing with superglue or cement.

STEP 3 Attach the other end of the ½-inch (1.2-cm) bushing to one end of the pipe, again using your glue.

STEP 4 Sharpen the pointed ends of your skewers, and round or blunt the back ends. If you are using metal skewers, you may have to cut off a ring or handle first.

STEP 5 Measure out several inches (at least 10 cm) of string and glue it to the end of a wooden skewer, about an inch (2.5 cm) up from its base.

STEP 6 Pull a couple of long tufts from a cotton ball, lay half of their length against the back of the skewer, and wind the string around them to pin them in place. Continue adding tufts of cotton, tying them on, until you have a tail on your skewer.

STEP 7 Trim off excess string and glue the end so it does not unwind. Make sure the dart can be placed snugly into the blowgun but does not entirely block air flow. Once you have the right size, you can make more darts the same way.

230 Use What's Close

When it comes to defending yourself or your property, take a cue from some common items.

THINK GALVANIZED Every kid who ever played knights in armor knows about using the lid of a trashcan as a shield. It won't stop a bullet, but it will stop a machete or a hatchet and will most certainly deflect a punch.

CLIMB A LADDER You can even pick one up to keep attackers at bay. Improvised weapons aren't always offensive; when it comes to protecting yourself from physical assault, anything that keeps an aggressor at more than arm's length is good. A lightweight ladder can easily be grabbed to put space between you and an intruder. In the event the assailant is of the four-legged variety, a ladder is invaluable in keeping you from being bitten.

SPRAY AWAY A spray bottle is useful for more than simply watering plants or using pesticides. Chances are, it already contains something you'd rather not have in your eyes. If not, just pick up an extra one and fill it with common ammonia. Set the nozzle to "stream," and don't hesitate to use it in an emergency situation. A well-aimed squirt of ammonia is usually all that's needed to keep you safe, especially with small animals.

TOOL UP Household tools make for good weapons. Look at the weaponry of medieval peasants: pitchforks, spades, hammers, and more. There is almost always a weapon within reach, especially if tools are kept where they are most often used rather than in one central location.

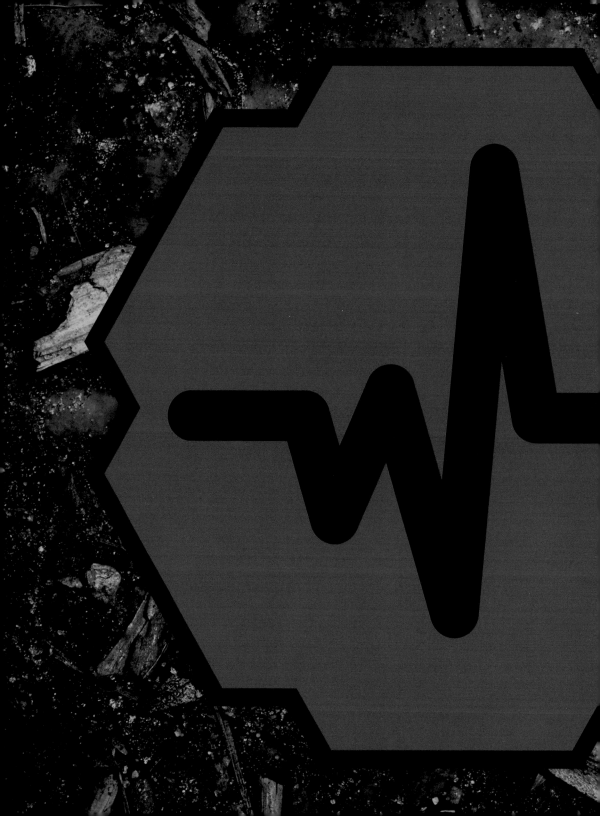

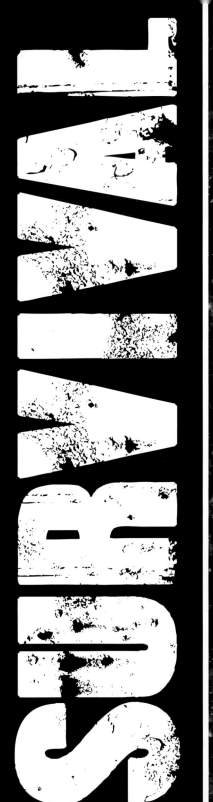

You've gotten the right gear and you've picked up some new skills. Now there's only one thing left to do: survive. In the uncertain world of emergency preparedness, it's nearly impossible to predict which chain of events will unfold in front of you. With this chaos in mind, it's time to delve into the long-term survival strategies that will help you to achieve even greater levels of self-reliance and safety.

This third chapter will address some specific emergencies like natural disasters, EMPs, and economic collapse. We'll discuss diversifying your food strategies with trapping, fishing, hunting, and preservation. It's also time to tackle some scarier situations in which you may be on your own, like handling your own medical care, figuring out when and how to bug out, and honing techniques for surviving with just the clothes on your back. And in the case of a future where things never really come back (or take a very long time to do so), you'll find guidance on bartering, blacksmithing, and even making your own gunpowder.

But first, a word of caution.

These scenarios are not to be viewed through the fantasy lens of survival movies. There's nothing glorious about striding down a highway with a BOB on your back—it means your life is in shambles and your home is gone. And while I'm on the subject, walking down the highway is a good way to get robbed of your supplies. There is no chance that you're going to be living some sort of idealized "little house on the prairie" lifestyle after a disaster, either. A lack of modern resources will not bring back historical morals and civility or make your kids and neighbors behave better.

This section is not for those who would roll over and die in a crisis. It is for the hard-wired survivor who won't quit. There are many different traits that can make up this survivor's mentality. It may be a positive attitude in the face of adversity, a mental toughness that allows him to tolerate the intolerable, the creativity to make something from nothing, or maybe the burning motivation to see friends and family again. And these are just a few of the positive traits that I hope this chapter will cultivate in you.

231 Chart Your Survival Priorities

Getting your priorities out of whack can have dire consequences. Deal with the most dangerous things first, then start working your way down the list until you are safe.

THE THREAT	FIRST PRIORITY	SECOND PRIORITY
WILDERNESS SURVIVAL	Find or make a safe shelter to stay in while awaiting rescue.	Locate and disinfect your drinking water; store some if possible.
EARTHQUAKE	Get to a safe spot when you feel the first signs of an earthquake.	Stay in that spot until it's safe to leave.
FLOODING	Listen to live TV or radio for flood warnings if bad weather is predicted.	Evacuate the area or seek higher ground, if instructed to do so.
TORNADO	Listen to live TV or radio. You may only have seconds to react.	Get into a storm shelter or an interior windowless room.
HURRICANE	Listen to live weather reports if a hurricane is predicted.	Batten down to ride out the storm, or evacuate the area, if instructed.
VOLCANO	Listen to live TV or radio for instructions.	Evacuate, or shelter in place after sealing off doors and windows.
PANDEMIC	Avoid public places and those who have been in public places.	Shelter in place, and quarantine any late arrivals. Listen to the news.
DIRTY BOMB/ CHEMICAL EMERGENCY	Evacuate or shelter immediately. Toss clothes that may be contaminated.	Seal off your windows and doors with tape and plastic sheeting.
NUCLEAR WAR	Get to a stocked bomb shelter as fast as possible and listen to news.	If exposed to radiation, take potassium iodide for your thyroid.
POWER GRID FAILURE	Shelter at home, relying upon stored food, water, and supplies.	Devise ways to safely resupply your food and water.
EMP (ELECTRO-MAGNETIC PULSE)	Shelter at home, relying upon stored food, water, and supplies.	Try to locate functioning communications equipment.
ECONOMIC COLLAPSE	Shelter at home, relying upon stored food, water, and supplies.	Come up with ways to provide your own food, water, and supplies.
GOVERNMENT COLLAPSE	Shelter in place, hopefully with a group of trusted friends and family.	Set up security measures against looters and lawlessness.

THIRD PRIORITY	FOURTH PRIORITY	FIFTH PRIORITY
Build a fire and begin signaling for help in numerous other ways.	Look for safe food sources; prepare and store some food if practical.	Leave the area to look for help only if rescue isn't likely.
Turn off your utilities (gas, water, and electricity) after the quake.	Seek refuge until your home is declared safe to return to.	Be mentally and physically prepared for an aftershock.
Take water and all vital supplies from your home.	Monitor the media for updates and additional warnings.	Return when the "all clear" is given, but don't drive through water.
Ride out the bad weather by sheltering in place.	After the tornado, get out of the building if there's structural damage.	Seek a safe place until the building is inspected for structural safety.
Rely upon stored food, water, flashlights, etc. during the storm.	Don't go outside during the storm unless it's a medical emergency.	Get the building inspected for structural damage after the storm.
Wear tight-fitting safety goggles and respirators to protect from ash.	If sheltering, rely upon stored food, water, flashlights, etc.	Be prepared to abandon the area once travel is deemed safe.
Rely upon stored food and water; continue to avoid the public.	Wear gloves and surgical masks both in home and outside.	Take immune system supplements and stay isolated until it's over.
Listen to live TV or radio for evacuation or shelter instructions.	If sheltering, rely upon stored food, water, flashlights, etc. Don't go out!	Be prepared to abandon the area for good once travel is deemed safe.
Dispose of clothing or supplies that may have been contaminated.	Shelter in place, relying on stored food, water, flashlights, etc.	Evacuate the area when radiation levels reach a safe level.
Use cash and barter to obtain the things you need.	Use alternative energy and power systems.	Learn to make do without a lot of modern conveniences.
Learn what has happened and what the authorities are advising.	Use cash and barter to obtain the things you need.	Be prepared to revert to a low-tech lifestyle.
Take security measures to be prepared for desperate people.	In a neutral location, use barter to get things you need.	Be prepared for tough times and tough choices.
Rely upon stored food, water, and fuel.	Figure out safe ways to replenish vital supplies.	If your area is hostile, head for a safe haven in an armed caravan.

232

Assess and Respond to an Emergency

Who is the true hero in an emergency? It's not necessarily the action-star type who comes in swinging. In real life, someone who is calm, cool, and collected is much more likely to save the day. Silly as it may sound, practicing strategies to remain calm may very well set you up to succeed when the chips are down. For example, do you get infuriated when someone cuts you off in traffic? Freak out when the bathtub starts overflowing? Get squeamish at the sight of blood? In each of these cases, take a moment, assess the situation, ask yourself if your reaction is helping to make things better, and, if not, find something constructive and helpful that you can do. If you train yourself to handle life's little emergencies, you'll be much better at dealing with life-threatening events. Here are some basic concepts to keep in mind.

DON'T PANIC Take an extra moment to breathe deeply and calm yourself before taking any action.

BE REALISTIC Assess what you can realistically do to make a situation better. Prioritize your own health and safety and that of your family.

USE LOGIC Don't think about what you want in an ideal world, or what *should* happen, or what you hope you can talk others into doing. What's the best, most logical course of action based on your skills, abilities, and resources? Do that. Worry about everything else later.

233 Survive Anything

People with no skills and no gear have survived seemingly insurmountable scenarios, simply because they had the right mindset not to become a casualty.

MENTAL TOUGHNESS The strength of your will and the toughness of your mind can trump physical prowess in survival situations. You must learn to tolerate the intolerable, suffer through the insufferable, and overcome your weakness and your desire to give up.

> **BE AWARE: PANIC** Panic is one of your worst enemies. Panic costs people their lives because it blocks logical thinking and allows the disconnection of your imagination from reality—which can be dangerous during traumatic events. Stay positive and maintain a firm grip on the situation. Carefully monitor yourself and other survivors for depression, anger, frustration, hyperactivity, feelings of intense guilt, ideas of suicide, and irrational behavior. Lend others as much support as you can, and don't let a negative mental state sneak up on you or worsen your situation.

MOTIVATION What motivates a person to stay alive when everything has gone wrong? Many survival stories speak of the survivor's devotion to a higher power or their intense desire to get back to family, friends, and loved ones. Motivation is the mental aspect that keeps people going beyond all hope or reason.

> **BE AWARE: IGNORANCE** Despite the wealth of information available to the world today, there are a lot of people who couldn't survive even a minor emergency. Most people assume that survival skills are easy because they look easy on TV, and so they overestimate their own abilities. You need to know what to do, how to do it, and you need to have done it before in order to really possess the skills to survive.

ADAPTABILITY Adaptability and survival have always been closely related. The ability to adapt to changing events, situations, and environments is one of the most impressive and necessary parts of a survivor's mind-set. You must be able to recognize what's worth continuing and what needs to be abandoned.

> **BE AWARE: STUBBORNNESS** Stubbornness can be a real stumbling block for some people, and it's often confused with tenacity. Don't be afraid to change your mind. If something isn't working, change it up. Don't let your stubborn side get you or someone else killed.

234 Obey the Rule of Threes

A great way to categorize dangers is by using the Rule of Threes. This time-honored teaching tool breaks down dangerous hazards in increments of time. There are a lot of variables that could change these numbers, but this chart will give you a good framework of issues and survival tasks.

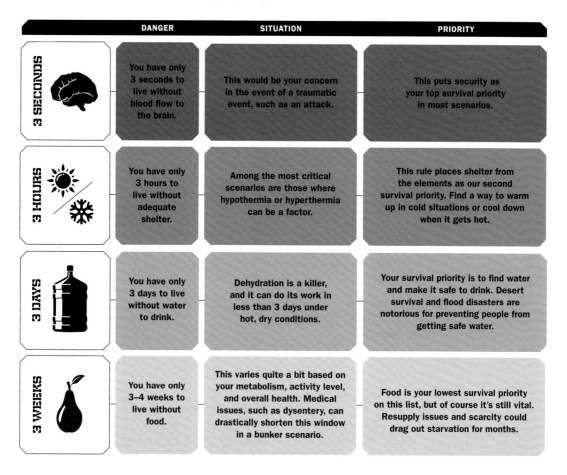

	DANGER	SITUATION	PRIORITY
3 SECONDS	You have only 3 seconds to live without blood flow to the brain.	This would be your concern in the event of a traumatic event, such as an attack.	This puts security as your top survival priority in most scenarios.
3 HOURS	You have only 3 hours to live without adequate shelter.	Among the most critical scenarios are those where hypothermia or hyperthermia can be a factor.	This rule places shelter from the elements as our second survival priority. Find a way to warm up in cold situations or cool down when it gets hot.
3 DAYS	You have only 3 days to live without water to drink.	Dehydration is a killer, and it can do its work in less than 3 days under hot, dry conditions.	Your survival priority is to find water and make it safe to drink. Desert survival and flood disasters are notorious for preventing people from getting safe water.
3 WEEKS	You have only 3–4 weeks to live without food.	This varies quite a bit based on your metabolism, activity level, and overall health. Medical issues, such as dysentery, can drastically shorten this window in a bunker scenario.	Food is your lowest survival priority on this list, but of course it's still vital. Resupply issues and scarcity could drag out starvation for months.

235 Develop an Attitude

An upbeat, positive attitude can be a major asset in an emergency situation. In this case, "positive" doesn't mean "irrationally cheerful" but rather a levelheaded calm with an optimistic spin.

That said, there's room for a more aggressive stance, especially when trouble or danger looms.

Of course, we're not suggesting you go berserk on anyone, just noting that a dose of properly harnessed aggression can give you a wellspring of energy in a survival emergency. Get mad. Get mean. Let nature know that you're not going to lie down and take it, you're going to fight to stay alive.

236 Decide Whether to Stay

Whether to stay put or bug out could be the toughest and most important decision you make in times of disaster. While much writing about survival focuses on bugging out, in reality many, if not most, situations are best ridden out in a secure, well-provisioned home or place of business. That said, sometimes things are so bad that hitting the road really is the best (or only) choice. How do you know what to do when things are scary? Here are a few things to consider when you're trying to decide if it's time to get out of Dodge.

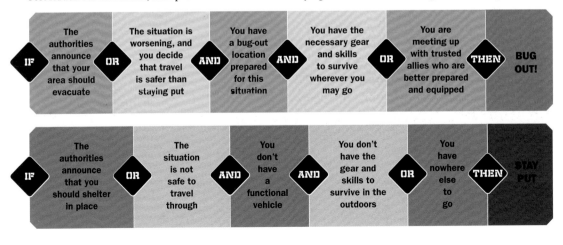

IF The authorities announce that your area should evacuate **OR** The situation is worsening, and you decide that travel is safer than staying put **AND** You have a bug-out location prepared for this situation **AND** You have the necessary gear and skills to survive wherever you may go **OR** You are meeting up with trusted allies who are better prepared and equipped **THEN** BUG OUT!

IF The authorities announce that you should shelter in place **OR** The situation is not safe to travel through **AND** You don't have a functional vehicle **AND** You don't have the gear and skills to survive in the outdoors **OR** You have nowhere else to go **THEN** STAY PUT

237 Ask for—and Give—Help

Disasters and emergencies can bring out the best in people—and the worst. Whether you decide to stay put or to flee, you may well need to get some help from others. And others will ask you for assistance. Remember, there is strength in numbers, and you can get more done through cooperation than by going at it alone. But you don't want to be a patsy. Here are a few basic guidelines.

SAY IT RIGHT If you go to your neighbor asking for something during a crisis, you'll probably be rebuffed. But if you go to her offering something, you'll almost always have a warmer reception. Tell the neighbor who you are, that you'd like to help her. Tell her that you're not in charge of anything but you're asking everyone to rally at a certain time and place to discuss the crisis at hand. Get as many neighbors together as you can, and then let nature take its course. Leaders will emerge and plans will form—all because you were the catalyst.

HELP OTHERS, BUT GUARDEDLY Even if you are the biggest prepper hoarder on Earth, you're not going to have enough supplies to take care of everybody. Keep your own safety and security in mind as you help others. No one should know how much food, water, and supplies you have—or where they're located. It's outstanding that you want to help others, and you should. But remember that the

person you helped today may be desperate tomorrow—and feeling justified as he or she is taking your stuff by force.

238 Share Your Skills

There are some skill sets that are useful almost anywhere, such as medical training, wilderness survival skills, and so forth (see item 263). However, you never know what other skills might come in handy. For example, if you're dealing with an epidemic, doctors, nurses, and other medical professionals are obviously crucial. But what if you need to quarantine a group of children in order to keep them safe? A kindergarten teacher would be worth her weight in gold if you needed to keep the youngsters calm and under control. That guy whose hobby is home brewing? His basement full of booze would be a treasure trove of trade goods. The basic lesson here is that you'll do well if you get to know your neighbors, and encourage everyone to share their skills and interests—whether they seem immediately relevant or not.

239 Plan Your Bug-Out Camp Supplies

What would you do after bugging out? Take the time now to consider what it would take to build a base camp outside your home in the event that some emergency sent you packing. In addition to your normal BOB and its supplies, you can fill two plastic bins with these additional items to help you fulfill your needs while surviving in the outdoors.

SHELTER A tent, a few tarps, and lots of thin rope will supply what you need for shelter construction.

WATER One quart (1 l) of bleach and a large collapsible water carrier will create a camp water supply.

KITCHEN A large cooking pot, metal spoons and bowls, and stored items like rice, beans, salt, and sugar are the basics for camp cooking.

HYGIENE Antibacterial dish soap and three 1-gallon (4-l) tubs can be used for washing dishes and to help maintain the health and hygiene of the camp.

LATRINE You'll need toilet paper, hand sanitizer, and feminine hygiene products—for obvious reasons.

OTHER Also consider the following: a battery-powered lantern with spare batteries, a first aid kit, a hatchet, a camp saw, a multitool, a sharpening stone, a radio with spare batteries, a flashlight or headlamp with—you guessed it—spare batteries, a camp shovel, one box of 1-gallon (4-l) zip-top bags, three lighters, several bars of soap, a manual can opener, kitchen knives and spoons, duct tape, trash bags, and a solar cell phone charger or battery backup.

240 Embrace the Plastic

A few extra tarps can serve as shelters, firewood coverings, rain ponchos, ground cloths, hammocks, and a host of other useful items. The more tarps you have, the better off your camp will be. The large trash bags in your gear list can also serve many functions. They can be used to create improvised rain gear and small tarps, and you can even fill them with leaves to make a DIY sleeping bag.

Perhaps the greatest use of these plastic panels is as a rain catch. Just a small amount of rain over a limited area can yield buckets of water. Hang up a tarp over your shelter, and you've also made a rain catch. Just set up the tarp on an angle, with a low spot on one side where the water will pour off. Set your bins and buckets under the lowest point of the tarp during the next rain shower.

241 Create Order with Areas

The camp kitchen, tent sites, dishwashing area, latrine, and other critical camp features should be planned with safety and sanitation in mind (i.e., don't put the camp toilet next to the cooking area).

THE LATRINE Dig a latrine trench a good distance away from camp—and downwind. Leave the dirt that you dug up in a pile, and use a can as a scooper to cover up after each use. Keep some of your toilet paper handy in a waterproof zip-top bag. Maintain a little dignity and respect camp privacy by using a tarp to screen off the latrine area. If you cannot spare the tarp, then select a latrine area shielded by brush, big rocks, or other natural cover.

THE KITCHEN Set up your campfire cookpot using bricks, cinderblocks, rocks, or whatever else you have handy to create a safe and stable fireplace. Scrounge up a grill or an oven rack to make an even better cooking setup. The fireplace must be stable. If the pot falls over, a good amount of boiling water can scald anyone gathered around the fire.

THE WASHING AREA Dirty dishes can spread everything from dysentery to spinal meningitis; don't take shortcuts with camp cleanliness. Use a three-tub system—the first tub holds plain water to get the majority of food off the dishes, the second tub has a little dish soap to get the rest of the food off, and the third tub has a little bleach to rinse off the soap and disinfect the dishes. The final step is to air-dry the dishes in the sun.

242 Make Camp Life Easier

Add these elements to your camp for safety and efficiency.

CLINIC Have a designated area for your field hospital. You should select an area where the waterproof first aid kit will reside and where wounds will be tended. This should not be near the kitchen area.

TRASH PIT Dig a hole for trash, but only if animals are not a local problem. If you have bears, feral dog packs, or other wild animals, then you'll have to shift strategies and burn all your garbage. Create a burn pit at least 100 yards (90 m) downwind of camp in an area that is not prone to wildfires.

FOOD STORAGE In areas with no bears and few scavengers, you can use one of your empty bins to serve as a food and cooking equipment storage locker. However, in bear country or areas with bold scavengers like rats and raccoons, you'll have to "bear bag" your food by hanging it up in a tree at least 15 feet (4.5 m) up and 100 yards (90 m) downwind from camp.

TOOLSHED You don't need to build an actual shed to make use of the tools you added to your supplies, but just make sure that your group keeps the multitools and duct tape in one spot so you can find them when you need them.

243 Signal to Rescuers

No matter how you attract attention, when it comes to signaling your best bet is to get to the largest clearing at the highest elevation. Certain situations may require you to be a bit stealthier, but for now, let's assume you're simply out in the wilderness and you need to signal to a rescue party. There are a few different ways to do this.

FIRE Probably the easiest and most well known way to signal is with fire. In a large clearing, you can build your signal fire ahead of time, then wait until you are certain someone is within sight of the smoke, which is the most visible part of the fire. Light a hot blaze, then cover it up with plenty of greenery. If there's a lone dead tree standing in that clearing, sacrifice it and turn it into a torch visible for miles.

FLARES Add these to a survival kit. Pen flares—part of a pilot's survival vest—will fire a small signal flare several hundred feet (over 100 m) into the air. Larger flares or flare guns can achieve even greater heights with a more visible flare. Don't discount the big guns as overkill; treat them as essential, and learn how to use one before you need it.

MIRRORS Reflective materials are some of the easiest survival tools. If you have a mirror designed specifically for signaling aircraft, follow the directions on the back of the mirror (or see item 245). For another mirror or reflective material, hold it at an angle that allows you to see the reflected light on the ground, then slowly bring it up to eye level and aim at the target. For best results, try tilting or rotating it slightly, which will flash to a search party.

GPS OR RADIO Technology can make the difference between life and death in the wilderness. Consider investing in a GPS that can transmit your location. These aren't cheap, and frequently require a subscription, but they can really pay off. A satellite phone or short-range radio can also call for help on emergency frequencies. Learn how to use them both before you need them.

244 Turn On the Radio

You may already know that the best way to get yourself rescued or receive crucial information during emergencies is through the use of a radio. Most shelters have a reliable radio, but in extreme situations, your basic AM/FM radio may prove useless. In a worst-case scenario, have a backup plan.

CB RADIOS CBs are great in many situations but have limitations: They only transmit a few miles, and channels may be chaotic during genuine emergencies. If you live in a rural area, one could be a godsend. But anyone can own and operate a CB, so the information you hear might not be the best.

WALKIE-TALKIES These can help small groups of people stay in touch with each other, but their range, like the CB, is limited. They also run on battery power, so you may have to ration their use if you're stranded or lost for a longer period of time.

SCANNER RADIOS These are great for receiving information, but that's all they do. Sorry, no two-way communication. This makes them ideal for listening in on emergency broadcasts, assuming services are available, but they won't necessarily be any help if you need to summon a rescue.

HAM RADIO A ham radio is your best option by far. Ham radios are a more powerful option for two-way communication in emergencies. They can reach incredible distances through the use of repeaters, and the fact that ham radio operators require FCC licenses means you'll have much more experienced operators spreading information, especially in large-scale disasters like hurricanes. They do require a heftier output of cash, and you have to jump through a few hoops to get licensed. But the ability to stay connected in even the worst circumstances is well worth it.

245 Use a Survival Mirror

The MK-3 signal mirror is almost universal to all survival kits. Using it is easy with a little practice.

STEP 1 Reflect light onto a nearby surface, such as a raft or your hand.

STEP 2 Slowly bring the mirror up to eye level and look through the sighting hole. You will see a bright spot of light. This is the aim indicator.

STEP 3 Hold the mirror near the eye and slowly turn and manipulate it so that the bright spot of light is on the target.

STEP 4 Even if a rescuer is not in sight, continue to scan the horizon with the mirror, as signal flashes may be visible from a long distance away.

246 Don't Get Caught Without: SPACE BLANKETS

Sure, wrapping up in a space blanket can keep you warm, but this item is far from a one-trick pony. Space blankets have the ability to morph into many different survival staples. These reflective Mylar blankets usually only cost a few dollars, which makes them a great investment for a lifesaving tool. At a minimum, keep these blankets in your first aid kit, survival kit, and vehicle.

① SLING

A busted arm can be cradled in a sling improvised from the space blanket. Fold it into a large triangle shape and tie it around the patient's neck to make a warm and effective support.

② WATER CARRIER

Line a container with a space blanket to make a water transport. You can line baskets, backpacks, bags, and pretty much anything else.

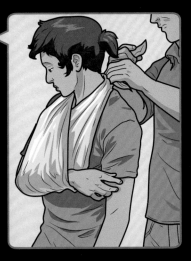

③ TRAIL MARKER

Cut the space blanket into short strips and tie them onto tree branches, bushes, or weeds to mark trails and create paths for your group, and for potential resucuers.

④ BANDAGE

Make a sucking chest wound suck a little less with a small piece of space blanket. Cut off a piece of the blanket and encircle it with duct tape around the wound.

⑤ RAIN CATCHER

The waterproof nature of this plastic blanket makes it an ideal rain harvester. All you have to do is dig a hole, line it with the blanket, and wait for the skies to open up.

⑥ PONCHO

Using the blanket as a piece of rain gear can be a game-changer—especially in places where precipitation is abundant and your supply of rain gear is low.

⑦ SIGNAL

The reflective or colored side of the space blanket can be staked out on the ground as a signal panel or hoisted onto a pole to create a highly visible, portable signal flag.

8 TENT

Tent and shelter configurations abound when you're dealing with a strong, flexible piece of rectangular material. Use a large blanket as an A-frame shelter, a wedge-shaped hut, or a dome tent.

9 BLANKET

Use the blanket for its intended purpose: Wrap up in it to stave off the cold, treat shock, and manage hypothermia.

10 ROPE

Cut a few long, thin strips off the sides of the blanket and twist or braid them into pieces of cordage. You can also fashion longer ropes by cutting a spiral pattern from round or oval blanket sections.

247

Understand Major Blackouts

Blackouts are caused by all sorts of mundane factors, from overuse of the electrical grid to natural disasters such as hurricanes or tornadoes knocking out power lines and flooding substations. These blackouts can take anywhere from a few hours (due to minor storms or technical failures) to several weeks (in the case of a major event like Hurricane Katrina) to remedy. However, there are a few even worse scenarios that could potentially send our tech-dependent world back to the beginning of the Industrial Revolution. Are these situations likely? No, but they're possible.

ELECTROMAGNETIC PULSE
Non-weaponized EMPs can be caused by lightning, power surges, malfunctioning circuits or electric motors, and other nondrastic events caused by man or nature. However, a "massive EMP" generally refers to the effects of a nuclear bomb or other weapon. For more info, see item 252.

SOLAR FLARES These instances of rough "space weather" can be predicted (to some degree), though the effects are uncertain. Solar flares have knocked out regional power grids in recent years, and a big one in 1859 disrupted the fledgling telegraph system across the entire Northern Hemisphere.

248

Create Flare Contingencies

Solar eruptions of varying sizes can have a negative impact on the Earth, especially the fragile new technologies of the planet's dominant species. Let's take a look at our usually friendly sun's adversarial side with the three classes of solar eruptions.

CLASS C These flares are the weakest and really don't do anything. They happen all the time and are little more than a hiccup from the sun.

CLASS M These flares, which are moderate, give us more radiation and more particles than a C. They are responsible for the northern lights traveling outside their normal territories. Class Ms are still not a doomsday scenario.

CLASS X But then there are Class X flares, which are strong enough to cause disruptions in satellites, communication systems, and electrical grids. What happens to our very information-dependent way of life if our communications get knocked out? How would you make sure your friends and loved ones are OK? You should plan a place and time to meet your friends and family if communications go out, and you should have a backup time and secondary site, as well as a place to leave notes for each other. Solar flares (and other types of disasters) require communication plans with realistic backups in place at all times.

249 Don't Panic After a Pulse

If an EMP-producing weapon was ever employed against a modern high-tech society, there's no question that serious devastation would occur. However, it's all too likely that people's reactions would cause more harm than the actual weapon strike itself. After all, much lesser emergencies often lead to rioting, looting, and even murder. Imagine what would happen if all of a nation's electronics and power grid were permanently destroyed. "Civilization-ending" would probably be a fair description. So what could you do about it? You can keep a level head and try to prevent those around you from sinking into chaos. Self-sufficiency and the adaptability to revert to a low-tech lifestyle are your only other defenses. That, and praying that this scenario stays relegated to the realm of science fiction.

250 Laugh in the Face of Darkness

Want to be ready for an electricity-free world? Unless you require electrically operated equipment to stay alive (pacemakers, dialysis machines, etc.), electricity is a luxury. The majority of humans who have ever lived did so without electricity. You can, too, if you follow these steps.

STEP 1 Don't store so much food in your fridge and freezer. If the power goes, one can only eat so much ice cream in a sitting. Instead, stock up on canned goods and shelf-stable foods.

STEP 2 Have several different ways to cook your food and provide light in your home. These should work safely throughout all seasons. Flashlights are a safe and practical option—just make sure the rechargeable ones are charged in case of an EMP. Candles and light sticks will work no matter what.

STEP 3 In an event with power outage but no damage to electronics, have a way to charge your cell phone (see item 254). Solar chargers are nice, and AA-battery chargers are cheaper and more available. Also consider

keeping some two-way radios for closer communication.

STEP 4 Model yourself after low-tech cultures. The beauty and simplicity of less technologically dependent cultures will be very evident in a grid-down situation.

251 Employ People Power

No electricity to operate your fancy electric can opener? Good, shame on you for owning one. Stick to manually operated devices that work in all conditions. Check out camping and specialty catalogs—there are a surprising number of choices out there.

- [ ] Manual can opener—the P38 is a military classic, and it fits on a key chain.
- [ ] Hand-cranked radio for emergency updates and entertainment.
- [ ] Grain and meat grinders will make flour from whole grains or create "hamburger" from available critters.
- [ ] Crank coffee grinder for the coffee addicts.
- [ ] Windup flashlight for obvious lighting purposes.
- [ ] Butter churn—milk cow, separate cream, churn butter, enjoy.
- [ ] Hand-powered water pump to get water out of a well or cistern.
- [ ] Well sleeve (well bucket)—see item 114.

252 Understand EMP Danger

On the long list of very bad things that you'll hopefully never have to worry about, a massive, weaponized EMP would rank somewhere on the scale as less likely than a global epidemic but more likely than the zombie apocalypse. An EMP on any scale, whether caused by a natural event or a deliberate attack, can fry power grids, destroy personal electronic devices, and in general wreak havoc on anything that uses electricity (including cars, airplanes, factories, and even satellites). Massive solar flares (see item 247) can have similar effects.

All nuclear bombs create a local electromagnetic pulse with their blast, but the greatest danger would be from a device designed specifically to emit a massive EMP. Experts theorize that a large device detonated 25 to 250 miles (40 to 400 km) above the Earth's surface could be devastating to electronics across entire continents. For example, a large EMP bomb detonated high above the center of the U.S. could knock out most of the nation's electronics. Should you worry? As we see it, it makes sense to be prepared for power outages, as they're common around the world for any number of reasons. Staying vigilant in case of a high-altitude EMP may be going a bit far, but there's no harm in taking precautions.

253 Protect Electronics with a Faraday Cage

If you're worried about the fate of your Game Boy after the Bomb drops (or, more likely, about communications hardware or medical equipment), there is a simple home solution to keep your electronics ticking.

A Faraday cage (named for the 19th-century inventor, Michael Faraday), is any conductive structure that protects its contents from electrical pulses. Your simplest option is to use a microwave oven or a tightly sealed metal garbage can (other easy options include an ammo can or a metal safe). However, if you've got a fair amount of equipment to protect, or you just like the idea of doing it yourself, a simple Faraday cage is easy to build.

One caveat is that due to the fact that these principles haven't been tested with modern electronics, it's not actually known how badly things would be damaged and what might survive unshielded. All we can do is rely on informed best guesses.

STEP 1 Determine what size box you're going to need. Gather up everything you want to shield and see how much space you need. Likely items include shortwave radios, walkie-talkies, a couple of prepaid cell phones, any crucial medical equipment, such as a glucose meter, and spare parts for your generator and car. Note that batteries are not affected by EMP so don't need to be included.

STEP 2 Choose a box that closes as securely as possible. Any gaps will render the ground ineffective.

STEP 3 Wrap your box securely in aluminum foil. Be sure the body of the box and its lid are totally encased.

STEP 4 Tape every seam down firmly. You can use regular cellotape for this, although aluminum or copper tape provide better security.

STEP 5 Line the inside of the box with cardboard to ensure that your electronics do not contact any of the foil or metal tape.

STEP 6 Place your items inside and close the lid firmly.

254 Charge a Cell Phone in a Blackout

While not a long-term solution to loss of the power grid, this DIY battery system can charge a cell phone enough to give you several days' worth of phone use. Sometimes, just that much can be a lifesaver.

Note that this system requires a marine battery, which is similar to a car battery but safe to use indoors (car batteries give off harmful fumes). Purchase a 55-aH 12-volt "advanced glass mat" (AGM) battery, widely available at home improvement or boating stores.

You'll also need: a battery wall charger, a cigarette lighter adapter, a cell phone car charger, and a voltmeter.

Always wear safety goggles and take great care when working with batteries. While AGM batteries are less toxic than car batteries, they do contain acid and will hold a charge.

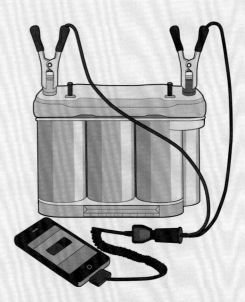

STEP 1 Be sure your battery is fully charged using the voltmeter (basically just jumper-cable style clips that go to an electrical plug). When you store your battery, be sure to check it every three months with the voltmeter. If it drops below 12.4 volts, charge it up so it'll be ready to go when the lights go out.

STEP 2 Attach the clip-on cigarette lighter port to your battery (it's easy—the port is attached to wires with jumper cable–like clips).

STEP 3 Plug in the phone charger, just like you would in

your car, and charge your phone. Results will vary based on your phone and the battery, but you should be able to recharge your phone fully for more than a week with this system.

STEP 4 Periodically insert the voltmeter into the cigarette lighter adapter to check on your voltage, as you don't want to run your battery down too far. As when it's in storage, never let it drop below 12.4 volts.

255 Hack Your C-Cell

Sometimes you're stuck in a situation where you need a D-cell battery, but all you have are Cs. These tricks will get you through until you can stock up.

INVEST IN SOME COINS You can pad out C-cell batteries to fill in somewhere that D-cells are needed— just place some quarters into the space between the battery's terminal and the contacts.

FOIL YOUR FLASHLIGHT If you need to power one of those long flashlights, wad up tinfoil as tightly as you can and use it to fill the space between one of the C-cell batteries and the contact on the flashlight's lid.

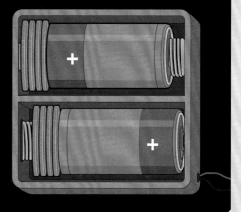

256 Be Ready for Storms

During horrific storms and tornadoes, all of your preparedness can be irrelevant. Bodily harm is often the biggest danger from these intense natural disasters. Have all the supplies as directed in this book, but keep in mind that they could all be blown into the next county. Head for a basement, root cellar, or, ideally, a buried storm shelter if you hear about an impending storm. If those locations aren't an option, hide in a closet in your home's interior, keeping the clothes there with you as protection from storm-driven projectiles. You could also lie in a bathtub, covered in protective piles of towels, clothes, or bedding.

257 Prepare for Hurricanes and Cyclones

Getting ready for a hurricane can be a little intimidating, but it accomplishes two vital things. First, preparing for trouble removes some of the helplessness that many people feel when an emergency is imminent, putting you in the right mind-set: to be a survivor, not a victim. Second, prepping forces you to gather the supplies and make the plans that can help you adapt to the changing environment of a disaster. This can even arm you with the security and resources to help others as you put the pieces back together after a storm.

As you prepare for a hurricane, consider that you may lose power, which obviously takes away many of our modern conveniences. Make sure you have plenty of easy-to-fix, no-cook foods on hand and ample sources of lighting. Lean toward battery-operated lights instead of candles to reduce the hazard of fire. Also, make sure you know the routes to evacuate inland, away from the hurricane's path.

Gather at least a 72-hour supply of water and food for each person in your home, plus flashlights, first-aid supplies, hygiene items, and something to pass the time for each person (books, board games, coloring books for the kids, and other electricity-free items). Get your cell phone charged up, and have a backup power source for it, like a car charger or external battery packs. Also have a battery-powered radio so you can stay alert to evacuation notices, disaster news, and other instructions.

258 Fight Back Against Flooding

Staying safe during a flood takes a combination of proper planning and quick thinking. Be aware of flood hazards no matter where you live, but especially if you're in a low-lying area, near a river or bay, or downstream from a dam. In low-lying or flood-prone areas, a NOAA (National Oceanic and Atmospheric Administration) weather radio with an alarm can be a lifesaving investment.

BE READY If you have a day or more to prepare, move important things to the highest and driest location in your home. Pack any and all important and irreplaceable papers, photos, files, and data to take with you if you evacuate.

BE AWARE Stay very alert to flood watches and warnings for your local area and the areas upriver and upland from your location.

MOVE FAST If you only have minutes to get out, don't waste time gathering possessions. Things can be replaced—lives cannot. Don't wait to be told to move to higher ground if authorities say flash flooding is possible.

STOCK WATER Contamination can be a big deal during and after a flood, so make sure you have a safe supply of a gallon of water per person per day—both in your home and if you evacuate.

BUG OUT RIGHT Prepare to evacuate well in advance, and be sure your car is stocked with plenty of cash, no-cook foods, spare clothes, sanitation items, your cell phone charger, rain gear, and other essential supplies in case you have to provide for yourself and your family for some time.

DON'T DIG IN Never decide that you're smarter than the experts and that you can ride out the storm. If you are told to evacuate: DO IT! And as you go, beware of streams, ditches, drainage channels, canyons, and other low-lying areas. Flash floods can happen in these places even far away from the rainstorms.

DRIVE SAFELY Never drive through even shallow floodwaters—turn around and find another path. Even seemingly safe water can pick your car up and sweep it away.

259 Find a Quake-Safe Spot

Since earthquakes are so unpredictable, you never know when one's about to hit. So the best way to prepare is the same as for other disasters. Stock up on food, water, and medical supplies. Make sure to locate the safest place in your home to ride out a quake, and at your office, too, in case you're on the job when disaster strikes.

FIRST CHOICE Get to a place outside where nothing can fall on you.

SECOND CHOICE Get under structurally reinforced areas like doorways (one you know is secure) or near load-bearing walls.

THIRD CHOICE Get next to a heavy table, desk, or large piece of furniture to deflect anything that might fall around you.

FOURTH CHOICE Get in an interior room with no windows.

FIFTH CHOICE Get in a closet in the center of the structure.

These last two options are dicey, as you can get buried with few paths of escape. But they beat getting crushed to death. Your best bet is to be outside, safely away from tall trees and buildings.

WE WERE AS READY AS WE WERE GOING TO BE. WE HAD OUR SUPPLIES AND GEAR, PLUS AXES AND FLARES TO AVOID GETTING TRAPPED IN THE ATTIC.
BUT THERE WAS NO TELLING IF THE ROOF—OR THE HOUSE—WOULD HOLD, AND WE COULD HEAR IT GROANING UNDER THE ASSAULT FROM MOTHER NATURE.
KREEEEEEERK
SKREEEEEEEEEEEKKK
BY MORNING, IT WAS OVER. THE HOUSE WAS ONE OF THE FEW STILL STANDING. TWO HUGE TREES HAD FALLEN IN MY BACKYARD—THE WIND HAD BEEN SO LOUD I HADN'T EVEN HEARD THE CRASH.
I GRABBED AN OLD SHOTGUN TO SCARE THEM OFF. IT WAS COMPLETELY UNUSABLE, BUT THEY DIDN'T KNOW THAT.
NOW THE REAL ADVENTURE BEGAN—SHARING SUPPLIES AND HELPING OUT OUR NEIGHBORS.

261 Get Ready for a Fall

TEOTWAWKI (The End of the World as We Know It) certainly sounds ominous and un-survivable. But if we look back into history, we can see that many "worlds" have ended, only to give rise to a different culture or civilization—not without growing pains, but with plenty of survivors. The fall of Rome, two World Wars, the Crusades, and many other historical events have been game changers, ending some lives and changing the survivors' lifestyles immensely. Could the modern world suffer from a similar kind of collapse? Here are some ways it could happen.

SOCIAL COLLAPSE Sometimes people just can't see eye to eye. Civil wars, religious conflicts, and class wars have taken countless lives over the centuries and affected entire continents. On a smaller scale, race riots, gang wars, and rioting have immobilized entire cities. When civility is lost between neighbors, societies have a hard time continuing as normal.

GOVERNMENT COLLAPSE Throughout recorded history, many governments have fallen apart due to a variety of stressors. When a government system fails to be sustainable or fails its people one too many times, leaders can topple.

ECONOMIC COLLAPSE Zimbabwe's economy collapsed in 2008 due to hyperinflation, among other factors. Argentina's economy fell apart a few years before that when the country defaulted on international loans. The economic bubble popped for many in America in 2008, leading to a recession—a downturn that reminded old-timers of the Great Depression some 80 years earlier.

262 Stock Up for the Crash

The ideal lifestyle after a currency collapse is one that doesn't require money. But few folks today have the skills and the land to be completely self-reliant. In the event that a currency fails, bartering goods and services can fill the void until a new monetary system is established (see item 298). So you'll want to be the one with the possessions and skill sets that would be valuable in a time without money. You'll also want to conceal the location of these things—and guard them with your life.

263 Build a Team

In the crime-ridden aftermath of a collapse, being surrounded by like-minded individuals with complementary skills could be your best plan of action. Living in close proximity to each other could offer great advantages to all of you. Try to make friends with folks who bring these skill sets to the table.

- ☐ Military and law-enforcement backgrounds
- ☐ Medical and dental skills
- ☐ Food production experience
- ☐ Vehicle repair experience
- ☐ Building and fabricating skills
- ☐ Firefighting background

264 Hail the New Chief

A government collapsing on its own is a fairly rare event in history. More often, you see piecemeal changes occur over time. Unless you're planning to take the throne yourself, the best advice during a government collapse is to get as far away as possible. It may take years for a stable society to emerge from the chaos after coups, assassinations, invasions, and the like. If you cannot flee, or refuse to become a refugee, you'd better get on board with your new leadership if you wish to survive.

265 Understand the Real Threat

The two biggest threats during a social, government, or economic collapse are violence and an inability to provide for your basic needs. The issue of violent crime is by far the most dangerous by-product of unrest and an ever-present reality during instances of community meltdown. The rates of murder, theft, arson, rape, and home invasion have always increased in these scenarios. Regardless of the type of collapse, take the steps to protect yourself, your friends, and your family.

HIDE YOUR WEALTH Your wealth may come in the form of money, water, food, ammunition, animals, or any other kind of desired commodity. Don't flaunt it, and don't let anyone outside your circle know what you have or where it is—even before a collapse.

GET ARMED An armed person is a lot more daunting to a predator. Firearms, knives, machetes, axes, or even a baseball bat can help to protect you and yours.

GET TRAINING A tool for self-defense is good, but the training to go with it is great. Find a local business that offers self-defense training with different weapons. Train regularly, and make sure that your family members have some skills as well. You can even take lessons from former police officers for a stiff dose of reality and an insight into the criminal minds they have faced.

HAVE A PLAN Devising plans within plans may keep you up a little longer at night, but isn't that better than going to sleep with your head in the sand? Believe in the old adage, "Failing to plan is planning to fail."

266 Choose the Right Leader

Leadership is one of those survival skills that rarely gets recognized for its importance. Having a leader is also an inescapable reality when acting as a group. Choosing one may seem tricky in the abstract, but you'll find that there are natural-born leaders among us all. A good leader is decisive and steadfast, but willing to listen to dissenting voices and consider a range of options, including unpopular ones. He or she should be calm, courageous, and positive yet realistic. Don't worry about what a potential leader does for a living in his or her regular life. Maybe they don't have a critical leadership position as a day job, but given the chance, can finally play the role they were born to play. And in case you hadn't noticed, this isn't regular, everyday life anymore—this is an emergency, and good leadership is more important than ever.

267 Don't Screw It Up

If you're in a leadership position, be aware of the fact that power is clearly a corrupting force. The news is full of accusations of wrongdoing in politics, from the lowest functionary to the highest office. Don't fall victim to the same slipups that topple regimes and end careers in public office. Stay focused and knowledgeable about your position, and don't lie or use your power to take what's not yours. Don't take bribes or show favoritism. Don't let your vices, demons, and flaws out of their cage. Don't turn your group into some kind of cult. And finally, remember your place. As a leader during a crisis situation, your job is to augment and assist the local government, police, and military—not replace them.

268 Lead Like the Great Ones

History is full of examples of great leaders—and plenty of horrible ones. Understand that there is much more to being a leader than making a few plans, barking out orders, or trying to keep everyone pacified. If the mantle of leadership falls on your shoulders during a bad situation, emulate the strongest leaders you know. Here are a few tips to keep in mind for your new role.

PLAN AHEAD Being a solid leader requires a great deal of thought, planning, and consideration for the best interests of the group and the individuals in it.

MAINTAIN THE FOCUS Remind everybody (often) that they are all on the same team with the same goal—the survival of the whole group.

LEAD BY EXAMPLE Hold yourself to a higher standard. Set and maintain high moral and ethical bars, and don't ask anyone to do anything that you wouldn't do.

SET GOALS Set realistic targets for your group and put the right person in the right job.

TELL THE TRUTH Be honest and unapologetic. Do the things that must be done. Be open about your actions, and don't back down when you've made the right decision.

LAY DOWN THE LAW Have a group-approved plan ready ahead of time because, under stress, people will steal, lie, and fight. Don't forget the existing laws of the land, either.

PREPARE FOR THE WORST Expect all hell to break loose at some point. Hopefully it won't, but you will have made a few plans if it does. Have a plan ready for each possible issue that you and your group can imagine.

LISTEN Pay attention to your group and listen to what they say. Maybe they're talking nonsense, but give it a listen anyway.

MEDICATE Try to get your hands on a bottle of aspirin, too—you're going to need it.

269 Spot a Sociopath

Tough times can bring out the best in people—but they can also bring bad guys out of the woodwork. There's a certain sort of sociopath who lives to wield power over others. These folks often appear charismatic, smart, and competent at first. Don't jump to conclusions, but don't be misled either. Here are some traits to watch out for before throwing your support behind that charismatic newcomer.

CHARMING Sociopaths are often incredibly charming, seeming like born leaders. In fact, they are excellent con artists, using charm to manipulate and control others.

ENTITLED Sociopaths believe that they are better than others and will stop at nothing to prevail, as they genuinely believe they deserve it.

LACK EMPATHY Sociopaths can be nice and helpful when they need to, but they lack true, deep emotions. Similarly, they show no remorse for their actions. If you get an apology from a sociopath, it's because he or she wants something from you. Sociopaths have few or no real friends and don't tend to have romantic relationships.

BLAME OTHERS Nobody likes to mess up, but most folks will admit error and move on. The true sociopath always manages to pin the blame on someone else. They can often be bullies, intimidating or manipulating people to get what they want—or just for fun.

270 Pick a Compound

Taking over an abandoned prison facility might work on television, but if you're looking to legally and rightfully create a system of defenses, you're better off fortifying what you have. You will be most within your rights defending your own home, wherever that may be. But depending on the nature of the emergency and whether you are welcome in other places, you may want to carefully consider where else to set up your defenses.

FARM COMPOUND Open fields for clear visibility and existing barbed-wire fences are the best defensive assets a farm can offer. But this high visibility can backfire. If your farm is full of delicious-looking animals, the gates and fences might slow intruders, but they won't stop them. Desperate folks will do what they must to get fed. This makes a farm less ideal than you'd think in most short-term and long-term disaster scenarios.

NEIGHBORHOOD COMPOUND Urban and suburban streets and cul-de-sacs that are full of homes can be marshaled into a compound, provided your neighbors are willing, absent, or otherwise indisposed. Neighborhoods are full of resources that a building would lack, and they're not an obvious food source like a farm. The neighborhood stronghold has plenty of vulnerabilities, however, as it's large, sprawling, and hard to seal off from foot traffic. Neighborhoods are also very prone to looting and door-to-door robbing in the aftermath of a disaster.

BUILDING COMPOUND A stand-alone building, preferably with minimal entrances, has the potential to be a surprisingly good base. Small high-rises, office buildings, and warehouses are generally well built and offer a number of defensive possibilities. Again, your neighbors need to be on board (if the building is a dwelling), and you'll also need to shore up the first floor, as every door and window is a point of entry for those who would try to break in.

271 Remember the Basic Tenets

An improvised defensive compound isn't really all that defensive. That's why the careful actions of its defenders can be a matter of life and death, especially in a situation that requires a compound. Keep these basics in mind and don't let all those action movies go to your head.

DO maintain a house or building inside your defensive perimeter as a headquarters.
DON'T allow strangers into your group or neighborhood. Anybody coming in should have verifiable business there.

DO consider a dependable water source when you set up the boundaries of your perimeter.
DON'T expect to rely upon precipitation for your compound's water supply.

DO rely upon the sharp senses of dogs, particularly protective breeds. They can hear and smell people sneaking around way before you could.
DON'T forget to make sure that everybody in your compound is identifiable to each other, preventing false alarms and friendly fire.

DO be patient with neighbors who don't want to participate in the defense of the neighborhood. If things get ugly, they'll probably change their tune.
DON'T scare the police or military with your compound. Imagine their point of view as they encounter a group of armed individuals who have blocked off a road during a disaster. Keep your ID handy to prove that you live there, and keep your weapons out of your hands and out of sight when dealing with the authorities.

272 Build a Defensive Perimeter

During social unrest and mayhem, you won't have the time or resources to build walls and guard towers. However, there are still some things you can do almost anywhere to create a more defensible position.

STEP 1 Decide what you are willing to defend. Basically, you are marking the boundaries of your protected area. Consider the role existing walls, waterways, buildings, and fences can play in your defense.

STEP 2 Establish a controlled entry/exit point for the neighborhood. This may mean blocking off a street with derelict vehicles (if things are really that bad). If vehicles are operational, several could be parked to create a "gate" to keep out other vehicles.

STEP 3 Enhance existing defensive structures. This can be anything from locking gates in fences to boarding up windows and doors around the perimeter. Look at your perimeter from the outside, try to figure out ways in, and do your best to seal them off.

STEP 4 Set up a fallback position. This would be a place of refuge if you had to retreat within your perimeter, like the strongest and most defensible home within the neighborhood. Keep it well supplied with water and food, in case you have to spend a few days waiting out rioters.

273 Create Observation Posts

The eyes and ears of your defensive perimeter, observation posts are places where guards can see people trying to breach your boundary. Stop trouble before it starts with the following tips.

Outside corners of the neighborhood are good spots for observation posts, as they can allow you up to a 270-degree field of vision.

A bird's-eye view of the area can allow you to see and hear many things. A balcony can create a ready-made OP, as can a window. A kid's tree house could be the best of all.

The observation post should be both defensible and escapable. Utilize existing structures as much as possible to allow the OP guard to take cover if he or she is fired upon or threatened. If your guard is up in a tree that is difficult to climb, how well can he or she climb down if needed? Pick OPs that allow for a safe, quick exit.

Communications are a must. The observation post is useless if the guard can't communicate what he or she is seeing. If two-way radios or cell phones work, great. Otherwise, be prepared to yell!

274 Build a Basement Bunker

If you have a basement, this humble and musty part of your home could be a refuge in the event of tornadoes, robbery, and other life-threatening events. However, it has to be modified for this kind of use. Here is some work to consider doing before it's too late.

REINFORCE Install steel doors with multiple locks and reinforced steel doorframes to be able to seal off the basement from the inside.

CALL THE PLUMBER If the plumbing doesn't exist already, install a toilet and sink in the basement. One notable exception, however, is if you are the lowest house on your street and all the houses are on a city sewage system. A power outage, line blockage, or waste-water treatment plant malfunction could allow all of your uphill neighbors' sewage to back up into your basement.

COVER UP Create window covers for any basement windows—ideally one for each window exterior. The best covers are tough, steel shutters that can be locked in place during an emergency.

GET STOCKED Unless you live in a flood-prone area, store a large percentage of your food, water, and supplies down in the basement bunker so that it is well stocked if the need arises. Make sure your things are packed in watertight containers in case of minor flooding.

275 Make a Bucket Bathroom

A 5-gallon (19-liter) bucket (or two) with a tight-fitting lid, a box of small trash bags, a case of TP, and some sawdust are all you need to put together an emergency port-a-potty if your basement bunker lacks a functional toilet. Is it pleasant? From experience, I can tell you that it most assuredly is not. But it gets the job done. For optimal use, consider a "pee bucket" and "#2 bucket" for easier cleanup. The pee bucket can be the friendly receptacle for urine, which can be easily poured out somewhere and put back into service. There's no need for a liner or bag, but a swish of bleach water can work wonders. The #2 bucket can be lined with a trash bag and used for solid waste and toilet paper. If a little pee does end up in there, it's not going to be a deal breaker. Just sprinkle a little sawdust, cat litter, or other absorbent material after each use. Some baking soda or some other deodorizer to add could be a lifesaver, too. Tie the bag shut after several uses, and escort it off-site for a proper burial.

276 Create Layers of Security

Your basement bunker door should be your last line of defense, not your first. Build in layers of defensive obstacles outside your home to keep out rogues. Install defenses in your home that an intruder would have to tackle to get to the basement. Locks on interior doors are a good place to start, and an attack dog roaming the halls couldn't hurt. More advanced tricks could include the concealment of the basement door and other acts of in-home camouflage. Remember to reinforce the walls, as well—that steel-bolted door won't do you any good if the thief can punch through the drywall next to it.

277 Keep It Breathable

The air quality in a bunker can drop quickly if numerous folks are seeking refuge there. Low air quality, over time, can lead to a condition called hypoxia, which is characterized by irritability, poor judgment, memory loss, inattentiveness, and a loss of motor skills and coordination. Grab some of these easy fixes to keep your bunker air breathable.

Houseplants in the basement windows will enrich the air—and even if the windows are boarded up, keeping the plants down there will swap some of the unwanted carbon dioxide for much-needed oxygen.

Air filters can remove a lot of the dust particles and mold spores, provided you have electricity to run them, and oxygen tanks are available from medical-supply companies. You can periodically crack the valve, if there are no open flames in the bunker, and help everybody breathe a little easier. Just remember that even a little flame like a pilot light on a water heater can turn your whiff of pure oxygen into a lethal fireball.

279 Keep It Dry

Mold and mildew tend to flourish in moist basement environments. Try these different approaches to achieve basement bunker dryness.

DEHUMIDIFIER An electric dehumidifier is your best insurance against a damp basement. It can be run year-round and is capable of pulling large amounts of water out of the air in a 24-hour period.

DESSICANT This product is usually some variety of silica gel or crystals, which absorb water from the air and diminish moisture. These work fine in the average basement, and they can even be used to prolong the life of seeds by adding them to your seed vault.

SUMP PUMP If your basement is prone to wet floors, install a sump pump. This device makes a "well" in the basement floor to draw in water so that it doesn't seep up through the concrete. Sump pumps are emptied by an electric pump, but in the event of a power outage, the lid can be removed and the water can be dipped with a bucket to be poured outside.

278 Have Some Comms Handy

If you are going to invest in bunker upgrades, communication equipment should be high on your list. CBs, a spare cell phone, or a ham radio can provide vital communication during an emergency. If these are out of your price range, an old stereo tuner or some other radio in your basement can at least keep you informed of outside events. Being out of the loop is one of the hazards of hunkering in a bunker, and communications equipment will be a step in the right direction.

Here's Kirk Lombard, a transplanted Atlantic fisherman who came to California and learned how to really catch a fish—or an eel—in a way that would make a fisherman out of any urban survivor facing post-disaster food gathering.

280 Catch a Weird Fish

My poor fishing skills when I first moved to California were not helped by the fact that my only how-to sources were a dossier on coastal fishing dated 1932 and the half-forgotten conversations I'd had as a child with my fish-crazy grandfather. I spent every Sunday crawling around on rocks, casting out into the waves, and fruitlessly attempting to catch my dinner.

Six months after the move, I had a sum total of five minuscule surf perch to show for my efforts, and, what's worse, I had virtually carpeted the floor of the Pacific Ocean with fouled line, hooks, and lead sinkers. No one had prepared me for how many snags I would get fishing along the California coast.

And then one foggy Sunday in June, as I stood defiantly atop a giant boulder just outside the Golden Gate, I spied a middle-aged Asian guy scrambling along in the tide pools like a human shore crab—with a long bamboo stick in his hands. I was initially far less interested in what he was doing than in the size of the burlap sack—which was teeming with fish—that was slung over his shoulder. He made his way over toward me, and I was then forced to suffer the indignity of watching as this salty sea dog pulled one fish after another from under the rock I was standing on. Six months of casting as far as I could from a rock, and the fish had been right under my feet.

Now the happy part. I climbed down from my high perch above the ocean and introduced myself to the fisherman. He introduced himself to me as "Cambodian Stan." To this day, he occupies a special place in my personal pantheon of great fishermen. He told me that the method he was using was called "poke poling" and that despite the fact that he had a full sack, his main quarry had eluded him that day.

Stan was speaking of the flavorful and strangely named monkey face eel. He then patiently explained his technique, showed me how to make a poke pole, shook my hand, and stepped out of my life.

Since that day twenty years ago, I have caught a lot of coastal fish, including the state record monkey face eel, thanks to Stan's technique. And I haven't experienced a fishless fishing trip since.

Poke poling (also called "sniggling") is the best way to catch coastal species like rockfish, cabezon, and eels. It's also quite possibly the simplest method of fishing, requiring only a stick, a short line or wire, and a hook. If you were on your own or in dire circumstances and had to get your own protein from the ocean, poke poling would be the best way to go. And you might set a record in the meantime.

281 Poke Pole for Eels

STEP 1 Eels feed more consistently on the incoming tide than the outgoing, so find a rocky, seaweed-strewn shoreline and show up 2 hours before the tide bottoms out—then fish until it's too high to reach the rocky holes where the eels live.

STEP 2 Use squid for bait, or grab a mussel off a rock and use the tough "rind" just inside the shell. (Learn the seasonal restrictions on mussels first.)

STEP 3 Take your poke pole (a straightened wire hanger with a hook at the end will do) and a landing net. Bait the hook, and lightly poke it under rocks and in cracks. Then hang on—a big eel will make you think there's a human pulling on the other end.

STEP 4 After the fish bites, set the hook and pull it wriggling from the hole. It helps to have a landing net as many of these species, especially monkey face eels, are adept at squirming off the hook. Then take the eel home, skin it, gut it, and fillet it. *Bon appetit!*

282 Follow Kirk's Foraging Tips

GATHER TURKISH WASHCLOTH This red algae is a great source of agar, meaning you can use it to make your own ice cream.

SIPHON GHOST SHRIMP Using a rubber ball, a threaded rod, and a piece of PVC, make your own siphon to suck shrimp out of the mud.

PICK DOCK MUSSELS Simple enough: Go down to the docks, search around a bit, and grab some mussels.

NET FISH Throw nets on schooling fishes.

PULL FISH OUT OF DRAINS Many drains in coastal cities are positioned over ocean-access waterways, meaning the fish in the bay are the same ones in the sewers.

GO CLAMMING IN MUDFLATS Dig monster clams out of the local mudflats.

SCRAPE SNAKES You can scrape them off of breakwaters.

MAKE YOUR OWN CRAB SNARE Construct a simple snare, and you'll be eating a five-star meal while the other postapocalyptic wanderers are eating rats and pigeons.

SPEAR A BAT RAY Huge bat rays come into the shallows during low tide. Spear one with a homemade spear.

283 Select Your Trap

Low-tech animal traps like natural-fiber snares and rock deadfalls can be built with natural materials in the wild. Modern traps like cable snares, leg-hold traps, and body-grip traps can deliver even greater success rates. And let's not forget live-catch cage traps. In urban areas and wild places, traps can generate food, and you don't even have to be there for it to work—it's like getting other people to hunt for you.

SNARES These can be primitive and entirely set with gathered materials. You can even weave your own string from bark fibers. But there's lots that can go wrong (for instance, a possum chewing through your hand-woven cord and getting away). Cable snares made from braided steel cable are more secure, although you'll have to bring them with you.

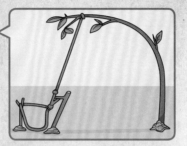

FOOTHOLD TRAPS Commonly used for the past century and a half, foothold traps are clamping jaws that restrain an animal by the foot should they step on the trigger. These do not have the potential to kill (like a body-grip trap), but modern trappers still frequently use them. The trapped animal is usually then shot with a firearm.

BODY-GRIP TRAPS These are like oversize rat traps minus the wooden board. Two heavy springs move the trap bars together, snapping necks, breaking backs, or strangling. These put the animal out of its misery quickly but are treacherous to set. Many modern trappers who have broken hands and fingers can attest to that fact.

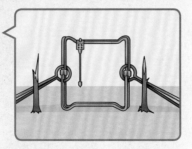

LIVE-CATCH TRAPS The typical cage trap is a live-catch trap. This forgiving trap allows you to release animals that you didn't intend to catch, and it's ideal for homebound settings. They do, however, bring home the reality of killing animals for food. Since the trap doesn't do the job, you'll have to—typically by shooting it through the cage.

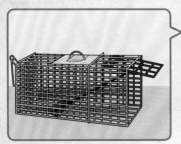

284 Cover Your Scent

Though trappers use many different types of traps, they all have the same problem: They've got human scent all over them. To have any luck when dealing with wild animals, you need to fool their noses. Follow these tips to de-scent your traps and hands with nature itself.

USE MUD Start by washing your hands and any questionable trap parts in the local waterway. Use sand, clay, mud, or silt as an abrasive and oil absorber.

POWDER WITH BLACK CHARCOAL As your hands and trap parts are drying, you can wipe them with powdered black charcoal from the campfire. Don't use the white or gray ashes, just grind black charcoal chunks into a powder and apply it.

LAYER WITH PLANTS Use a strong-smelling local plant as another cover scent. Crushed pine needles, wild onions, mints, and other pungent plants can hide your stink. Just stay out of the poison oak.

GET DIRTY The final touch in this layering system is fresh, damp, local dirt. Rub it generously on your hands and the trap parts as a final cover and scent absorber.

285 Build a Deadfall

One of the best traps is the Paiute deadfall, dating back to the early Paiute Indians. Like all deadfalls, there is some type of weight and a trigger system to hold part of the rock up in the air until your future meal gets under there. What makes this deadfall different is the stronger, more sensitive trigger that can be fashioned without a knife. Just break a few sticks into the right sizes, scrounge up a bit of string, and grab a flat rock.

STEP 1 Gather the sticks and other supplies. For an average-size rodent, you'll need the following: a Y-shaped stick thicker than a pencil and about 8 inches (20 cm) long; a straight stick thicker than a pencil, about 9 inches (23 cm) long; a 2-inch (5-cm) stick that is a little skinnier than a pencil; a slender bait stick half the diameter of a pencil and about 12 inches (30 cm) long; about 8 inches (20 cm) of string; appropriate bait for your critter of choice; and a flat rock that weighs 5–10 pounds (2–5 kg).

STEP 2 Take your 9-inch (23-cm) straight stick (this is called the lever) and tie one end of the string to it. Tie the other end to the 2-inch (5-cm) stick (the toggle). Square knots are fine. Wipe or skewer the bait on one end of the 12-inch (30-cm) bait stick.

STEP 3 Set the trap by laying the rock down on a hard patch of ground. Stand up the Y-shaped stick (the post) by the edge of the rock. Put the string-less end of the lever in the fork of the post, with a small portion of it sticking out toward the rock. Place the rock on the tip of the lever. You should be able to hold the weight of the rock by only holding down the string end of the lever. Now wrap the toggle halfway around the post. Place the baited end of the bait stick between a rough spot under the stone and the tip of the toggle. When you can let go of the trigger stick and the rock stays up, you know you did it right.

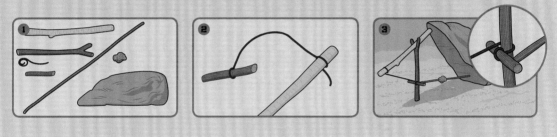

286 Bait Your Trap Correctly

When it comes to trapping, you need to use the right bait. Herbivores and carnivores will obviously go for different things—and even omnivores can be tricky.

BAIT FOR HERBIVORES There are plenty of vegetarian baits to choose from. Groundhogs go for sweet apples cut into pieces so their fragrance is released. Squirrels are very fond of whole peanuts, and they have a hard time resisting crushed sweet pecans and hickories. Just don't try using them under a tree full of those nuts. The animals won't go for the human-tainted bait when there is plenty of the same food lying nearby.

BAIT FOR OMNIVORES Omnivores, by definition, will eat anything. This can make them either easier or harder to bait. For raccoons, you can use canned tuna or sardines. The fouler and cheaper the fish are, the better. You can often trap for raccoons alongside creeks and streams, pouring the tuna juice into the creek so they'll follow the creek to get their fishy treat. Possums love lunchmeat, hot dogs, and other processed-meat foods.

BAIT FOR CARNIVORES Meat eaters do have their preferences. Coyotes love beaver meat. Foxes love rotten, hard-boiled eggs. Mink, ermine, and fisher cats love fish. Bobcats love fresh organ meat like liver and lung. You can also use various scent baits—it doesn't have to be food. Coyote and beaver scent can be used for coyotes. And coon urine can be a useful cover scent against other animals as well as for attracting raccoons.

287 Know Your Neighborhood Animals

The suburbs and nearby urban areas have a surprising amount of resources and can be a treasure trove of fat and happy wild game. Here are just a few of the creatures that can be utilized for food, should the need arise.

DEER These omnipresent critters represent the largest game meat payout, unless you have a neighborhood bear, elk, or moose. Take down an urban buck or doe with your rifle and you'll feed your crew for days.

RABBITS Your local bunnies and hares are quick and well-camouflaged animals, but they can be successfully hunted and trapped. The tender, chickenlike meat could turn a non-wild-game eater into a true believer.

SQUIRRELS They can be abundant around developed areas, often gorging themselves at people's bird feeders. These lightning-quick rodents are hard to trap; but they are as tasty as rabbit and are easy enough to hunt with a rifle, shotgun, or even a high-powered air rifle or BB gun.

RACCOONS AND OPOSSUMS Coons and possums are often lumped together, as they have similar diets and roam similar haunts. Both are omnivorous scavengers and can be hunted or trapped. Use caution if you eat raccoon—they are a prominent carrier of rabies.

GEESE AND TURKEYS Gamebirds can be found in many suburbs and agricultural areas. Neither is likely to fall for a trap, but waterfowl and turkeys are attracted to grassy feeding areas, where they can be hunted.

288 Bag a Backyard Buck

Those annoying deer that devour your garden can be an important source of wild game meat in a crisis. But don't assume they are tame or easy to hunt. Whitetail deer use their sharp hearing, sight, and sense of smell to remain undetected in the suburbs. To increase your chances of a successful backyard hunt, spend some time observing the deer. Look for their trails, hoofprints, scat, and other signs to give you an idea of their movements. Also watch where they travel at dawn and dusk, for a better chance of getting a deer in your sights. Be careful when hunting around homes and businesses. Use a tree stand or high vantage point to shoot downward, and never shoot toward areas where people could be. Remember that trees, brush, and fences are not a safe backstop for bullets or arrows.

289 Break the Law (If You Must)

Many ancient hunting techniques are frowned on by today's sportsmen and wildlife officials—in fact, they're illegal, and with good reason. But in a true state of emergency, if you need to survive by any means necessary, be aware of these outlawed tactics.

BUILD A FUNNEL Large fences with funnel-shaped openings once dotted America's eastern woodlands. These were used in conjunction with an animal drive to concentrate animals into one "kill zone."

SET A DEER NOOSE Using your strongest rope, create a large noose at a deer's head height in a well-worn trail. Tied to a strong tree, it confines a live deer in one area, allowing the hunter multiple shots.

CATCH THEM IN THE WATER A number of hunters working together can drive game toward a large river, where gunmen in boats can paddle alongside for point-blank shots at big game.

290 Hunt Better with Bait

Baiting animals is a highly controversial and often illegal strategy. Use this technique only after checking whether it's even legal in your area. And if you decide to break the law, do so only in a true life-or-death situation.

BAIT	PROS	CONS
FRESH MEAT	Brings in the picky carnivores like bobcats.	Can attract scavengers of all kinds, even birds.
BAD MEAT	Lures bottom-feeders like skunks or raccoons.	Won't last in the heat; draws flies.
PROCESSED MEATS	Heaven to raccoons.	You might need those canned goods yourself.
NUTS	Chief bait for squirrels, especially if exotic.	No drawbacks; peanuts are a sure thing.
FRUITS	Beloved by herbivores like rabbits.	Will draw scavengers as well as prey.
DOE SCENTS	Get the attention of local bucks.	Limited draw.
BEAVER CASTOR	Will draw beavers from miles away.	It's a smelly mess and may draw predators.
RACCOON URINE	Can draw raccoons as well as calm deer.	See above.

291 Catch Live Critters

Don't turn your nose up at smaller game—they can add up quickly if you find a good method, and a live-catch box trap can be your most effective and practical means. As an added bonus, you can safely release anything that you didn't intend to catch (like the neighbor's cat in the 'burbs). You can purchase these traps in a variety of sizes and styles. All are wire-cage bodies, so that the animals can't chew their way out. Small traps will catch rats and chipmunks, while large ones can catch dog-size animals.

292 Tan Your Hides

Tanning is the process of turning a raw pelt into leather. Properly tanned hides can be a valuable commodity, as a barter item or craft supply, and can increase your return on investment in raising animals.

STEP 1 Remove the hide and wet it immediately with cold water, then thoroughly wash the fur to remove any blood. You can use a mild detergent, but be sure to rinse it out very well. If you can't tan the hides immediately, put the sleeved hide (rolled, fur on the inside) in a plastic bag and stick it in the freezer.

STEP 2 When the skins have cooled, soak them for 48 hours in a tanning solution of 1 cup (0.2 l) coarse, granulated salt (noniodized), 1 cup (0.2 l) common alum, and 2 gallons (7.5 l) room-temperature water. Use a plastic tub that can be easily sealed.

STEP 3 Rinse the hides in cold water and flesh the skins with a flensing tool or kitchen knife. Rabbits have a clearly visible layer of fat that needs to be removed as close to the derma as possible. Be careful not to expose the root hairs when fleshing the hide. Start with the rump section of the pelt and you can usually peel off the entire layer of fat in one complete sheet.

STEP 4 Make a second tanning solution. Insert the pelts one at a time into the solution and soak thoroughly. Seal the container for seven days at room temperature, stirring twice a day.

STEP 5 Test for doneness by cutting a small piece of hide and dropping it into boiling water. If it curls or hardens, return the pelt to the solution. A well-tanned pelt won't change in boiling water.

STEP 6 Wash the pelts with a mild detergent and rinse thoroughly. Hang the skins on a line in the shade to dry (6–48 hours). When the pelts are slightly damp, give them a rough comb to help fluff up the hair.

STEP 7 Break the skins by pulling the still-damp leather in all directions. Don't pull too hard as you stretch, or you risk tearing the skin. If the leather is too dry, dampen it with a wet sponge. Broken hides can be tacked to a board or frame to dry flat.

STEP 8 Rub mink oil into the skin of the pelts for a soft, velvety feel, and brush the fur with a fine hairbrush. Store the tanned pelts in a cardboard box so they can breathe. To keep insects and pests away, put a bar of sweet-smelling soap in the box.

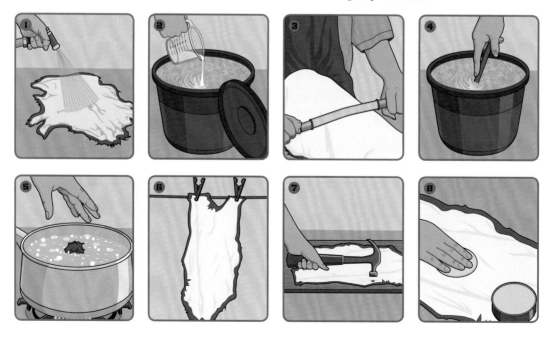

293 Use Your Brain

Long before toxic chemicals and tanning solutions, humans tanned hides using the naturally occurring elements in the animal's brain. The brain of every animal contains the perfect balance of conditioning oils to tan its own hide. All you need is your animal hide, the brain of the animal, a blender, a bath towel, and firewood. If you want a lot of tanning solution, you can buy brain from your local grocer.

After fleshing and drying the pelt, blend the brain with warm tap water on the liquefy setting. Look for the resulting liquid to be the consistency of hand lotion. Next, microwave the solution 2–3 minutes to warm it up. Lay the pelt on a flat surface and use your fingers to work the brain solution over the skin until thoroughly covered. Dampen the towel and wring it out. Roll the skin up in the damp towel and set aside for a couple of hours. Then hang it on a clothesline to dry. When slightly damp, stretch it in all directions to break up the skin.

294 Smoke Tanned Hides

Smoking a tanned hide won't waterproof it, but it will help it return to normal if it does get wet. To do this, you'll need to make a simple frame over a small firepit from which to hang your hides. A teepee shape works well.

Start by turning your skin fur side out and sewing up the sides to make a sort of bag. In a shallow pit, build a fire and let it burn down to coals, then add some rotted, punky wood. Watch out for flareups, as you want a lot of smoke but no heat. When you have a good amount of smoke going, stretch the pelt over the constructed frame and let it smoke for 30 minutes. Carefully remove it, turn it inside out, and smoke the other side for another half hour. Voila! You now have a sturdy, durable hide.

295 Enjoy Sun-Dried Foods

Food dehydrators are easily available as a kitchen appliance—but they're not much use when the power's out. And anyway, there's just something cool about growing your own tomatoes and making sun-dried snacks right there in the same backyard. Dried fruits and veggies are long-lasting and a great way to perk up dreary winter meals when the growing season's over. Here's how to make your own solar-powered snack machine.

YOU'LL NEED

- ☐ Three cardboard boxes
- ☐ Box knife
- ☐ Black paint or black plastic sheeting, clear plastic wrap
- ☐ Four dowels that are at least 2 inches (5 cm) longer than your box is wide
- ☐ Cloth screen, enough to make two shelves and to cover the box
- ☐ Duct tape

STEP 1 Gather your cardboard boxes—they can be any size, provided they fit together nicely, as shown (you can make as many shelves as you like).

STEP 2 Cut one box down to be your reflection tray, or use the lid from a banker's box or similar. Cut ventilation holes in the two long sides, and paint its interior black, or coat in black plastic sheeting, then cover in clear plastic.

STEP 3 Cut holes through your large box, and thread through dowels as shown. Stretch screen over them and tape down firmly.

STEP 4 Cut a vent in the bottom of your larger box, and use duct tape to attach the reflection tray, so the sun's heat flows into the interior.

STEP 5 Set the main box on a second to elevate it (you can also place it on a small table or chair). Angle the reflector so as to collect maximum sunlight.

STEP 6 Add fruit or veggies and cover the box with more screening. Your fruit is done when it has a leathery texture; vegetables when they become brittle.

296 Dry It in the Dark

If you live in a region where a solar dehydrator just won't get it done thanks to weather, sunshine, or humidity patterns, consider these old-school, sunshine-free drying techniques instead.

HANG 'EM UP Thread peeled, seeded, and sliced pieces of fruit or veggies onto a sturdy cotton string, cover with a thin cloth to keep off flies and dust, and hang above a radiator or stove top.

HIDE YOUR HERBS Herbs shouldn't be dried in the sun, anyway, so for those of you shrouded in gloom and darkness, find a dry, dark place in the house, tie the stems into bouquets, and hang upside down.

297 Whip Up Some Hardtack

What makes a good survival food? First, you need to be able to store it for long periods of time. Second, it needs to be nutritious. And third, it should taste good. Tasting good is not really a necessity, but it sure is nice if you end up living off the stuff for a long time.

Hardtack satisfies all three conditions. Once it's dried thoroughly, it will keep for years, provided it stays dry and away from pests. If you make it with natural, healthy ingredients, it's very nutritious. And if you know how to prepare it, it tastes delicious. Because it is completely dehydrated, it is relatively light and easy to transport, but because it is so dense, it packs a lot of nutrition in a small package.

Hardtack has actually been around since the time of Egyptian sailors, but you probably know it better from the Civil War period. During the war, squares of hardtack were shipped to both the Union and Confederate armies, making it a staple of a soldier's rations. Typically made six months beforehand, it was as hard as a rock when it actually got to the troops. To soften it, they usually soaked it in water or coffee. Not only would this soften it enough for eating, but any insect larvae in the bread would float to the top, allowing the soldiers to skim them out.

YOU'LL NEED

- 4–5 cups (480–600 g) flour
- 2 cups (0.5 l) water
- 2–3 teaspoons (10–15 g) salt

DIRECTIONS Mix the flour, water, and salt, making sure the mixture is fairly dry. Then roll it out to about $^1/_2$-inch (1-cm) thickness, and shape into a rectangle. Cut it into 3x3-inch (8x8-cm) squares, and poke holes in both sides. Place on an ungreased cookie sheet, and cook for 30 minutes per side at 375°F (190°C).

298 Make Your Own Pemmican

An ancient forebear of the modern survival ration, pemmican was originally prepared by North American Indians as a traveling food and cold-weather snack. Traditional pemmican is a blend of dried meat pounded into a powder, then blended with warm animal fat and often supplemented with dried fruits, berries, or other available foods. This mixture can be rolled into balls, pressed into a loaf or formed into cakes, or added to a pot of boiling water to make a greasy soup base.

YOU'LL NEED

- 8 ounces (0.2 kg) lard
- An 8-ounce (0.2-kg) cup packed tight with powdered jerky
- 8 ounces (0.2 kg) dried fruit
- Optional: flour, chopped nuts, spices

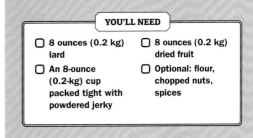

GET READY The lard, jerky, and fruit are essential ingredients. Some folks add a little bit of flour for extra carbs, a handful of chopped nuts for fat, or spices to make this mess taste a little better. Keep an eye on the temperature—cold lard won't incorporate well with the other ingredients, and melted lard will cook the jerky slightly, leading to dangerous spoilage. Get the lard to a soft state, below 100°F (38°C), by warming it slightly or stirring it aggressively.

MIX IT UP Add the lard to a bowl containing all the other ingredients and stir until well incorporated (about 2 minutes).

STORE IT Loosely wrap the pemmican in wax paper, and store it in a cool, dry, dark place. It can last for months before the fat turns rancid, especially in cold weather. Just make sure to store it out of the reach of pests, too. Once you get used to the odd feeling of grease running down the back of your throat as you chew pemmican, you just might start to enjoy this ancestral superfood.

299 Make a Good Trade

If the economy goes into total collapse, you may have to fall back on a barter system. Just like using precious metals, humans have been trading goods and services for ages; currency has just simplified the process. If your money's no good, it may be worth it to consider negotiating the relative value of a box of ammo or a live chicken, or the expertise needed to fix a broken pipe or pull a tooth.

How does it work? Anything can be traded for anything, if both parties agree. After a good trade, each person walks away with something valuable and a willingness to trade with that partner again. After a bad trade . . . well, let's just say you don't want to make a bad trade. The chart that follows will help you negotiate these tricky waters.

VALUE	$	$$	$$$
OPTIONS FOR TRADE	½ dozen eggs	1 pack of seeds	1 laying hen or 2 roosters
	1 can of vegetables	1 can of soup	3 fish
	1 beer	3 beers	1 rabbit
	½ pound (230 g) salt or sugar	1 bottle of wine	10 pounds (4.5 kg) potatoes
	1 bar of soap	1 pound (450 g) nails or screws	1 pair shoes
	1 baseball bat	1 knife	1 pepper spray
	10 rounds of .22	10 rounds of .223, .40, or 9mm	10 12-gauge shells
	5 cigarettes	1 pack of cigarettes	½ gallon (2 l) kerosene
	1 roll of toilet paper	1 first aid kit	1 potted medicinal plant
	1 hour of unskilled labor	1 hour of skilled labor	1 hand tool

300

Get Your Balance

Like most things, there are pros and cons to making trades. Here are a few of the benefits and drawbacks of the barter system.

⬆ You can trade your goods or services as you see fit.

⬇ Both parties must desire something that the other party possesses.

⬆ The barter system works under any conditions, regardless of a failure of utilities or infrastructure.

⬇ It can be hard to determine "prices" or fair trades.

⬆ You can trade different combinations of services, goods, and supplies.

⬇ Some things are difficult or impossible to divide without losing value, like a pair of shoes.

⬆ Barter can transcend language and cultural boundaries.

⬇ Bad trades and barters can make for bad neighbors.

$$$$	$$$$$	VALUE
1 pig	10 pigs	
2 goats	1 cow	
15 laying hens	1 horse	
20 meat chickens	1 pallet of food	
1 water filter	2 body-armor vests	
1 handgun	5 firearms	
100 rounds of small-arms ammo	1,000 rounds of ammunition	
5 gallons (19 l) gasoline	1 50-watt solar panel	
1 course of antibiotics	1 medic's bag, stocked	
1 week of unskilled labor	1 month of unskilled labor	

OPTIONS FOR TRADE

My connection to this particular survivalist is pretty obvious. We may not learn everything from our parents, but with a dad like this one, it's hard not to pick up a few things here and there.

301 Survive Like Dad

I was born on a farm in the middle of the Great Depression. When I was about 4 years old, we were robbed of two full barrels of flour and cornmeal as we slept one night. I still remember the white flour all over the grass—they had spilled it in their hurry. It was a crushing loss of riches. By the time I was entering school, World War II had impacted our family greatly. My parents and each family member had a ration book full of stamps for coffee, tea, sugar, and other items. We kids still have our ration books. During that same time, we had to move several miles away from our farm, as the Marine Corps purchased large tracts of the area to serve as training grounds. Our original farmhouse, barn, and outbuildings were eventually used for target practice, with marines shelling them until they were completely blown up. But I did manage to save a few bricks from the old farm.

On our new farm in Virginia, I grew up working with my hands. We raised livestock and grew our own food, canning and preserving it ourselves. We had no electricity or running water, and we dipped our water from a hand-dug well with a bucket. I was about 11 before our area began to have access to electricity.

During the Great Depression and World War II, people found ways to survive. Since a high percentage of Americans were farmers and rural people, they knew how to produce food and were able to do so. Now, a high percentage of Americans do not know how to produce food—and it's the number one skill that people should learn.

4

UNITED STATES OF AMERICA
OFFICE OF PRICE ADMINISTRATION

WAR RATION BOOK FOUR

864070 BZ

Issued to

Complete address

In accepting this book, I re...
States Government. I will...
authorized by the Office of...

Void if Altered

It is a cr...

OPA Form R-145

WAR RATION BOOK No. 3

958068 ER

Identification of person to whom issued; PRINT IN FULL

(First name) (Middle name) (Last name)

Street number or rural route

City or post office

AGE SEX WEIGHT HEIGHT
lbs. in.

SIGNATURE State
Ft. in.

OCCUPATION

Issued by
LOCAL BOARD ACTION
Street address (Local board number)
City

(Date)

NOT VALID WITHOUT STAMP

302 Learn an Art

Our family was self-taught in the ways of fixing things and making repairs, which seems like a lost art now. Some people paint pictures—that's art. Some people weld metal, and that's an art, too. I learned about cutting torches and acetylene torches as a teenager repairing farm equipment. Later, I turned these skills into a career as a professional welder.

Today, few people seem to know how to fix and repair their own things. Compared to Americans in the 1930s and '40s, we would be in far worse shape if an economic collapse or a world war were to occur today.

People need to take the time that they're wasting on electronic gadgets and learn how to produce and preserve food, and how to survive under harsh conditions. My greatest concern is people's lack of ability to do things for themselves. This is not rocket science, it's simply going back in time and learning the skills of our grandpas and grandmas, repeating the practices of self-reliance that allowed large families to survive very well—during some very tough times.

303 Develop New Skills

After spending many years as a welder, I became interested in fuel production. For many years, we produced ethanol fuel from our farm, and I've recently been branching out into biodiesel (all without any college education or engineering degrees). Here are some basics that anyone can master.

IT'S VERSATILE Anything that will ferment—not just corn—will produce ethanol, and anyone can learn this process.

IT'S ADAPTABLE Any oil seed (like soybeans, sunflowers, peanuts, coconut, canola, and many more) can be turned into biodiesel fuel. Every bushel of soybeans can be turned into 1.5 gallons (6 l) of vehicle fuel or home-heating oil.

IT'S GOT POTENTIAL This type of energy production does not have to be in the hands of big business. If the public got serious about it, we could have tens of thousands of people safely producing their own fuel in a sustainable manner.

IT'S POSSIBLE Solar is another great form of energy. I recently built a solar home-heating panel that heats air to 120°F (49°C) on sunny days, and my next project is to build a system that will stockpile some of this heat for use at night.

304 Spark It Up

Firestarters and tinder are survival basics. While tinder can be almost any dry, flammable substance, some options are better than others. Here's a guide to some flammable bounty found in nature—or in your pack.

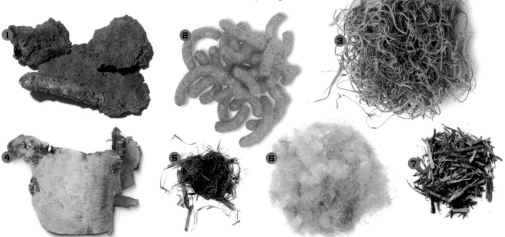

1 TINDER FUNGUS In northern areas, look for bulbous blotches of blackish wood on live birch trees. The inside of the fungus, which is reddish-brown, can easily catch a spark. Crumble it for a quick start to a fire or use chunks of it to keep a coal alive.

2 SNACKS Cheese curls are dry, crunchy stuff soaked in fat. No surprise that they burn nicely.

3 SPANISH MOSS Peel this from trees and it's a great tinder, but be careful—it's also a great home for chiggers and other nasty critters.

4 BIRCH BARK Strip ribbons of bark from downed trees; it works just as well as bark from live ones and is already nice and dry.

5 CEDAR BARK Mash the bark up with a rock and then pull it apart

with your fingers to make nice ignitable strands.

6 CATTAIL FLUFF Pull out the fluffy insides of a cattail and ball them up to catch a spark. Have more tinder on hand, as they'll go up fast.

7 ROTTEN WOOD Shave off small pieces of dry, rotten wood with your knife; they'll flame right up with a good spark.

305 Make Fire from Rocks

Archaeological evidence suggests that few of our ancestors could make fire with stones prior to the invention of flint and steel. This unlikely method can still work today if you have the right materials. To make a "fire stone" set, you'll need pieces of iron ore, such as bog iron or marcasite. You'll also need extremely fine tinder charred to improve its ignition abilities. Shavings of true tinder fungus (*Fomes fomentarius*) are a great choice, if you can find it.

You'll need to scrape the tinder fungus with a sharp tool and place the fuzzy scrapings into a bundle of dry tinder.

Once you've done this, strike one piece of iron ore against the other briskly and quickly. You could also use a sharp piece of flint against the ore. Strike your sparks right over your tinder. If everything is just right, one of the tiny iron sparks will catch in the tinder, which can then be blown into a fire.

306 Build a Fire Like a Pro

Matches and lighters should be your primary fire makers, but it's also smart to have some redundancies built into your survival gear. Add these backup methods and you'll always have a way to build a fire.

MAGNESIUM BARS Magnesium fire starters are common, inexpensive, and long lasting. The main section of the bar is magnesium, a soft metal that is meant to be scraped into shavings with a sharp tool. Some products include a tool for this job and for making sparks. As you scrape the attached ferrocerium rod to produce sparks, aim them at your pile of metal shavings sitting in a nest of dry tinder. When the sparks hit the shavings, the little pile will burn "white hot," thus igniting the tinder.

STEEL WOOL Steel wool can be incredibly effective when combined with a small-voltage electrical source. A 3-volt (or higher) battery and some fine-grade steel wool will quickly produce a burning ball of steel fibers—just touch a tuft of steel wool to the positive and negative battery posts at the same time. Then place the burning steel in tinder. Use steel wool with grades from 0 to 0000, and batteries with the "+" and "-" terminals close together.

LENSES With a simple magnifying lens, you can concentrate a point of sunlight on tinder to create fire. The larger the lens, the better this will work. Find a sunny spot, flatten a spot in some fluffy tinder, and focus the light in a white-hot pinpoint. Once you have the perfect, blinding dot of light and the tinder is smoking, blow gently across the tinder to help it burn. Keep blowing steadily until the tinder flames up.

307 Use a Fire Plow

The basic rule of firemaking is this: You need to create friction—and you need something easy to ignite. This method uses what you may have at hand (rotten wood) to provide both necessities.

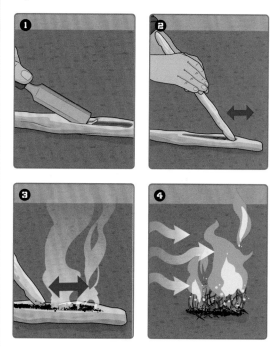

GET WOOD You'll need to find two pieces of dead, dry wood that is soft but not rotten. Cedar, yucca, basswood, aspen, and many other softwood species can work. You'll need a large piece to lay on the ground and a smaller piece to use as the "plow" to move back and forth.

MAKE A GROOVE Lay the bigger piece on its side on the ground. You can pre-chisel a groove if you have the tools (1). Also carve or sand a chisel-shaped point on the plow stick. Rub this aggressively, in short strokes, on the side of the bigger wood piece (2). This should begin to groove into the bigger piece and start to smoke.

GET IGNITED Once a groove is formed, rub the plow stick even harder, back and forth, to create chocolate brown dust in the groove you have burned (3). If the dust pile still smokes after you have stopped plowing, then you have an ember. Scoop the ember out of the groove, place it in tinder, and blow it into flame (4).

308 Make Charcoal from Firewood

That stuff you use for summer cookouts is basically a form of coal; it's wood that's had the moisture and various other impurities slowly burned out of it. With a little work, you can make your own, and you'll have something that's more compact, lasts longer, and provides more heat than plain old firewood.

STEP 1 Prepare the drums: Cut an opening at the bottom of the 80-gallon (300-liter) drum large enough to fit pieces of firewood inside, about 10 inches (25 cm) high by 18 inches (45 cm) wide. Then punch several holes into the bottom of the 30-gallon (110-liter) drum.

STEP 2 Place the bricks inside the bottom of the large drum, stacking two on either side of the opening. Put the smaller drum on top of the bricks, and fill with the wood you want to make into charcoal (roughly fist-size pieces). Put the lids on both barrels, leaving both of them slightly opened for air flow.

STEP 3 Light a fire inside the bottom opening of the larger barrel, beneath the smaller barrel within. Continue to feed wood to the fire, letting it burn for about 3–4 hours.

STEP 4 Remove the larger drum's lid, completely seal the smaller drum's lid, and replace the larger lid, again leaving it slightly opened. Continue to let the fire burn for another 4–5 hours.

STEP 5 Once the fire is burned out, let the drums cool, and carefully remove the lids to take the charcoal out of the smaller drum. The wood will have reduced in size by about half and should be hard, black, and brittle.
   Keep your load of charcoal somewhere dry, and use it for your cooking, blacksmithing (see item 310), or possibly black powder (see item 309).

309 Mix Your Own Gunpowder

Gunpowder, or black powder, has been around for centuries, and while modern firearms use newer propellants, it still sees use in some older-style guns, fireworks, model rockets, and more. This fiery stuff is made from three ingredients: charcoal—not commercial briquettes, but the stuff made from wood only (you can even make your own, as shown on the opposite page); sulfur, which can be bought from chemistry suppliers or garden stores (it's usually used to fertilize roses and kill soil mites); and potassium nitrate or saltpeter, which can be bought from the same places (it's often sold as a type of tree stump remover).

These ingredients are separately ground down to a fine powder—sulfur is often sold powdered, but saltpeter is usually granular, and lump charcoal definitely needs to be ground down. Small amounts can be ground in a mortar and pestle or in a blender. Larger amounts are ground using a special mill or other technique. Whether small- or large-scale, never use tools that generate sparks or heat, to avoid igniting any of the ingredients.

The typical ratio, by weight, is 75 percent saltpeter, 15 percent charcoal, and 10 percent sulfur. The finer the ingredients are ground, the faster they will burn (black powder for guns is made from the finest consistency). An optional process, called "corning," involves adding water to the components to make a claylike substance, then pressing the dried mixture through a series of fine sieves; the powder will burn even more efficiently when processed this way.

310 Build Your Own Backyard Forge

When the power goes off and the barbarian hordes of Cincinnati arise, learning to become a blacksmith might just come in handy, whether you're making tools and utensils or forging weapons to fight zombies. With these instructions and some parts, you can put together your own coal-fed blacksmith's forge.

STEP 1 Drill holes in the bottom of the grill and bolt on the floor flange. Drill or cut a hole to match the opening of the floor flange, too.

STEP 2 Thoroughly coat the inside of the grill's dish with fireplace cement, leaving the floor flange hole uncovered. Let it dry and set.

STEP 3 Thread the iron pipes and tee connector together, then screw into the floor flange.

STEP 4 Attach the rubber coupler hose to the base of the tee and secure with metal hose clamps. Attach the bellows to supply air to your forge. (As an alternative option to the bellows, you can use the nozzle of a hair dryer.)

STEP 5 Screw the pipe cap onto the bottom of the tee to seal off the assembly. This will keep air directed upward into the forge and trap ash. (You can also place the pipe's end in a water-filled bucket if your forge doesn't use the ashes.) Fill the forge with charcoal, fire it up, grab your tools and anvil, and get hammering!

311 Forge Your Own Knife

There are plenty of projects you can do with a blacksmith's forge and tools, but one of the simplest and most useful ones—and a good traditional way to get some practice—is making a blacksmith's knife. All you'll need are a few tools and a piece of steel (like an old file, a railroad spike, or a bit of leaf spring from a truck's suspension).

YOU'LL NEED

☐ Steel piece
☐ Tongs
☐ Hammer or small sledge
☐ File or grinder
☐ Oil
☐ Sharpening stone
☐ Forge and anvil

STEP 1 Fire up your forge and heat the steel in the coals until it's at about 2,200°F (1,200°C). It will be a pale yellow-white color.

STEP 2 Using tongs, pick up the metal and hammer it on the anvil to flatten it and begin making one side of the knife's edge.

STEP 3 Reheat as needed, and work on both sides to prevent distorting the steel. Save a good chunk at one end for a handle.

STEP 6 Refire the forge and heat the blade until it's very hot as in Step 1, then dip into a pan of oil to harden. Let the blade rest in low heat for about an hour to temper the metal.

STEP 5 Once you have a rough blade shape, reheat to red-hot a few times and let cool, then leave it to cool overnight as the coals die down. Grind or file the blade into shape.

STEP 4 Continue forging the blade's point by hammering in small taps to shape the metal, and then give the opposite side a bevel by hammering near the point.

STEP 7 Wrap the metal handle in leather, wire, or paracord, or attach shaped wood pieces for a grip. Sharpen the blade's edge with a file, whetstone, and even a leather strop for a very fine edge.

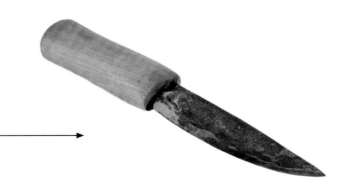

312 Heat with the Sun

If the grid is down in chilly weather, an emergency can leave the modern home or apartment dangerously cold. Death from hypothermia is a very real threat to your safety, especially in subfreezing temperatures coupled with a utility outage. Managing the sun coming into your dwelling is an easy and safe way to gain heat in a cold-climate catastrophe. Yes, a home heating solar array on your roof would be a good idea for frosty locales, but you can still get a warming effect with smart use of the assets that you already have. Take advantage of passive solar heat during daylight hours by staying in a room with south-facing windows. Lay out dark-colored blankets and rugs on the floor and furniture to help absorb the heat from the sunlight. Thick drapes or improvised insulation can block the chill coming off the windows after sunset.

313 Warm Up Safely

Don't replace one danger with another by swapping hypothermia for a house fire. Rely on these safety tips to keep a bad situation from getting worse.

FOCUS ON ONE ROOM Pick one area, preferably a smaller room with a low ceiling, to be your main living area during the emergency. Don't even try to heat every room in the house—it's a waste of time and resources.

VENTILATE You're just begging for carbon monoxide poisoning if you use a propane heater, a grill, or a gas stove for a heat source indoors. Even a kerosene heater needs to have some fresh air. Don't use combustion without ventilation.

TAKE CARE WITH CANDLES Candles are a problematic heat source, commonly causing home fires in already troubling emergency situations. Limit their use—if you have enough candles to create warmth in a room, you also have a serious fire hazard. Always make sure you have a working smoke alarm with a carbon monoxide detector.

314 Use Bricks and Stones to Heat Your Home

While you can't heat a room with hand-warmer packs, you can certainly heat yourself up by keeping a few of them in your pockets. Building on the concept of portable radiant heat, you can also turn rocks and bricks into small, heavy space heaters.

STEP 1 Safety first! You'll need to set up a heatproof platform in the room you intend to heat. A 2-foot (0.6-m) square of bricks on the floor will work fine. Then get some rocks or a few bricks from a dry location.

STEP 2 Fire up the grill or build a fire outside, and throw the rocks or bricks in the fire to heat them up. Heat for about 45 minutes and then scoop them out with a shovel. Get all the coals and sparks off of the bricks or rocks before continuing.

STEP 3 Drop the bricks into a stainless-steel cooking pot. Other types of pots can be damaged by the heat, and galvanized buckets can release toxic vapors with heat exposure. Stick with the steel pot.

STEP 4 Carefully bring the hot rocks or bricks inside and set the pot on your fireproof, heatproof platform. Repeat as needed every few hours.

315

Consider These Heaters

If you live in an area prone to cold winters and frequent power outages, you may want to plan ahead with backup heaters like these.

WOOD STOVE If firewood is abundant in your region, a wood stove could be the perfect solution for winter heating. They can heat a small house and even slow-cook meals on their hot, flat top. If you can cut your own wood, this becomes an inexpensive way to heat a home or building.

KEROSENE HEATER Stinky but easy to use, kerosene heaters can be burned indoors (if the particular model was designed for indoor use—check the instructions or labels). Just crack a window for a little ventilation and stock up on kerosene before bad weather hits (it's available at many gas stations).

PROPANE HEATER WITH CATALYTIC CONVERTER These small heaters offer carbon monoxide–free combustion and can run on small propane cylinders (like the ones for camping stoves) or on larger bottles (like your grill tanks). These devices are safe for use in homes, tents, cars, and other closed spaces, with only a tiny bit of ventilation.

316 Master 6 Advanced Knots

In the world of knot tying, everybody has his or her favorite. One knot can serve multiple purposes, and the basics will get you through most situations. But for those of you who have already mastered the beginner and intermediate knots that we've discussed (see items 65 and 191), consider expanding your skill set to include these more advanced techniques. After all, any good sailor, mountain climber, Boy Scout, or lumberjack already has them on lockdown, and you never know what kind of emergency situation might call for a specialty hitch.

SQUARE LASHING

This lashing has been used to build everything from camp chairs to towers and bridges—but you can also use it to secure two poles or planks together, as shown.

HOW TO TIE Tie a clove hitch to one of the poles, near the place where the two cross. Wrap your line around the junction, going under the lower pole and over the upper. Wrap outward five or six times, then wrap between the poles, biting onto the previous wraps to tighten them. Use a square knot to tie the free ends.

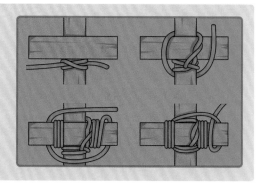

TRUCKER'S HITCH

This hitch provides a unique mechanical advantage for tightening up a line. It's great for tying down tarps and shifting loads and, though a little complex, it's worth it.

HOW TO TIE Start off this knot by tying a figure 8 knot with a loop of the line. Then pass the free end of the line around the object to be secured and pass the line through the loop. Next, pull the free end tight, and secure the free end with two half hitches just below the loop.

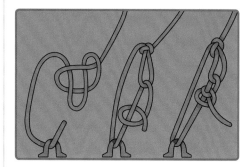

TRIPOD LASHING

This lashing is commonly used for shelters.

HOW TO TIE Start with your three poles lying on the ground side by side. Tie a clove hitch to one of the end poles, then wrap around all of the poles five or six times. Wrap the line between the poles—twice between each one—working back toward the original clove hitch. Finish by tying the free end of the line to the free end from the clove hitch that started this whole thing. Spread the legs for a handy tripod.

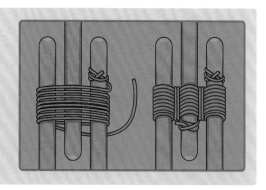

SHEEPSHANK

This may seem like half magic trick, half knot, but it shortens a line without cutting it, keeping our long ropes in one piece.

HOW TO TIE Fold the rope to the new length you need. Create a half hitch in one end of the continuing rope, and drop it over the nearby loop. Make a half hitch in the other standing end, drop it over its adjacent loop, and then tighten the whole thing slowly.

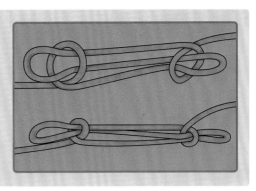

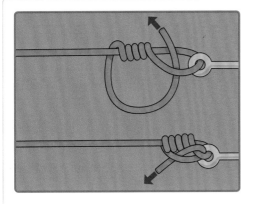

IMPROVED CLINCH KNOT

You can use rope, or, better yet, slippery monofilament fishing line, when tying this knot.

HOW TO TIE Pass the free end of the line through or around the object to be secured, like the eye of a fishhook. Then wrap the free end of the line around the other side of the line five or six times. Pass the free end of the line through the triangular opening next to the object and then through the large loop you just created by going through the small triangle. Tighten the knot, trim off any extra line, and enjoy your day fishing.

BARREL HITCH

This hitch has been used in sailing and construction work for centuries. It allows you to secure a barrel or other cylindrical object and lift it in a balanced position.

HOW TO TIE Place your barrel or other object to be lifted on top of your rope. Then tie an overhand knot across the top of the barrel. Open up the overhand knot until it wraps around the top sides of the barrel. Tie the ends of the rope together with a square knot and then lift. This knot makes a fine bucket handle when the wire handle finally breaks off.

SAFETY WARNING: For safety and stability while hoisting barrels, the rope around the barrel needs to be high above the center of gravity on the barrel but pose no danger of slipping off the top of the barrel. FYI, beer has an excellent center of gravity.

Don't Get Caught Without:
BEER

It's true: Beer can save your life. In survival situations, that can of local brew is able to transcend its sullied reputation to become a piece of malleable, versatile metal filled with calories. Here are a few uses for your stalwart can of beer.

❶ BOILING WATER

The trick to boiling raw water in cans is to set it next to the fire, in the ashes. Don't place the can in the center of the fire, as the metal will break down more quickly. Boil for 10 full minutes to be safe.

❷ CHAR CLOTH For a

one-shot deal, cut the top off the can and pack the inside with fibrous tree bark or cotton cloth. Fold the can shut and throw it into the fire for five minutes. It will produce usable char cloth.

❸ PERIMETER ALARM

This trick is ideal for bear country. Throw a few small rocks in an empty beer can and set it up where it can fall down with a crash. Tie a string to the can, and then run the string around your camp, about 1 foot (30 cm) off the ground. Just one bump of the line from man or beast will send the can tumbling down and give you a head start.

❹ FISHING REEL

You can make a reel out of almost anything cylindrical, but the beer can also makes a fine spool for storing the fishing line. Tie the monofilament to the pull tab, or through a small hole, and wind the line around.

❺ FISH HOOK

For survival fishing only: Break off the pull tab, cut part off, sharpen the tip, attach your line, and bait. Let the fish swallow it whole, and retrieve during the gutting process.

❻ FIRE STARTER

Polish the can so the light of the sun can be reflected off the can's concave bottom. Select a fine, fluffy, dark-colored tinder. Play with the zenith and azimuth angles of the can until you get some smoke coming from your tinder.

❼ FIRE SOCKET

Find a small concave spot on a crushed beer can, and it will act as the top socket for a bow and drill fire starting set. This socket won't need lubricant, and it will get hot up there!

❽ SURVIVAL STOVE

Cut a can in half, add a few ounces of alcohol to the bottom, and you've got a camping stove. You can also prowl the Internet for how to build a can stove with jets around the top lip, to increase the stove's efficiency.

❾ CANDLE LANTERN

I love a good, cheap camp lantern. Cut a line down the side of the can, plus two more so the cuts form a capital I. Fold open the double doors and drop in a tea light, or add some sand and a candle nub.

❿ REFLECTIVE SIGNAL

If your beer can isn't shiny on the outside, cut the thing in half to expose the metallic interior. It's not going to be as shiny as a signal mirror, but it can still reflect light to signal for help. You can also hang it up and let it twist in the wind.

318 Multitask Your Meds

Let's start out by saying that this kind of playing doctor is a very bad idea. You should not be diagnosing yourself or others without proper training, and you should certainly not be messing around with drugs. However, it can be helpful to know how versatile some prescription meds are, if only so that you can discuss options with any medical professionals you encounter in the post-event landscape. A surprising number of drugs have multiple approved uses and/or are used "off label" in ways that are effective but not FDA-approved. Here's a small sampling.

MEDICATION	GENERIC NAME	APPROVED USES	OFF-LABEL USES
ADDERALL	Dextroamphetamine	ADD, narcolepsy	Depression, obesity, aphasia, OCD
CYMBALTA	Duloxetine	Depression, diabetes, anxiety, fibromyalgia, nerve pain, urinary incontinence	Chronic knee and back pain, smoking cessation
DEPAKOTE	Divalproex sodium	Epilepsy, bipolar disorder, migraines	Borderline personality disorder, PTSD, OCD, alcoholism, anxiety, cocaine addiction, sleep disorders, schizophrenia, Alzheimer's
EFFEXOR	Venlafaxine	Depression, anxiety, panic disorder	Bipolar disorder, hot flashes due to cancer therapy, migraine prevention, chronic fatigue, tension headaches, ADD, fibromyalgia, anorexia nervosa, osteoarthritis, binge eating
ENBREL	Etanercept	Rheumatoid arthritis, chronic spinal pain, psoriasis	Investigated for use in Alzheimer's and vasculitis, among other conditions
NEURONTIN	Gabapentin	Epilepsy, pain from shingles, restless leg syndrome	Neuropathic pain, HIV/AIDS-related neuropathy, phantom limb pain, anxiety, bipolar disorder, migraines, depression, PTSD, sleep disorders, multiple sclerosis, chronic fatigue, menopausal symptoms, cocaine abuse
PROPECIA	Finasteride	Fighting baldness	Preventing prostate cancer

319 Stockpile Essential Meds

If you have a prescription that you need in order to survive, that's your number-one concern. But it's also wise to keep a stock of the following versatile and essential over-the-counter remedies.

IBUPROFEN (Motrin, Advil) This incredibly versatile anti-inflammatory can be used not just for headaches and cramps but for earaches, sore throats, sinus pain, stiff neck, muscle strains, arthritis (including gout), and back pain. It is also effective at reducing fever and is generally safe for kids.

ACETAMINOPHEN (Tylenol) Useful for the same conditions as ibuprofen, though generally less effective. High doses can cause liver damage, so be careful.

LOPERAMIDE (Immodium) The best medicine for diarrhea, which can be deadly in a survival situation.

PSEUDOEPHEDRINE (Sudafed) An anticongestant, this drug is used to treat respiratory infections, allergies, chemical irritation, and mild asthma or bronchitis.

DIPHENHYDRAMINE (Benadryl) Mainly used for sniffles caused by allergies or respiratory infections, it can also treat rashes (including poison oak or ivy), hives, and nausea. It also makes many people very drowsy and can be used as a safe sleep aid.

MECLIZINE (Dramamine) Relieves nausea, vomiting, motion sickness, and vertigo, and may work on anxiety. Can also be a safe sleep aid.

RANITIDINE (Zantac) Mainly used to treat heartburn, ulcers, and other stomach issues, it can also relieve hives.

HYDROCORTISONE CREAM The strongest steroid cream available without a prescription can treat painful or itchy rashes such as eczema, poison ivy, diaper rash, and minor genital irritations.

CLOTRIMAZOLE (Gyne-Lotrimin) This antifungal can treat athlete's foot, ringworm, and diaper rashes.

320 Repurpose Street Drugs

You shouldn't take illegal drugs for lots of reasons, including that they're, well, illegal. And not very good for you. That said, if you're truly desperate and happen upon someone's stash, many illicit substances have surprisingly licit uses (after all, many of them started out as medicine long ago).

MDMA Used in treating PTSD and for other therapeutic purposes, this "party drug" is being investigated as a treatment for Parkinson's.

COCAINE A potent topical anaesthetic, cocaine was once used in surgery and dentistry. It can also be used to slow or stop bleeding. Coca leaves are often chewed to treat nausea and altitude sickness.

MARIJUANA The kingpin of medicinal drugs, weed is legal in many places for medical use and has been approved for treating nausea, insomnia, chronic pain, anxiety, and epilepsy.

LSD Both LSD and mushrooms in *very low doses* have proven effective in treating debilitating cluster headaches and other severe pain. Once again: *Very. Low. Doses.* Otherwise, you'll likely have a very interesting view of the End Times.

HEROIN The original opiate painkiller, it's more effective than morphine, Vicodin, or OxyContin. Also more likely to kill you, of course.

AMPHETAMINES Useful in treating some severe allergic reactions, as well as narcolepsy and ADD. Studies show some evidence of efficacy in helping stroke victims recover.

321 Deliver a Baby

An expectant mother may go into labor at an inopportune moment, and you might wind up assisting in the delivery. It's a trying ordeal, but humans have been having babies as long as humans have been around. Pay attention to these instructions and you can make yourself useful in an urgent situation.

STEP 1 Stay calm and assess your situation. Call for emergency services (they may be able to stay on the line and help you over the phone while you wait), and prepare for the delivery. If the mother is experiencing contractions that are 2 minutes apart or less, delivery is imminent.

STEP 2 Thoroughly wash your hands and arms and be sure the birthing area is clean and covered in sheets or towels. If you have a delivery kit, open it and make use of the gloves, drapes, suction bulb, and other tools.

STEP 3 Help the mother assume a comfortable position during labor (see right for some suggestions). For delivery, reclining is traditional but not the most effective position; instead, some mothers may be on hands and knees, squatting, or even standing.

STEP 4 Give assistance only if needed. When the baby's head is showing, gently cup and support the head as it emerges. If the umbilical cord is around the neck or head, gently slip it off. Be ready to catch the rest of the baby, too—he or she will be slippery!

STEP 5 Gently wrap the baby in a towel and clean off blood and fluids; this motion also stimulates the baby to begin breathing if he or she hasn't already (don't spank the baby—that only happens in the movies). You can also use the suction bulb to help clear the baby's mouth and nostrils. Give the baby to the mother to hold (skin contact is good), and keep them both warm.

STEP 6 Wait for the umbilical cord to stop pulsating and apply clamps—one about 12 inches (30 cm) from the baby's abdomen, and another 6 inches (15 cm) past the first clamp.

STEP 7 Await delivery of the placenta about 15–30 minutes after the baby. You can gently encourage this by massaging the mother's lower abdomen in slow circles. Do not pull on the cord or placenta. Once it is delivered, examine it carefully to see if it is fully intact (if not, the mother may experience more bleeding and may need additional medical care). Your delivery kit may also include a bag to carry the placenta to a doctor.

STEP 8 If the mother is still bleeding, use sanitary pads or dressings to help reduce or stop bleeding. Take her and her newborn to see a skilled medical professional as soon as possible.

Gently rock back and forth while sitting.

Hands-and-knees position can relieve stress on your spine.

Squatting helps to open the pelvis.

Straddle a chair to relieve back pain.

322 Use an EpiPen

Anaphylaxis is a rare type of severe allergic reaction that can be triggered by anything from certain foods to insect stings. Milder reactions can be unpleasant and sometimes a little harmful to the victim, but anaphylactic shock can be lethal if untreated. The allergic reaction can take place within minutes, with the victim experiencing severe swelling and rashes, difficulty breathing, and dangerous changes in blood pressure and heart rate.

If you know a person is experiencing this sort of reaction, it can be countered with epinephrine (the same stuff as adrenaline) administered by a pen-shaped auto-injector. If you stock a few in your medical kit, make sure they're kept in a stable-temperature environment and are within their expiration date.

STEP 1 Remove the cap from the end of the injector.

STEP 2 Grip the shaft firmly in your hand, with your thumb on its back, and aim for the victim's thigh muscle. (You can even use the pen through a layer of clothing.)

STEP 3 Jab down firmly against the muscle, keeping

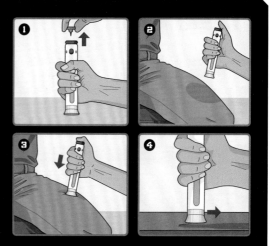

the shaft of the pen perpendicular to his or her limb. Hold the injector in place for at least 10 seconds to allow the needle to deploy and the medicine to be administered.

STEP 4 Remove the needle from the victim's thigh, and carefully dispose of the injector and/or bend the tip to avoid being stuck with it.

STEP 5 Monitor the victim's condition and get him or her to skilled medical treatment.

323 Apply a Tourniquet

There are progressive steps for controlling bleeding. Cover the injury with a dressing, elevate the wound above the heart, apply direct pressure, and use arterial pressure points (see item 337). But if the injury is so severe that those methods aren't stemming the flow of blood, it's time to consider using a tourniquet. The victim may lose the use of a body part due to lack of circulation, so this is a last resort to save life at the expense of limb.

Use a strong, broad, flexible object, such as a rolled-up shirt, thick cord, rope, or belt. It should not be so thin as to cut into tissue and cause further injury or bleeding. Ideally, you should be trained in using a tourniquet, and you should get the victim's

permission (in writing if at all possible).

Wrap the tourniquet around the limb as close to the injury as possible, and tie it off as tightly as you can. Alternatively, you can tie the tourniquet around the limb in a loose loop, then tie a handle such as a short, strong stick inside the knot of the loop. Turn the handle several times to twist and tighten.

Whatever method you use, you should secure the tourniquet so that it does not come unwound. If possible, dress and bandage the wound, mark the victim's forehead with a T and the time the tourniquet was applied to alert the pros, then get the victim to medical care as soon as possible.

324 Don't Try This at Home

You may not be able to handle some medical emergencies on your own, even if you have a decent amount of first-aid or EMS experience. Unless you happen to be a doctor, nurse, or military medic, the sorts of emergencies discussed on the next few pages will definitely require the help of someone with professional training. In a truly critical situation, with no medical help available, you may have to act. Here's what to do in those circumstances, but we sincerely hope you never have to. Some things really should be left to the professionals.

325 Save a Toe (or Finger, or More)

A lost digit (or worse, appendage) is definitely a major trauma to the body. The victim will obviously lose the use of that body part without immediate intervention.

First, assess and treat the patient's injury and stop the bleeding; remember, it's life before limb. A tourniquet may be necessary on larger injuries. For smaller injuries like a toe or finger, wash the site of the injury and the severed digit itself. Apply dressings and bandages to the wound.

The severed part should be thoroughly insulated— wrap it with moistened gauze bandages, seal it in a plastic bag, and place it in a container of ice or cold packs. Get the patient and the body part to a medical facility immediately.

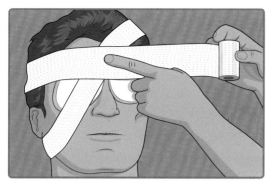

326 Save an Eye

An eye injury is never anything to take lightly, and a serious one needs to be taken care of right away. If small particles or fluids are splashed in the eyes, immediately begin rinsing with cool water. Use as much as there is on hand, and, if possible, flush the victim's eyes for at least 15 minutes. If the victim has contact lenses and they are not washed out during the rinse, make sure to remove them.

If the victim's eye has a larger foreign body or has been impaled by something, do not try to remove the object. Stabilize it, and carefully cover both eyes (both eyes move at the same time, so covering both helps keep an injury to one from being worsened by movement of the other). The next step is—you guessed it—seek skilled medical help immediately.

327 Don't Spill Your Guts

If someone has been so badly injured that her internal organs are exposed, she is definitely in need of serious skilled medical care and long-term treatment. The most important thing you can do in the short term is to limit further damage and reduce the risk of infection.

Any organs that are exposed should be carefully immobilized; do not try to push them back into the body. Cover the area with a trauma dressing soaked in saline, keep the area guarded against any further injury or impact, treat the victim for shock, and get help immediately.

328 Open an Airway

When a victim's airway is blocked, an absolute last-resort measure is to surgically open the airway, a procedure known as a cricothyrotomy or emergency airway puncture.

STEP 1 Extend the neck and find the soft area between the Adam's apple and the cricoid cartilage. Keep your finger there as a guide.

STEP 2 Hold the skin taut and carefully make an incision, about 1/2 inch (1 cm) long and 1/2 inch (1 cm) deep.

STEP 3 Puncture the membrane beneath and enlarge the hole with a gloved fingertip.

STEP 4 Insert a rigid tube (like a pen barrel) into the hole, allowing the victim to breathe.

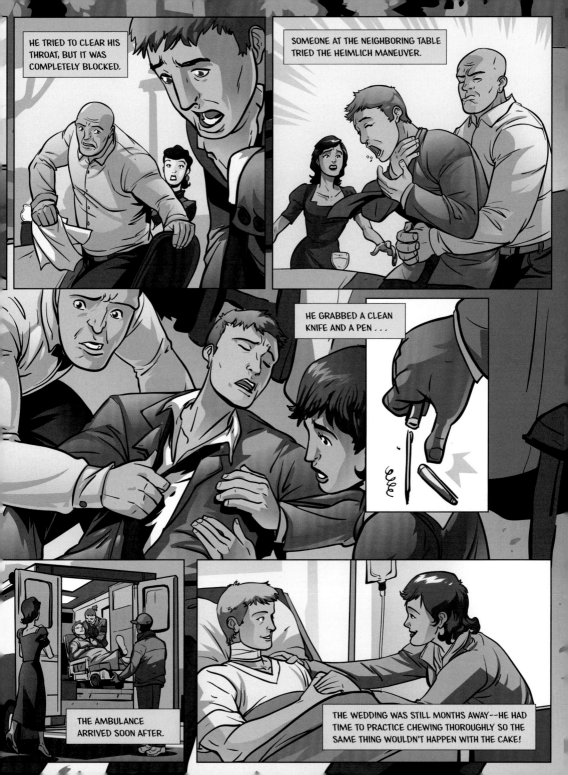

330 Survive a Gunshot Wound

As with all of these scenarios, getting medical help is crucial. If it's not forthcoming, here's what you can do in the event of a gunshot wound.

Short-term survival means stopping bleeding and praying that nothing too important, like an organ or an artery, got hit. Put pressure on bleeders, elevate wounded limbs, stay calm, and watch the patient's blood pressure and pulse for symptoms of shock.

Long-term survival after a noncritical gunshot wound, with no help coming, boils down to one thing: preventing infection. Those bits of clothing, skin, and hair that the bullet dragged into the wound are going to cause trouble, so keep the wound clean. Surviving the injury is all about dealing with the pain, letting your body mend itself, and—again—preventing infection. Keep potent antibiotics in your bug-out bag, and carry a product called QuikClot, which (as you'd imagine from the name) helps to stop bleeding fast.

331 Take Care of an Impaled Victim

One of the most serious injuries is when a person is impaled by debris or objects. Whether it's embedded in soft tissue, an eye, or an organ, it needs to be well taken care of.

First things first: Leave the object in place. Removing it without the proper skill may worsen the injury or leave debris behind, and in some cases the object may actually be keeping the victim from bleeding out.

Next, stabilize the affected area. Carefully cover any exposed tissue with a saline-moistened dressing, then immobilize and wrap the object and the injury with bandages. Transport the victim to a medical facility as soon as possible.

332 Decompress a Chest Wound

A tension pneumothorax, also known as a sucking chest wound, occurs when air or gas fills the chest cavity (usually after a chest injury), which prevents a lung from properly expanding. An emergency chest decompression may be necessary in some cases to keep a victim breathing, but it's also high on the list of things you really shouldn't do unless you know exactly (and professionally) how.

STEP 1 Remove a stopper from a syringe and apply a sterile needle.

STEP 2 Locate and clean the insertion site (between the second and third ribs, above the nipple).

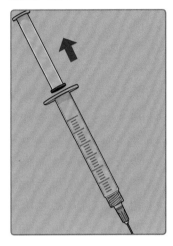
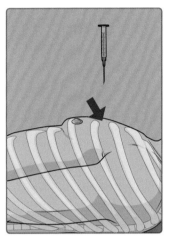

STEP 3 Insert the needle straight into the chest, and feel for a pop as the needle penetrates into the pleural sac (around the lung).

STEP 4 Listen for a hiss from the needle and let air escape. Apply an airtight bandage or other sterile covering over the wound.

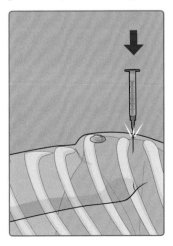
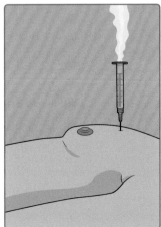

333 Suture a Wound

Suturing an open wound can speed healing, reduce infection, and reduce chances of reinjury.

STEP 1 Clean the wound thoroughly with water and an antiseptic solution rinse.

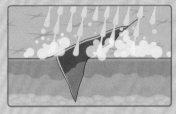

STEP 2 Carefully align the edges of the wound.

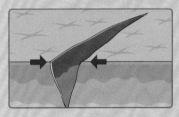

STEP 3 Using sutures, needle, and forceps, stitch the wound shut, from about $1/10$ to $4/10$ inch (0.1 to 0.3 cm) around and beneath the cut.

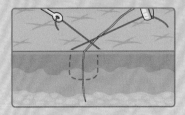

STEP 4 Tie off with square knots and cover with dressings.

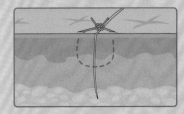

334 Survive with Nothing

One of the worst survival scenarios you may face is a situation in which you have to survive with only the clothes on your back (or less). This could happen in wilderness survival or a bug-out gone horribly wrong. However your story may unfold, you've got to have the skills to turn nothing into something.

The first step is take stock of your situation. If you lost your gear because an angry mob tore off your BOB, then escape and evasion are your tools for safety. If people are threatening you in postdisaster lawlessness, then self-defense will be your top priority. Arm yourself as best you can—in the wilderness, in your home, or in the wreckage.

335 Know Your Lines of Shelter

Your clothing is your first line of shelter from the elements. Each extra layer is like another insurance policy to keep you safe, so insulate if you can. Seek shelter from heat or cold as best as you can. You don't need tools to build insulated nests from castoff materials—think of the nests you've seen in nature, and create one that you can just squeeze into. Make it open and breezy to combat the heat, or make it thick and fluffy to fight the cold.

Without your gear, lighting a fire will be a monumental task. Considering the myriad of uses of fire, from boiling water to heating, lighting, and cooking, it makes sense to become a friction-fire-building master. Or you can take a shortcut by carrying multiple fire-starting methods on your person. Keep a lighter in your pocket, even if you don't smoke, or get a survival bracelet with a spark rod in it. Know how to make a fire by concentrating light through your glasses. When your backups have their own backups, your lost gear won't matter so much.

336

Scrounge for Nourishment

Catching rainwater and locating a natural spring are two safe ways to get wholesome drinking water without any tools or materials. What you don't want to do is emulate the TV survival gurus who demonstrate drinking water out of puddles and waterways without disinfecting it. This is the fast track to dysentery, which can kill a healthy person in a short (or long) few days. Look for helpful garbage, like bottles and cans, which can be used as boiling vessels if you are able to get a fire going.

Foraging for food can be a pleasant experience, yielding delicious results when you're at your leisure with a full spread of cooking methods and condiments to work with. But all those gourmet sensibilities go out the window when you are scavenging just to stay alive. If you don't know how to definitively identify the local wild edible plants, stick with animal foods. Freshwater fish, worms, crickets, and many other critters are safe for human consumption. Just make sure that you cook them thoroughly in case they are loaded with parasites or disease-causing pathogens.

337 Diagnose and Treat Ailments

With no first aid kit, medical care becomes a whole lot more difficult. A lack of clean dressings or antibiotic products is a sure recipe for infection. Still, medical aid can be rendered if you have a working knowledge of the skills.

You can diagnose ailments like heat exhaustion and dehydration without supplies, and identify pressure points to slow bleeding. If severe bleeding does not stop with direct pressure and elevation, switch tactics and apply direct pressure to the right artery.

When you apply pressure to an artery, you stop bleeding by pushing the artery against bone. There are specific major arteries in the body where pressure should be placed (see illustration). Press down firmly on the artery between the bleeding site and the heart, closer to the heart. After bleeding stops, do not continue to apply pressure to an artery for longer than 5 minutes.

In short, you're performing medicine as our ancestors once did. Use what you have to make what you need.

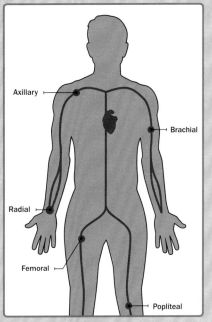

338 Keep It Positive

An upbeat, positive attitude and a generous streak of mental toughness can be literal lifesavers, especially under the dire circumstances outlined here. Surrounded by an emergency and bereft of gear, it would be easy to give in to despair and cease fighting for your life. If you can find little ways to maintain your morale and remain motivated to survive, seemingly insurmountable odds can be fought, and, for the lucky, fought and overcome.

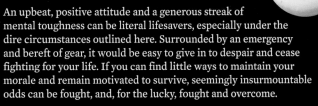

NOW IT'S TIME TO GET TO WORK.

You've read, researched, planned, and imagined your way through hundreds of survival topics and situations. This is great, but you're not done yet. You still have to put it into practice. You should make a list of the most likely emergencies that could happen to you, your family, and your friends—and a list of supplies you would need in those scenarios. Make it realistic. Look at the things that governments and big businesses worry about. Storms, earthquakes, floods, and terrorist events are some of the most likely situations to address. Aliens, zombies, pole shifts, or sliding into a black hole? Not so much.

Next, start gathering supplies to provide for yourself and those in your care. Don't break the piggy bank; you can get these things step by step. Buy things that you know you will use. Grab a couple of factory-filled water cooler jugs on your next trip to the store. Buy a few extra cans of food on your next grocery trip. Make your vehicle and workplace ready for emergencies, too. Don't go into debt; just get your supplies before you need them.

Your third task: Become less dependent on the complex (and vulnerable) modern systems that sustain the First World lifestyle. Electricity, communications, Internet commerce, and clean running water are luxuries; you may have to do without them at some point. Become more independent by going without electricity periodically, making your own power, camping out for a vacation, and growing your own food (yes, even in the city; see the urban gardening section). Practice makes perfect—or at least close to it.

Your final task is the easiest, and yet some people find it difficult: Don't let preparedness consume your life. It's easy to get carried away with worry. You've probably spent time watching survival shows or reading about calamities. If you've actually lived through a disaster, many things in this book may have hit home, possibly dredging up painful memories. But you have to move onward and live your life. If you spend all your time in a bunker, fearing every new day, you'll miss the things that make life great. You *can* plan for the worst and still hope for the best. The tenacity of the human spirit is one of our greatest survival tools. If you've made your preparations and done all that seems reasonable, you can rest easy, because you're better prepared than ever before. You are ready.

Semper paratus, sine metu. "Always prepared, without fear."

Tim MacWelch

INDEX

A

air compressors, 83
alcohol, 75, 187–190, 193
arithmetic, as basic skill, 86
arrows, making, 222
attitude, mental, 233, 235, 338
automobiles, 79–84
   maintenance of, 86
   manual transmission in, 86

B

baking soda, 121
bartering, 262, 299, 300
batteries, 11, 12, 21, 82, 84, 196, 197, 199, 200, 254–255, 257
beer
   brewing, 187, 189
   repurposing cans, 317
bicycles, 79, 86, 197
biodiesel, 201–209, 303
birthing, 321
blackberry wine, 190
bleach, as disinfecting agent, 46, 112, 239
blowguns, 229
BOBs (bug-out bags), 11, 13, 239
boots, 50, 51
botulism, prevention of, 32, 33, 179
bows
   arrows for, 222
   making, 221
   shooting, 223
brewing, home, 187–190
bricks, heating with, 314
briquettes, recycled, 78
bug-out options and supplies. See BOBs; evacuation
bunkers, 274–279

C

calories, in food supplies, 35
camps, emergency, 239–242

candles, 195, 250, 313
canning, 170–179
carbohydrates, 30
carbon monoxide, 313
cars. See automobiles
cash. See money
cell phones, 19, 123, 250, 254
char cloth, 56, 103, 317
charcoal, making, 308
chemical protection suits, 48
chickens, raising, 149–154, 157, 158
chimneys, residential, 118
chlorine, as disinfecting agent, 40, 46, 47, 112, 136
cigarettes, 13
cleaning agents, 121
clothing
   boots, 50, 51
   hazmat suits, 48
   shoes, 50, 51
   survival-kit list of, 52
   wool, 49
coconut water, 37
coffee, brewing, 198
cooking
   as basic skill, 87
   sardines, 105
cooperation, in emergencies, 237–238, 263
CPR, 96
cyclones, 257

D

deer hunting, 288–289
defensive compounds, 270–273
diesel fuel, types of, 202
dried food, 178, 295–296
drugs, 318–320, 322
ducks, raising, 155
duct tape, 11, 53, 84, 90, 105, 125, 222, 224

E

earthquakes, 6, 231, 259

economic collapse, 231, 261, 262, 299

   See also money

electricity supply. *See* power supply

emergency drills, 10

emergency plan, 9, 232, 236

EMP (electromagnetic pulse), 231, 248, 249, 252

energy drinks, 13

EpiPens, 322

evacuation

   camp supplies for, 239

   in floods, 258

   fuel stockpiled for, 74

   of pets, 127–129

   versus staying put, 236

F

Faraday cage, 253

feed, for livestock, 158

fertilizer, 134, 135, 138, 149, 167

fire

   emergency drills for, 10

   prevention of, 16, 118

   signaling with, 243

   starting, 14, 56, 88, 101–104, 304–307, 317, 335

   types of, 17

firearms

   basic skills for using, 88

   safe handling of, 62, 225

   stances for shooting, 226

   trigger control for, 227, 228

   types of, 61

first aid, 89–100, 324–333, 337

   for allergic reactions, 322

   as basic skill, 88

   birthing, 321

   controlling bleeding, 93

   CPR, 96

   in emergency camps, 242

   first aid kit, 89, 242

   Heimlich maneuver, 100

   improvised supplies for, 90

   training in, 89, 91, 324

   treating broken bones, 98

   treating burns, 99

   treating shock, 97

   treating wounds, 94–95, 323, 325–327, 330–333, 337

fishing, 280–282, 317

flares, 243

floods, 81, 231, 258

food supply

   basic, 28

   in BOBs (bug-out bags), 11, 13

   calories in, 35

   canning, 170–179

   carbohydrates, 30

   dried food, 178, 295–296

   dried fruit, 178

   in evacuation camps, 239

   foraging for, 180–181, 336

   hardtack, 297

   in hurricanes, 257

   jams and jellies, 177

   jerky, 186

   luxury items, 31

   nonperishable items, 12, 21, 84

   pemmican, 298

   pickling, 176

protein, 29
in residences, 21
sardines, 105
smoked foods, 183–185
storage of, 32–34, 36, 38
in vehicles, 84
See also cooking; gardening
forges and forging, 310–311
fowl, raising, 149–158
fuel
biodiesel, 201–209
containers for, 71, 73
extending life of, 72
homemade, 193
stockpiling of, 74
storing, 72, 73
straight vegetable oil, 202, 204
substituting, 75
types of, 70

G

gardening, 132–145
as basic skill, 87
best location for, 133
best soil for, 134
canning produce from, 175
containers for, 136, 138, 144

fertilizer for, 134, 135, 138, 149, 167
grow lights for, 136
hammer for, 55
of herbs, 31, 143
pest control for, 142
plant choice in, 137, 139, 141
plant placement in, 135, 141
raised bed for, 140
urban, 136, 137, 138
water for, 135, 136, 144
gasoline, 70–72
geese
hunting, 288
raising, 155
generators, power, 74, 197, 199, 200
goat's-milk cheese, 168
government collapse, 231, 261, 264, 265
GPS, 88, 243
gunpowder, 309
guns. *See* firearms

H

hammers, 55, 84
handguns, 61
hardtack, 297
hazmat suits, 48
heaters and heating, 312–315

herbs, 31
    medicinal, 143, 146–148
Hill People Gear, 58–60
homes. *See* residences
home survival kit, 12
horse riding, 88
Hueston, Rick "Hue," 180–182
hunting, 288–290
hurricanes, 44, 117, 123, 257, 260

I

insurance, 6
iodine, as disinfecting agent, 40, 46

J

jams and jellies, 177
jerky, 186
jump-starters, 82

K

kerosene heaters, 315
knives
    fighting with, 215–218, 220
    forging, 311
    sharpening, 219
    types of, 64
knots, 65, 191, 316

L

latrines, 239, 241
leadership, 266–268
light sources, 192, 194, 195
livestock
    breeding, 166
        cattle, 168
        fowl, 149–158
        goats, 168
        rabbits, 158, 159–161, 163, 165
    slaughtering, 153, 163, 164
Lombard, Kirk, 280

M

MacWelch, R.P., 301
manual appliances, 251
maps, 88
martial arts. *See* self-defense
matches, waterproof, 15
mead, brewing, 188
medical care. *See* first aid
medicines, 318–320, 322
mirrors, as signaling tool, 243, 245
money
    cryptocurrencies as, 67
    for emergencies, 69
    in foreign bank accounts, 67
    gold, 67
    hiding, 67, 265
    managing, 66
    See also economic collapse

N

nuclear war, 231

P

pandemic, 231
paracord, 63, 85
pemmican, 298
PETE plastic, 32, 33
pets, 105, 125–130, 145

pheasants, raising, 155
pickling, 176
plumbing, residential, 119–120
power supply
    generators for, 74, 197, 199, 200
    hydroelectric, 199, 200
    outages in, 6, 231, 248–255
    solar, 76
propane
    heaters, 313, 315
    stoves, 77
protein, 29
PVC pipe, 221, 229

Q

quail, raising, 156

R

rabbits
    hunting, 288
    raising, 158, 159–161, 163, 165
radios, 243, 244, 258, 278

rainwater, collecting, 41, 136, 240, 246, 336
residences
    basic maintenance of, 117–121
    disaster-proofing, 22
    plumbing in, 119–120
    security for, 23–26, 122–124
    supplies for, 21
    survival kit for, 12
rifles, 61
rule of threes, 234

S

safe rooms, 122–123
salmonella, avoiding, 157
sanitation
    in bunkers, 276
    in emergency camps, 239, 241
sardines, 105
self-defense
    as basic skill, 88
    following social collapse, 265, 334
    using firearms, 61
    using fists, 212–214
    using improvised weapons, 230
    using knives, 215–218, 220
sewing, 87
shoes, 50, 51
shopping for supplies, 27
shotguns, 61
signaling
    with beer cans, 317
    with mirrors, 243, 245
situational awareness, 1–4, 211
skills
    basic, 86–88, 302
    sharing, 238, 263
slaughtering livestock, 153, 163, 164
smoked foods, 183–185
social collapse, 261, 265
sociopaths, spotting, 269
solar flares, 248, 249
solar heating, 312
solar lightbulb, 192
solar power, 76

solar still, 111
solar technique, for disinfecting water, 42
space blankets, 246
squab, raising, 155
squirrels
    cooking, 182
    hunting, 288
survival kits, 12, 13, 52, 105, 243, 245
SUVs, 79, 80
swimming, as basic skill, 88

T

tanning, 292–294
tarps, 239, 240
telephones, 19, 123
tents, 239, 246
tofu, smoked, 184
tools, 53–56
    automotive, 84
    basic skills for using, 86
    plumbing, 119–120
    as weapons, 84, 230
tornadoes, 20, 231, 256
tourniquets, 323
trading, 299, 300
transportation, types of, 79
trapping animals, 105, 283–286, 291
trucks, 43, 79, 80
turkeys
    hunting, 288
    raising, 155
types of crises and emergencies, 5–7, 231
Tyvek safety suits, 48

U

UV purifiers, 107, 108

V

vehicles, 43, 79–84
video surveillance, 124
vodka, 13, 57
volcanic eruptions, 6, 231

W

water-powered generators, 199, 200
water supply
    alternative sources of, 41, 45, 47, 336
    amount of, 39
    boiling, 108, 116
    containers for, 44
    disinfecting, 40, 42, 46, 47, 105–108, 116, 239
    distilling, 110–111
    in evacuation camps, 239
    filtering, 112
    in hurricanes, 257
    rainwater, 41, 136, 240, 246, 336
    residential, 21, 45
    in safe rooms, 123
wells as source of, 113–115
weapons. See blowguns; bows; firearms; knives
wells, as water source, 113–115
wilderness survival, 43, 210, 231
wood stoves, 315
wool clothing, 49
wounds, treating, 94–95, 323, 325–327, 330–333, 337

ABOUT TIM MACWELCH

Tim MacWelch has been an active practitioner of survival and outdoor skills for over 26 years. His love of the outdoors started at a young age while growing up on a farm in the rolling hills of Virginia. Eating wild berries, fishing, and learning about the animals of the forest were all part of country life. Tim became interested in survival skills and woodcraft as an offshoot of backpacking as a teen—out in remote areas, it seemed like a smart plan to learn some skills. The majority of his training has involved testing survival skills and devising new ones, but the biggest leaps forward have occurred as a result of teaching.

Tim's teaching experiences over the years have been rich and diverse, from hundreds of volunteer instructional hours to founding his own survival school with a busy year-round teaching schedule 18 years ago. He has worked with Boy Scouts, youth groups, summer camps, and adults in all walks of life, as well as providing outdoor skills training for numerous personnel in law enforcement, search and rescue organizations, all branches of the United States Armed Forces, the State Department, and the Department of Justice and some of its agencies. Tim and his wilderness school have been featured on *Good Morning America* and several *National Geographic* programs, and featured in many publications including *Conde Nast Traveler*, the *Washington Post*, and *American Survival Guide*.

Since late 2010, Tim has written hundreds of pieces for *Outdoor Life* and many other publications. Tim's current and past articles and galleries can be found at survival.outdoorlife.com and you can learn more about his survival school at advancedsurvivaltraining.com.

ABOUT OUTDOOR LIFE

Since it was founded in 1898, *Outdoor Life* magazine has provided survival tips, wilderness skills, gear reports, and other essential information for hands-on outdoor enthusiasts. Each issue delivers the best advice in sportsmanship as well as thrilling true-life tales, detailed gear reviews, insider hunting, shooting, and fishing hints, and much more to nearly 1 million readers. Its survival-themed Web site also covers disaster preparedness and the skills you need to thrive anywhere from the backcountry to the urban jungles.

A NOTE TO READERS

The information in this book is presented for an adult audience and for entertainment value only. While every piece of advice in this book has been fact-checked and, where possible, field-tested, much of this information is speculative and highly situation-dependent. The publisher and author assume no responsibility for any errors or omissions and make no warranty, express or implied, that the information included in this book is appropriate for every individual, situation, or purpose. Before attempting any activity outlined in these pages, make sure you are aware of your own limitations and have adequately researched all applicable risks. This book is not intended to replace professional advice from experts in survival, combat techniques, weapons handling, disaster preparedness, or any other field. Always follow all manufacturers' instructions when using the equipment featured in this book. If your equipment's manufacturer does not recommend use of the equipment in the fashion depicted in these pages, you should comply with the manufacturer's recommendations. You assume the risk and responsibility for all of your actions, and the publisher and author will not be held responsible for any loss or damage of any sort—whether consequential, incidental, special, or otherwise—that may result from the information presented here.

FROM THE AUTHOR

I am immensely grateful to everyone who helped me on the winding trail that led to Andrew McKean's fateful email: "Interested in writing a survival book?" Thank you to my wife Jennifer, daughters Megan and Kaitlyn, and my mom and dad for being supportive and patient while I hid myself away to write. Thank you to my survival students for giving me the opportunity to teach these skills, and to learn how to put them in a language that is easy to understand. I am also very thankful to my compatriots Wes, Hueston, Rob, Joe, and Ken for training with me, teaching with me, and helping me to push my skills to a higher level. Thank you to Johnny Cabrera for being my radio show producer, which sent me moving in the direction of outdoor-themed media. Thanks to Todd Smith, John Taranto, Alex Robinson, and Andrew McKean—for welcoming me into the *Outdoor Life* family and for giving me the time and guidance to become a better writer. And speaking of writing, I direct my deepest gratitude to Mariah Bear and Bridget Fitzgerald, the editors of this book. Their unending support and encouragement during the book writing process have been amazing. And thank you survival fans and book readers! Without your dedicated interest, I'd be out in the woods, talking to myself.

PHOTOGRAPHY CREDITS

Photography courtesy of *Shutterstock Images* except where otherwise noted: *501room / Shutterstock.com*: 258 *5-hour ENERGY*: 13 *Advil*: 89 (C) *Sarah Alban*: 297 *Banana Boat*: 89 (K) *Baofeng Electronics Co.*: 244, back cover (radio) *Benelli USA Corporation*: 61 (semi automatic) *Boker USA Inc.*: 64 (6), table of contents (knife), back cover (knife) *CRKT*: 3, 5 *Hang Dinh / Shutterstock.com*: 261 *DUKAL Corporation*: 327 *Enero Group Inc.*: 77 *falk / Shutterstock.com*: 299 *FEMA*: 237 *Getty Images*: Tim MacWelch opener *GunVault*: 62 *Sadik Gulec / Shutterstock.com*: 1 *Henry Repeating Arms*: 61 (AR-7) *Evan & Scott Hill*: 58, 59, 60 *Rick Hueston*: 180 *Alexander Ivanov*: 304 (1, 3–7) *Johnson & Johnson Consumer Companies, Inc.*: 89 (A, B, E, F, N) *Kimballstock*: 159 *Luster Leaf*: 134 *John Lee*: 28, 57, 84 (3, 17), 85, 89 (D, G, M), 105, 224, 246, 317 *Brian Liloia*: 195 *Kirk Lombard*: 281 *Tim MacWelch*: 301 (shots of R.P.), index (shot of R.P.) *Rod Morey*: 146 (shot of Rod) *Mossberg & Sons*: 61 (tactical) *Henrique Nogueira*: 306 *Ryan O'Donnell*: 187 *The Old Farmer's Almanac*: 176 *Anton Oparin / Shutterstock.com*: 236 *Orvis*: 50 (C) *Oxy-Sorb*: 32 (packets) *Pelican Products Inc.*: 14 *Presto®*: 172 *www.Petflow.com*: 126 *Travis Rathbone*: Cover *Dan Saelinger*: 61 (AR rifle, .308) *Joseph Schell*: 280 (photos of Kirk) *SOG Knives*: 64 (2) *The Southern Foodways Alliance*: 174 *Vincent Soyez*: (Tim MacWelch closer) *Slime*: 84 (6, 7) *Smith and Wesson*: 64 (1) *SteriPEN*: 107 *Stoeger Industries*: 61 (double-barreled) *Super Glue Corporation*: 94 *Lara Swimmer*: 201 *Gibby Zobel*: 192

Weldon Owen would also like to thank architect *Susan Jones / atelierjones* for the photograph in 201.

ILLUSTRATION CREDITS

Conor Buckley: 22, 78, 104, 115, 144, 161, 164, 183, 196, 200, 213, 218, 227–228, 295, 308, 310, 321, 328, 332, 337, back cover (diagram) *Tina Cash-Walsh*: 68, 307, 312 *Liberum Donum*: 43, 57, 63, 100, 105, 131, 210, 212, 224, 230, 245, 246, 260, 311, 317, 329, 331, back cover (middle, right) *Allister Fein*: 17 *Hayden Foell*: 25–26, 38, 54, 138, 140, 165, 168, 194, 219, 229, 254–255, 285, 292, 326 *Paula Rogers*: 226 *Shutterstock*: 79, 234 *Lauren Towner*: 65, 103, 110, 171, 189, 191, 216–217, 221–222, 283, 316, 322, back cover (left) *Bryon Thompson*: 99, 149, 333 *Paul Williams*: 92

weldon**owen**

PRESIDENT & PUBLISHER Roger Shaw
SVP, SALES & MARKETING Amy Kaneko
ASSOCIATE PUBLISHER Mariah Bear
ASSOCIATE EDITOR Ian Cannon
CREATIVE DIRECTOR Kelly Booth
ART DIRECTOR Allister Fein
ILLUSTRATION COORDINATOR Conor Buckley
ASSOCIATE PRODUCTION DIRECTOR Michelle Duggan
IMAGING MANAGER Don Hill

Weldon Owen would like to thank Marisa Solís, Katharine Moore, Andrew Joron, Rob James, Kirk Lombard, Evan Hill, Scot Hill, Rick Hueston, Wes Massey, Rod Morey, R.P. MacWelch, Bridget Fitzgerald, and William Mack for their work on the original version of this book.

Library of Congress Control Number on file with the publisher.

ISBN: 978-1-68188-297-0

10 9 8 7 6
2020 2021 2022 2023 2024
Printed in Canada

Weldon Owen
1150 Brickyard Cove Road
Richmond, CA 94801
www.weldonowen.com

Originally published in 2014 (ISBN: 978-1-61628-673-6)

OUTDOORLIFE

EDITORIAL DIRECTOR Anthony Licata
EDITOR-IN-CHIEF Andrew McKean
GROUP CREATIVE DIRECTOR Sean Johnston
MANAGING EDITOR Jean McKenna
EXECUTIVE EDITOR Gerry Bethge
SENIOR DEPUTY EDITOR John B. Snow
SENIOR EDITOR Natalie Krebs
ASSISTANT MANAGING EDITOR Margaret M. Nussey
ASSISTANT EDITOR Tony Hansen
EDITORIAL ASSISTANT Hilary Ribons
ART DIRECTOR Brian Struble
ASSOCIATE ART DIRECTORS Russ Smith, James A. Walsh
PHOTOGRAPHY DIRECTOR John Toolan
PHOTO EDITOR Justin Appenzeller
PRODUCTION MANAGER Judith Weber
FISHING EDITOR Gerry Bethge
HUNTING EDITOR Andrew McKean
SHOOTING EDITOR John B. Snow
DIGITAL DIRECTOR Nate Matthews
ONLINE CONTENT EDITOR Alex Robinson

2 Park Avenue
New York, NY 10016
www.outdoorlife.com